Arctic Politics

Arctic Visions
Gail Osherenko and Oran Young, General Editors

The Arctic has long appeared to outsiders as a vast, forbidding wasteland or, alternatively, as a storehouse of riches ready for the taking by those able to conquer the harsh physical environment. More recently, a competing vision paints the Arctic as the last pristine wilderness on earth, a place to be preserved for future generations.

Arctic Visions confronts these conflicting and simplistic portraits, conceived in ignorance of the complexities of the circumpolar world and without appreciation of the viewpoints of those indigenous to the region. Drawing upon an international community of writers who are sensitive to the human dimensions, Arctic Visions will explore political, strategic, economic, environmental, and cultural issues.

The Arctic has always been a place of human and natural drama, an arena for imperial ambitions, economic exploitation, ecological disasters, and personal glory. As the region gains importance in international affairs, this series will help a growing audience of readers to develop new and more informed visions of the Arctic.

Arctic Politics: Conflict and Cooperation in the Circumpolar North, Oran Young, 1992

Arctic Wars, Animal Rights, Endangered Peoples, Finn Lynge, 1992

ORAN R. YOUNG

Arctic Politics

*Conflict and Cooperation in the
Circumpolar North*

DARTMOUTH COLLEGE
Published by University Press of New England
Hanover and London

DARTMOUTH COLLEGE
Published by University Press of New England, Hanover, NH 03755
© 1992 by the Trustees of Dartmouth College
All rights reserved
Printed in the United States of America   5   4   3   2   1
CIP data appear at the end of the book

For Naomi,
who is growing up in
an Arctic household

CONTENTS

The purpose of this book is to launch Arctic politics as a field of inquiry capable of attracting the attention not only of those with specialized interests in the polar regions but also of those who will see issues of a more generic nature being played out in a particularly clear-cut or intriguing fashion in the Circumpolar North. In the following paragraphs, I endeavor to lay the foundation for this field of inquiry; the superstructure is contained in the substantive chapters that follow.

Natural scientists have long treated the Arctic as a distinctive region and have sought to broaden and deepen our understanding of its physical and biological systems. But the Far North has been slow to emerge in the thinking of policymakers and scholars alike as an area worthy of the attention of those concerned with political and socioeconomic matters. This is partly because the Arctic is sparsely populated, commonly viewed as a remote periphery of little relevance to mainstream issues, and frequently regarded as a region where human activities are sui generis. Under the circumstances, it is not hard to understand why social scientists have been content, for the most part, to leave the Far North to a small band of archaeologists, ethnographers, and naturalists who have all, in their own ways, highlighted the exotic and even unique features of the region.

Partly, this neglect is a consequence of the conceptual lenses we habitually and unreflectively employ to organize thinking about our world. We have trouble thinking coherently about the

Circumpolar North as a region, for example, because of the continuing influence of the Mercator projection, a perspective that
leaves the Far North strung out along one edge of the map and
makes it virtually impossible to conceptualize the Arctic as a region in geographical terms. As a result, most of us lack a mental
picture of the Arctic as an area of potential interest in regional
terms.

Yet the Arctic has become an area with much to offer students
of politics and political economy. A few examples will serve to
illustrate this proposition. In recent years, both the North American Arctic and the Eurasian Arctic have emerged as important
testing grounds for innovative approaches to constitutional issues, as local and regional governments seek to redefine their relationship to central governments, and for new thinking about
collective as well as individual rights, as indigenous peoples endeavor to protect their distinctive ways of life within overarching
political and legal systems premised on the ideal of equal treatment for all citizens. Similarly, the Far North, which is undoubtedly a storehouse of raw materials of great value to advanced
industrial societies, has become a critical arena, not only for those
desiring to reexamine the efficacy of traditional resource regimes
but also for those wishing to dig deeper in an effort to rethink
the bases on which we organize human/environment relations.
Somewhat unexpectedly, moreover, the Arctic has come into focus as an area of considerable interest for those endeavoring to
improve our understanding of the role of regimes or institutions
in achieving sustained cooperation at the international level.

As these examples suggest, my perspective on Arctic politics
has the effect of standing the usual argument for area studies on
its head. Those who devote themselves to European studies,
Asian studies, Latin American studies, or African studies normally argue that events occurring in those regions are profoundly
affected by the history, languages, and cultures of the areas in
question. On this account, both scholars and policymakers wishing to understand the politics of an area must steep themselves
in the relevant history, languages, cultures, and so forth. Only
in this way can they hope to explain the current state of affairs
or to predict events likely to unfold in the region during the foreseeable future.

Whatever the merits of this way of thinking (and there are serious arguments both for and against it), my own perspective on Arctic politics is informed by the converse of this point of view. To be sure, the Arctic has its share of unique features. The Inuit culture of the Northern American Arctic and the Saami culture of Fennoscandia, for instance, represent distinctive adaptations to an unusual natural environment. Soviet efforts to construct sizable urban centers north of the treeline are unparalleled. The various models of home rule government now flourishing in Alaska, northern Canada, and Greenland are unusual, at least in terms of their specific provisions.

But far more significant, in my judgment, are the opportunities that are now available to treat the Far North as a testing ground for varied approaches to socioeconomic and political issues and as an arena within which to develop new ideas relating to issues of generic interest. In thinking about the circumstances of the Arctic's indigenous peoples, for example, I see opportunities to contribute to our understanding of the conditions facing the world's roughly 200 million indigenous peoples locked into overarching sociopolitical systems they can never hope to control. The study of resource regimes in the Circumpolar North strikes me as providing an opportunity to broaden and deepen our understanding of these institutional arrangements more generally. The opening up of the Russian Arctic in recent years is exciting to social scientists precisely because it raises the prospect of being able to compare and contrast markedly different political and economic systems operating in biological and physical settings that are remarkably similar. The analysis of international relations in the Arctic is attractive because it offers a chance to test our ideas about the determinants of sustained international cooperation and to reformulate these ideas for further testing by others looking at different areas. To my way of thinking, then, it is the prospect of a two-way flow of ideas between the substance of Arctic issues and generic concerns, rather than the unique features of the region, that makes Arctic studies attractive to social scientists in general and students of politics in particular.

The substantive chapters of this book are grouped into three broad clusters: community studies, regional studies, and international studies. This way of characterizing the clusters arose, after most of the individual chapters were complete, from a workshop on Arctic social science held in Moscow in April 1991 and sponsored jointly by the National Academy of Sciences of the United States and the Soviet Academy of Sciences. But the substantive chapters included in the book fit remarkably well into this framework. Some deal with the problems and prospects facing the remote (predominantly indigenous) communities of the Circumpolar North. Although the details naturally vary from one part of the region to another, there are striking similarities in the underlying concerns of remote communities scattered throughout the region (for instance, the problem of avoiding or mitigating the dependence that typically arises in core/periphery relationships). Other chapters focus on Arctic issues that are regional in scope in the sense that they extend well beyond the level of the community and yet are not, fundamentally, matters of international relations. They deal with issues that involve states, territories, or autonomous regions (for example, the impact of oil revenues on regional governments), raise questions of intergovernmental relations (for instance, many Arctic resource conflicts), or concern the ways in which developments originating outside the region affect Arctic areas (for example, the impact of the animal protection movement on northern socioeconomic and political systems). The opportunities for comparative analysis in the study of these issues are particularly rich and rewarding. Still other chapters focus on the emerging role of the Arctic as an international region. They explore both the growing significance of the Arctic in strategic terms and the rising interest among governmental and nongovernmental entities alike in fostering sustained international cooperation in the Circumpolar North.

As will be readily apparent from the individual chapters, the bulk of my field research in the Arctic has involved Alaska and the marine areas adjacent to its coasts. Accordingly, I draw heavily on Alaskan cases, especially in examining the problems and prospects facing the region's remote communities. It is only fair to warn readers, therefore, to be alert to the possibility that my conclusions do not hold up well when applied to other parts of the Circumpolar North. Nonetheless, I have traveled widely throughout the Arctic and discussed the issues raised in this book on numerous occasions with colleagues from all of the Arctic countries. Although it is not difficult to pinpoint specific differences in the socioeconomic and political circumstances of various segments of the Arctic, these encounters have strengthened my conviction that the fundamental issues at stake are generic.

The original versions of the chapters included in this volume were written over the course of a decade. It is inevitable, therefore, that some of the factual material in individual chapters is dated. The financial crisis facing village Alaska during the late 1980s has eased, at least for the moment; the flow of public revenues available to the government of the state of Alaska has recovered somewhat from the drop caused by the collapse of the world oil market in 1986; the International Arctic Science Committee is now a going concern. I have made an effort to update important matters both by revising material included in a number of the chapters and by writing prologues for each of the three parts of this book. But I have not attempted to revise the individual essays drastically to take into account broader developments that have occurred during the time that has elapsed since the completion of the essays. Such an effort would not only be time-consuming; it also would not affect the basic argument of the book regarding Arctic politics as a field of study.

Even so, it is appropriate to put the reader on notice that specific facts (for example, the percentage of the oil produced in the United States that comes from Alaska or the composition of the Soviet/Russian Northern Fleet) may not be accurate as of the time the printed version of this book becomes available. More dramatically, the date on this preface coincides with the date of the official demise of the Soviet Union. This change will surely have profound implications for Arctic politics. The new Russia is likely to differ significantly from the Soviet Union both in its material capabilities and in its Arctic policies. Naturally, I have not been able to write extensively about the implications of this transformation in the chapters to follow. If anything, however, the upheaval now taking place in the former Soviet Union only reinforces my conviction that the Arctic offers numerous attractive opportunities for analysts to investigate topics of generic interest to students of politics.

Many individuals and organizations deserve acknowledgment for the contributions they have made to my thinking about Arctic politics. First and foremost, I want to record my appreciation for the contributions of many Arctic residents and members of the community of northernists or Arctic specialists both in this country and abroad. I have found Arctic residents to be unusually generous in sharing their insights. For its part, the community of northernists is, at one and the same time, highly diverse and close-knit, a combination that makes it both enjoyable to belong to and unusually stimulating in intellectual terms. More specifically, my work in this field has profited from my service as a member of the Polar Research Board of the National Academy of Sciences (and co-chair of the board's Committee on Arctic Social Sciences), an adviser to the U.S. Arctic Research Commission, and a director of the Arctic Research Consortium of the United States.

I began my work on Arctic politics during the 1970s while teaching at the University of Texas at Austin and the University of Maryland at College Park. For the most part, however, the essays that form the basis for the chapters of this volume are products of my years as co-director and then director of the Center for Northern Studies and as founding director of the Institute of Arctic Studies at Dartmouth College. Both organizations have proved congenial environments within which to think about Arctic politics in an interdisciplinary setting. Whereas my early efforts in this field were largely self-supported, I have been greatly assisted in recent years by generous grants from the John D. and Catherine T. MacArthur Foundation and from the Ford Foundation. I like to think that this increased support is a sign of the times with regard to the role of the social sciences in the field of Arctic studies.

An array of individuals too numerous to name individually have shaped my thinking and provided support both at home and in the field. A few individuals, however, deserve special notice. Leonard Rieser, a physicist and longtime director of the John Sloan Dickey Endowment for International Understanding at Dartmouth, was instrumental in the founding of the Institute of Arctic Studies. Nicholas Flanders, an anthropologist with broad experience in the North, has served as the Institute's associate director and has taken on many administrative duties. Gail Osherenko, an environmental lawyer who is both my wife and my collaborator on other projects, has made available her considerable talents as the Institute's director of studies. My secretaries over the past several years, Chrystel Buell and Nicki Maynard, have kept track of my comings and goings and provided admirable support for my endeavors. A number of students, both undergraduates and graduates, have stimulated my thinking by seeking my help with their own projects. To all of these people, I offer my sincere thanks.

Wolcott, Vermont   O.R.Y.
New Year's Day, 1992

Arctic Politics: Setting the Stage

The Arctic forms a cap on the Northern Hemisphere whose apex is the North Pole but whose southern boundaries vary considerably depending upon the criterion we use to demarcate them. At first glance, the Arctic Circle, a line girdling the globe at 66°33' north latitude, may seem the obvious candidate for this role. Yet this line does not direct attention to any important feature of Arctic systems—it merely marks the point at which the sun is above the horizon for twenty-four hours during the longest days of the year and below the horizon for twenty-four hours during the shortest days. Few of those concerned with Arctic matters have found this criterion useful as a basis for organizing their work.

Natural scientists interested in the Arctic have turned to a number of criteria pertaining to physical and biological systems in bounding their study area. These include the 10°C surface air isotherm for the warmest month of the year; the treeline separating the tundra biome from the taiga, or boreal forest, biome; the southern boundary of continuous permafrost; and the seasonal limit of sea ice during the winter months. Each of these criteria has something to recommend it, especially for specialists in particular scientific disciplines. But they identify substantially different southern boundaries for the Arctic region, a fact that has led many scientists as well as most science administrators to adopt a composite approach in terms of which the Arctic or the Circumpolar North is associated with a collection of ecosystems that most natural scientists can accept as being arctic or subarctic in nature.

Whatever the merits of this approach for those whose work focuses on physical and biological systems, it leaves much to be desired for social scientists whose work centers on the human systems of the Far North. Demarcating the Arctic's southern boundaries in a manner that bisects the human systems that are the objects of their study is an obvious liability for these scientists. Although the resultant definitional disparity made little difference in the past, it is emerging now as a matter of growing concern as scientists from many disciplines turn their attention increasingly to interactions and feedback mechanisms linking human systems with physical and biological systems in the Circumpolar North.

Social scientists engaged in Arctic studies have not succeeded in devising a precise formula of their own for demarcating the southern boundaries of the study area. In a rough-and-ready way, however, they have achieved a considerable measure of consensus about what to include in the Arctic. With regard to land, the Arctic of the social sciences encompasses Alaska (except for the area known as Southeast); the Yukon and Northwest Territories, Northern Quebec, and all of Labrador in Canada; all of Greenland; Iceland; the northern counties of Norway, Sweden, and Finland (known collectively as Fennoscandia); and all of what the Russians treat as the Arctic and the Russian North. This study area also encompasses the marine systems of the Arctic Ocean and its adjacent seas, including the Bering, Chukchi, Beaufort, Greenland, Norwegian, Barents, Kara, Laptev, and East Siberian seas. In this book, the terms *Arctic*, *Circumpolar North*, and *Far North* are used interchangeably to refer to this study area (see map).

Defined in this way, the Arctic includes an area of over 40 million square kilometers (16 million square miles) or about 8 percent of the surface of the Earth. This breaks down into some 15 percent of the planet's land area and 5 percent of the world ocean. Given the recent history of the Arctic, it is worth noting immediately not only that the region encompasses areas under the jurisdiction of eight states—Canada, Denmark/Greenland, Finland, Iceland, Norway, Russia, Sweden, and the United States—but also that

THE CIRCUMPOLAR NORTH

Jory Johnson 1989

well over 40 percent of the land area of the Arctic and almost half of the region's coastline lie within the jurisdiction of Russia alone. In an important sense, the opening up of the Soviet Union, and now Russia as its successor in the Arctic, has made possible the joining together of the two halves of the Circumpolar North. This development holds particular promise for social scientists because the social, economic, and political systems of the two halves of the Arctic differ markedly, whereas the physical and biological systems that form the environment within which those systems operate have much in common.

The Arctic is both large in physical terms and richly endowed with valuable natural resources. As of the end of 1991, the bulk of the oil and gas produced in Russia (or, for that matter, in the former Soviet Union as a whole) and about 25 percent of the oil extracted in the United States came from the Far North. Exploratory efforts in the Arctic continue to turn up major deposits of hydrocarbons, such as the giant Bovanenkovo gas field discovered by the Soviets on the Yamal Peninsula and the equally large Shtokmanovskoye and Rysanovskoye gas fields located in the Barents and Kara seas. But such efforts also provoke sharp controversy regarding their ecological and socioeconomic impacts, a phenomenon exemplified by the intense debate in the Soviet Union during the last several years of its existence about hydrocarbon development on the Yamal Peninsula, as well as the long-running debate in the United States concerning proposals to open the coastal plain of the Arctic National Wildlife Refuge to those interested in exploring for hydrocarbons.

Similar observations are in order concerning the renewable resources of the Arctic. Natural variations in ecosystems are, of course, substantial. But many northern marine areas rank high on global scales of biological productivity. The fisheries of the Circumpolar North (particularly those located in the Bering and Norwegian seas and along the coast of Labrador), for example, are unusually rich. In many recent years, the Bering Sea pollock fishery has ranked as the world's largest single-species fishery. Yet controversy surrounds the human use of these resources also, both because practices leading to stock depletions are common and because users and managers alike are not in the habit of focusing on the roles that specific resources play in the broader or more encompassing ecosystems, whose considerable value is difficult to express in utilitarian terms.

At the same time, the Arctic is remarkably small in terms of its human population. The region contains a mere fraction of 1 percent of the world's people, and a large majority of these reside in the northernmost parts of Russia, which encompasses all of the Arctic and northern lands of the former Soviet Union. Outside of a few urban centers that provide homes for as many as half a million people, such as Murmansk, Archangel, and Norilsk in Russia; Reykjavik in Iceland; and Anchorage in Alaska, the Circumpolar North is among the Earth's most sparsely populated regions. In much of the Far North, population densities are well under one person per square kilometer, and communities of five thousand to ten thousand people function as transportation hubs and regional administrative centers.

Even so, the region constitutes a homeland for numerous groups of indigenous peoples and their distinctive cultures. These include the Inuit (Eskimos), Aleuts, and Indians of the North American Arctic; the Saami (Lapps) of Fennoscandia, and an array of indigenous groups located in Russia and known collectively as the "small peoples" of the Soviet (now Russian) North. It will come as no surprise, therefore, that the Far North has emerged in recent years as a scene of sharp conflict between those desiring to exploit valuable natural resources or to protect threatened species on the one hand and those concerned with maintaining the integrity of the unique human cultures of the region on the other.

Arctic Politics: Benign Neglect and Nascent Interests

Long known for its dramatic landscapes, magnificent wildlife, and exotic cultures, the Arctic has a well-established reputation for captivating adventurers, naturalists, archaeologists, and ethnographers, who return to the region again and again, as well as many members of the general public, who exhibit a continuing desire to experience the Arctic in a purely vicarious fashion. There is a large and seemingly inexhaustible market for the works of those able and willing to write in a popular vein about Arctic ecosystems (for example, Barry Lopez), the Arctic's indigenous peoples (for example, Richard Nelson), the history of Arctic exploration (for example, Pierre Berton), or human/environment interactions in the Far North (for example, Farley Mowat).[1] Yet the region has seldom attracted serious attention on the part of social scientists interested in politics and public policy. Among those concerned with the processes through which societies arrive at collective choices or authoritative allocations of values, the Arctic is apt to be regarded as a sideshow, a subordinate system lacking in political dynamics of its own. To those endeavoring to assess the relative merits of policy options relating to national security, economic growth, public health, and other prominent items on public agendas, the Arctic generally appears as a remote area of no more than passing interest.

More specifically, four clusters of factors, taken together, have produced an attitude of benign neglect toward the Arctic among political analysts and policymakers alike:

• *The Arctic as an empty stage.* Because the region's human population is so sparse, it is easy to think of the Arctic as an empty stage on which the interests of various outside groups are occasionally played out. On this account, we must direct our attention to interactions unfolding elsewhere in order to comprehend events taking place in the Arctic.

• *Arctic exceptionalism.* There is a venerable tradition of accentuating the exotic and unique features of the Arctic, a practice that has the effect of setting the region aside from the mainstream concerns of most fields of study. The prospect of looking to the Arctic to obtain insights pertaining to generic issues is actually distasteful to some northernists.

• *Core/periphery relations.* Southern metropoles have long treated their own Arctic realms as resource hinterlands to be guarded jealously and exploited as secure storehouses of raw materials. From this perspective, there is little to be gained from viewing the Arctic as a whole or the Circumpolar North as a focus for analysis in its own right.

• *Cold War paralysis.* Through much of recent history, the superpowers faced each other across the Arctic Basin in a posture of mutual antagonism. Under the circumstances, most observers have long regarded the Far North as an unpromising area for initiatives involving international cooperation.

Despite these obstacles, recent years have witnessed a striking growth of interest in ideas that have the effect of encouraging practitioners and scholars alike to treat the Arctic as a distinctive region. Statesmen, led by Mikhail Gorbachev, have called for the establishment of an Arctic zone of peace.[2] Indigenous leaders have made great strides toward the development of a pan-Arctic aboriginal movement. Scientists have laid the basis for a concerted effort to protect the Arctic's environment and have come to focus increasing attention on the role of the Arctic in the feedback mechanisms driving global environmental change. As a result, thinking about the Arctic as an international region with its own dynamics, a practice that struck many as unwarranted as recently as the mid-1980s, no longer seems far-fetched.

Even so, any effort to establish Arctic studies and, more specifically, Arctic politics as a field of inquiry worthy of attention on the part of political scientists and policy analysts must address the four sets of factors outlined above, demonstrating that they should no longer be taken as evidence of the marginality of the Far North in political terms. In the discussion to follow, I endeavor to do just that. The argument is not framed in relative terms; I do not claim that the Arctic is more appropriate as a study area for those interested in politics and policy-making than other regions of the world or other functionally defined areas. Rather, I conclude that the Arctic is not only an area of considerable interest to political analysts in its own right but also that the region provides an attractive setting within which to develop and refine ideas about an array of political issues that are of broad, generic interest.

The Arctic as an Empty Stage

Those interested in the political dynamics of international regions typically focus on two sets of cases, which may be characterized as cockpits and arenas. What makes the Arctic interesting, in this connection, is that it exemplifies a third set of cases, which are less well understood than cockpits or arenas but which constitute an increasingly important cluster of cases for those interested in international governance systems. In the discussion to follow, I refer to members of this third cluster as shared resource regions.

In international cockpits, such as the Middle East, Southeast Asia, or Central America, conflicts indigenous to the region threaten to escalate in ways that embroil outside parties and, in the process, trigger wider international conflicts. The fundamental problem in such regions is to devise codes of conduct to minimize the frequency and extent of outside interventions (especially those of a competitive and escalatory nature) while seeking durable and preferably equitable solutions to the regional conflicts themselves. Because this problem is so difficult to solve, students of international politics have long exhibited an intense interest in the analysis of cockpits.

In international arenas, such as Antarctica, the oceans, or outer space, by contrast, outside actors are drawn to regional settings as attractive stages on which to pursue interests of their own. In such regions, which lie beyond the bounds of national jurisdiction and are frequently referred to as global commons, the central concern is to establish institutional arrangements or international regimes to regulate the interplay of outside interests in such a way as to protect the integrity of the commons without seriously interfering with efforts on the part of outside parties to pursue their own goals. The advent of technologies allowing for a continuous growth in human capacities to exploit global commons has led to a marked rise of interest among students of international politics in governance systems for such regions.

It is tempting to assign the Arctic to the second of these categories. The Circumpolar North is sparsely populated, and the region's principal human settlements are grouped into that part of the region located within Russia. This ensures that the Arctic will not emerge as an international cockpit or a scene of intense conflicts of an indigenous nature, even though the Far North is resource-rich, ecologically sensitive, and highly important to the great powers in geopolitical terms. Recently, this region has begun to loom larger in the thinking of those concerned with global environmental change. Yet this too has more to do with the reactive properties of Arctic systems than with events originating within the region itself. Increased levels of carbon dioxide in the Earth's atmosphere attributable to industrial production and the destruction of forests far to the south, for example, are expected to raise temperatures in the high latitudes of the Northern Hemisphere considerably more than similar temperature increases in the midlatitudes. This warming, in turn, is likely to trigger positive feedback processes in which the Arctic plays an important role, as the melting of sea ice lowers the Arctic's albedo, the melting of permafrost releases carbon dioxide stored in tundra ecosystems, and ultimately the melting of the Greenland icecap contributes to rising sea levels worldwide.

Nonetheless, the Arctic differs from global commons in two ways that have profound implications for the political dynamics of this international region. Even in an era of creeping jurisdictional claims affecting marine areas and other traditional commons, the sovereign authority of states reaches much farther into the Arctic than it does into Antarctica, the oceans, or outer space.[3] No one questions the sovereignty of the Arctic Rim states over the lands, including the various clusters of islands, lying in their respective sectors of the Arctic. The presence of ice makes the boundary between land and water particularly indistinct in this region, a fact that has motivated several Arctic states to take an expansive view of the geographical scope of their jurisdictional reach in the region. Though the sector principle, under which each Arctic Rim state would assume jurisdiction over marine as well as terrestrial areas lying within a wedge-shaped slice of the region, has received little support, expansive claims featuring the concepts of historic waters, enclosed or semienclosed seas, and straight baselines have made considerable headway in the Circumpolar North. Recent developments in international law, such as the ice-covered waters provisions of Article 234 of the 1982 Convention on the Law of the Sea, have reinforced this trend by identifying special circumstances that justify expansions in the jurisdiction of Arctic states regarding various functional matters (for example, marine pollution). Unlike the south polar region, where the Antarctic Treaty System has effectively frozen existing jurisdictional claims and restrained the growth of new claims, therefore, the Arctic is an area where any effort to solve regional problems must come to terms with the undeniable reality of multiple and, in some instances, expanding jurisdictions.

In contrast to genuine global commons, moreover, the Arctic is a homeland for a sizable collection of indigenous or aboriginal peoples who, even today, constitute the core of the region's permanent human population.[4] What is happening in and to the Far North is a matter of profound importance to these peoples, especially those anxious to protect distinctive cultures or ways of life. As the importance of the Circumpolar North in strategic, economic, and ecological terms grows, the region's future is increasingly affected by the actions of outsiders, who are seldom well informed about the concerns of the Arctic's indigenous peoples and who, in any case, have few incentives to make choices that are sensitive to those concerns. Despite—or perhaps because of—this development, however, the indigenous peoples of the Arctic are now experiencing a pronounced resurgence of cultural awareness that has stimulated a rising tide of interest in protecting their unique ways of life. The clash between these two trends is central to the political dynamics of the Arctic; it will undoubtedly play a key role in setting the agenda of Arctic politics during the foreseeable future.

Under the circumstances, the Arctic has emerged as an international region that cannot be understood either as an arena or as a cockpit and that is bound to suffer from any effort to force it into one or the other of these conceptual categories. Given the prominence of jurisdictional concerns in the region, it will come as no surprise that the growth of human activities in the Circumpolar North has triggered a rising interest in resolving jurisdictional ambiguities that the Arctic states were previously content to ignore.[5] Many of the resultant issues (for example, the Canadian/American Beaufort Sea boundary issue, the Norwegian/Soviet Barents Sea boundary issue, or the Danish/Norwegian Greenland Sea boundary issue) are straightforward problems of demarcating jurisdictional boundaries between opposite or adjacent states. Others, such as the status of the shelf area surrounding the Svalbard Archipelago or the status of the waters of the Northwest Passage, involve the interests of a number of states and arise either from lacunae in institutional arrangements established in earlier times (for example, the regime for Svalbard articulated in the 1920 Treaty Relating to Spitsbergen) or from difficulties in applying well-known legal concepts (for example, the idea of transit passage) under the conditions prevailing in the Arctic. Still others, such as Inuit claims regarding the right to use the sea ice, raise questions that are hard to deal with in conventional international terms because they involve the rights of "dependent nations" in their dealings with the states that constitute the principal subjects of international law.

As this last observation suggests, the Arctic has also emerged as a region that is increasingly characterized by interactions that cut across or transcend the boundaries of sovereign states and that involve actors other than national governments. Partly, this is a matter of the growing role of organizations (for example, the Inuit Circumpolar Conference or the Nordic Saami Council) representing the concerns of indigenous peoples for whom national boundaries have little cultural, economic, or political meaning. In part, it is attributable to the growth of transnational interactions on the part of subnational governments, such as states, provinces, territories, counties, and autonomous regions, that have discovered common interests that national governments are unlikely to pursue. Under the circumstances, it seems probable that the Far North will play a role of considerable importance during the foreseeable future as a setting for innovative initiatives involving international activities on the part of a variety of nonstate actors (for example, the Northern Forum established in 1990 to facilitate relations among subnational governments in the Arctic) and for new patterns of interaction that circumvent or simply bypass the traditional dominance of the state in international society. This may well lead to a reemergence of the diverse and rather fluid patterns of interaction that prevailed in the Far North prior to the systematic imposition of state sovereignty in the region from about the 1930s onward.[6] As such, this is a trend that cuts against the extension and clarification of jurisdictional authority described in the preceding paragraph. It follows that a tension between the forces of state sovereignty and the growing desire of nonstate actors to operate independently is almost certain to constitute an important theme of Arctic politics during the near future.

Above all, the emerging Arctic agenda features an array of increasingly significant issues involving the management of shared resources and ecosystems.[7] Actual cases range from relatively restricted bilateral concerns (for example, Canadian/American efforts to manage the Porcupine caribou herd, which migrates annually across the Alaska/Yukon border) through regionwide concerns (for example, the coordinated efforts of the five range states to manage polar bears) to global concerns (for example, efforts to understand and manage the feedback processes through which Arctic occurrences affect global climate change). But in every case, the fundamental problems at stake arise from the fact that the natural systems requiring management on a coordinated or unitized basis cut across political and legal boundaries. These problems differ profoundly from issues involving the design of regimes for resources or ecosystems lying largely outside the boundaries of state jurisdiction, such as krill in the southern ocean, manganese nodules on the ocean floor, or the electromagnetic spectrum in space.[8] Although these latter problems are both challenging and intriguing to students of international governance, there is a sense in which they are relatively simple compared with the more numerous situations in which it is necessary to devise governance systems for resources that range across two or more jurisdictional zones and therefore require sustained efforts to mesh the activities of public agencies belonging to separate governments and responding to distinct political cultures and administrative practices.

Without in any way depreciating the importance of the issues to be examined in conjunction with international cockpits and global commons, it seems accurate to say that issues relating to the management of shared resources and ecosystems are destined to occupy a larger proportion of our attention as we become more aware of the profound importance of the linkages between human systems and physical and biological systems. In this connection, it is pertinent to note that the Arctic is a member of a sizable class of shared resource regions. Other prominent members of this class include the Caribbean region, the South Pacific region, the North Sea/Baltic Sea catchment area, the Arabian Peninsula, the Mediterranean basin, the Amazon River basin, and the Nile River basin. It is probably correct to say that efforts to establish regionwide resource regimes or governance systems have advanced farther in several of these regions than have parallel efforts in the Arctic. The Mediterranean Action Plan, initiated in the 1970s as the initial offering of UNEP's Regional Seas Programme and the governance system for marine resources developed during the 1980s under the auspices of the South Pacific Forum are cases in point.[9] But recent years have witnessed a remarkable surge of interest in the establishment of resource regimes for the Arctic. It follows both that those seeking to enhance our understanding of shared resource regions have much to gain from a careful study of Arctic politics and that those endeavoring to solve problems of resource management in the Arctic stand to benefit from comparing and contrasting their concerns with similar issues arising in other shared resource regions.

Arctic Exceptionalism

There is a pronounced streak of romanticism in the thinking of many who take an interest in the Arctic, an attitude that encourages those affected by it to focus on the exotic and even unique properties of the physical, biological, and human systems of the region. The Far North is a vast area where the forces of nature (for example, extreme cold, raging storms, shifting sea ice) challenge human capabilities to the utmost. The region contains great expanses of wilderness whose extraordinary beauty has made them a rallying point for environmentalists and whose wildlife populations have led to the use of the phrase "Serengeti North" among those espousing protective measures for Arctic ecosystems. The great and, in some cases, notorious European and North American explorers of the Arctic have taken on larger-than-life proportions whether their efforts ended in success, as in the cases of Nordenskjöld, Nansen, and Amundsen; ultimately came to grief, as in the cases of Franklin, Greeley, and DeLong; or remain shrouded in controversy, as in the cases of Peary and Cook.[10] There is, as well, an idealized conception of human life in the Arctic that casts the indigenous peoples of the Circumpolar North as happy hunter/gatherers living a simple existence in harmony with the natural environment and uncorrupted by the forces of modernity. As a result, many outsiders visiting contemporary Arctic communities are offended by the realities of life in the Arctic and distressed by the resultant gap between their romanticized ideal and the actual conditions they encounter.

This Arctic of the imagination is well suited to the vicarious explorations widely available in the pages of glossy magazines (for example, *National Geographic*), picture books designed for coffee table use, and rousing tales of daring human exploits in the face of daunting challenges posed by nature (for example, the stories of Jack London).[11] In a sense, the region's appeal lies precisely in the fact that the Circumpolar North seems so far removed from the contentious and troublesome social issues that rage within and between the dominant societies of today's world, including battles among exponents of democracy and communism, capitalism and socialism, nationalism and internationalism. To those who find these conflicts wearisome, the romance of the Arctic is a source of welcome relief. For them, the fact that the Far North seems unconnected to the concerns of the modern world is one of its strongest attractions; they would be distressed to learn that the Arctic has social problems of its own or that these problems are in many ways similar to issues now arising in other parts of the world.

Understandable as the resultant Arctic exceptionalism may be, it has the effect of obscuring our vision of a range of issues that are both critical to various constituencies in the Circumpolar North and of great interest to social scientists as exemplars of concerns that are generic in the sense that they arise in every corner of the world. Some specific cases will serve to illustrate this emerging role of the Arctic as an attractive setting for the study of broader social concerns.

Consider, to begin with, the matter of cultural diversity, especially as it applies to the survival of the cultures of the world's approximately 200 million indigenous people. The generic argument for seeking to protect cultural diversity is much like the case for protecting biological diversity. In a rapidly changing world that is likely to present us with a variety of formidable but hard-to-predict challenges, we all stand to benefit from maintaining the full range of human cultural experience as a fund of ideas and social practices to draw on as we seek to solve a bewildering array of complex problems.[12] A particularly attractive feature of indigenous cultures in today's world is the rich collection of practices they encompass that are relevant to the achievement of sustainable human/environment relations. Increasingly, the indigenous peoples of the Far North have assumed a leadership role in efforts to devise strategies for preserving the integrity of indigenous cultures. The priorities they have established (for example, sustaining Native languages, protecting subsistence practices, enhancing aboriginal self-determination) are remarkably similar to those of indigenous peoples around the world. It follows that insights regarding the preservation of cultural diversity arising from the efforts of Arctic peoples will be of great interest to those located elsewhere and that ideas originating elsewhere will find application in the Arctic. In the end, the world's human population as a whole stands to benefit from the lessons emerging from the Arctic regarding the determinants of cultural diversity.

The Far North has also become a focus of attention for those interested in social institutions governing human/environment relationships and, more specifically, in the origins and operations of institutional arrangements, such as common property resource regimes, conceptualized as alternatives to the more familiar systems featuring structures of private property or public property. Long dismissed as a recipe for generating the dismal results associated with the tragedy of the commons, common property systems have recently become an object of renewed attention on the part of analysts who are interested in sustainable development and who harbor doubts about the results flowing from both private property systems and public property systems in these terms.[13] These analysts have produced a body of case studies from all over the world, including the Far North, demonstrating that common property systems can yield results, at least under some conditions, that are sustainable in terms of maintaining the productivity of ecosystems and of sustaining human communities over time.[14] A particularly interesting outgrowth of this line of inquiry is the idea of co-management or power sharing as an approach to resource management that combines elements of traditional indigenous practices and Western scientific procedures. The evolution of this idea, a development to which northernists have made major contributions, has led to the initiation of a number of institutional experiments in the Circumpolar North and elsewhere in which (predominantly Native) user groups and public authorities have joined together in the interests of creating mutually acceptable practices for the management of renewable resources (for example, whales, caribou, waterfowl).[15] Here, too, Arctic studies have made their way to the cutting edge of an intellectual development of generic interest.

Turning to issues closer to the mainstream concerns of politics and public policy, we encounter a growing agenda of questions involving intergovernmental relations and constitutional arrangements that hinge on the allocation of authority between central or senior governments and various subnational governments. Of course, recent events in the former Soviet Union have highlighted the tension between political centers and subsidiary units defined in geographical or cultural terms. But the issues at stake arise in many societies, making this topic a focus of worldwide concern. Though the scale may be small, the Circumpolar North has emerged as a remarkable microcosm in which a variety of interesting experiments with alternative constitutional arrangements are presently underway. Partly, this is an outgrowth of the drive to enhance self-determination or to achieve some measure of sovereignty on the part of northern indigenous peoples, who are concerned with collective rights in contrast to individual rights and who fear the assimilationist consequences of Western constitutional arrangements built on individualistic premises.[16] In part, it stems from a pervasive sense on the part of public governments in the Far North that their circumstances and concerns differ profoundly from those of subnational governments located elsewhere. The result is an array of emergent arrangements involving both new forms of public government (for example, the Home Rule in Greenland, the North Slope and Northwest Arctic Boroughs in Alaska, Nunavut in Canada) and new forms of Native government (for example, the Kativik Regional Government in northern Quebec, the Saami Parliament in Finland), which are not only altering the political landscape of the Circumpolar North but are also producing a body of experience of considerable interest to those struggling to solve complex problems of intergovernmental relations elsewhere.

Recently, the Arctic has emerged also as a focus of interest for those seeking to add to our understanding of the establishment and operation of governance systems or regimes under the anarchical conditions prevailing in international society. Interestingly, the Far North has long been a setting for geographically circumscribed and functionally specific regimes, such as the multilateral arrangement for Svalbard, the four-nation agreement concerned with the conservation of northern fur seals, and the agreement among the five range states covering the management of polar bears. But interest in the study of international regimes, in contrast to more grandiose alternatives centering on the creation of a world government, has risen rapidly in recent years among students of international affairs, especially those concerned with the dynamics of global commons and shared resource regions, such as the Arctic. Here too, the Arctic has proved attractive as a microcosm. Arctic cases figure prominently in the work of those seeking to formulate and test generic propositions about sustained cooperation in international society.[17] At the same time, a steady stream of Arctic initiatives involving localized arrangements (for example, the joint development zone for the resources of the seabed located between Jan Mayen, which belongs to Norway, and Iceland), subregional developments (for example, a series of interrelated steps dealing with the Bering Sea region), and regionwide initiatives (for example, the establishment of the Arctic Environmental Protection Strategy) have made the Circumpolar North an intriguing focus for those desiring to apply ideas about sustained international cooperation to issues on active policy agendas around the world.[18]

Adding to the attractions of the Far North as a setting in which to explore these and other concerns is the fact that the economic and political systems of the two halves of the Arctic—the North American Arctic and the Eurasian Arctic—differ considerably, even though the biological and physical systems of these subregions are remarkably similar. This facilitates efforts to hold some variables constant and therefore to devise field experiments designed to test ideas relating to the role of social institutions as determinants of collective outcomes in human affairs. To what extent, for example, do variations in structures of property rights account for observable differences in the extent to which human uses of renewable resources prove sustainable? Do differences in national decision cultures or practices relating to the choice and implementation of policies affect the nature or magnitude of the ecological and socioeconomic impacts arising from the exploitation of nonrenewable resources? These and other related questions are matters of increasing interest to students of politics and public policy. Under the circumstances, while those who espouse a more romantic vision of the Far North may mourn the passing of Arctic exceptionalism, the rising tide of interest in Arctic affairs on the part of analysts seeking to formulate generic propositions about human affairs constitutes grounds for optimism on the part of those working to lay the groundwork for the evolution of Arctic politics as a coherent and recognized field of study.

Core/Periphery Relations

It is no exaggeration to say that the politics of the Arctic have centered during most of this century on relations between industrialized southern metropoles and resource-rich northern hinterlands.[19] The principal features of this pattern of core/periphery relations—or, to use a more emotive phrase, internal colonialism—are now well known.[20] Core/periphery relations are highly asymmetrical both in the sense that peripheries are heavily dependent on the economies of the cores and in the sense that their fate is largely in the hands of central policymakers who have little knowledge of the specific conditions prevailing in the peripheries and few incentives to be responsive to the concerns of those located in the peripheries in any case. The result is a form of segmentation in which northern peripheries have had little direct contact with each other, despite the facts that many of their concerns are similar and that there are numerous opportunities to learn from each other's experiences.[21] To the extent that this pattern prevails in the Arctic, it is easy to understand why students of politics and public policy have seldom exhibited a sustained interest in the political dynamics of the region as a whole.

But in this regard, too, winds of change are blowing in the Far North; their impact is altering the political landscape of the region and, in the process, calling into question some of the central elements of the long-standing pattern of core/periphery relations in the Arctic. As a result, the Circumpolar North is emerging as a distinctive international region endowed with political dynamics of its own that are not only interesting in their own right but that are also suggestive for those seeking to understand the political aftermath of colonialism or internal colonialism in other parts of the world.

There is, to begin with, a remarkable process of devolution that is altering the political contours of the Arctic—except in the northern counties of the Scandinavian states or Fennoscandia. Greenland now has a Home Rule government possessing authority over most issues other than foreign affairs, defense, and the monetary system (its authority includes a veto over any plans for the development of nonrenewable resources on or around the island).[22] In Canada, public governments that are relatively independent from Ottawa have developed in the Yukon and the Northwest Territories; the closing days of 1991 produced a final agreement on a plan to subdivide the Northwest Territories to form a political entity that will encompass the eastern Arctic and be known as Nunavut.[23] Alaska achieved statehood in the United States as recently as 1959, and the experiments of the 1970s and 1980s with the creation of borough governments have left large areas, such as the North Slope and the Northwest Arctic, with considerable political autonomy vis-à-vis both the state and the federal government.[24]

Needless to say, the center of attention regarding devolution has now shifted to Russia, a vast realm encompassing all of the northern territories of the former Soviet Union. The success of Russia in wresting power and authority from the former Soviet Union has stimulated a growing interest on the part of those residing in distinctive areas within Russia (for example, the Chukotka Autonomous Republic, the Magadan Region, the Yamalo-Nenets Autonomous Republic) in seeking greater authority over their own affairs in dealings with the government of Russia. It is too early to say how all of this will settle out over time. But it is clear that the forces of devolution at work in Greenland and the North American Arctic are on the rise in the Eurasian Arctic as well.

Two additional factors complicate this picture and make it even more intriguing to those interested in problems of intergovernmental relations around the world. There is no guarantee that the political autonomy that devolution brings will be accompanied by economic independence. In a number of cases, in fact, newly created public governments in the Circumpolar North continue to depend heavily on the relevant central government as a source of public revenue. Denmark pays about half of the cost (in the form of a block grant) of running the Greenland Home Rule. The bulk of the operating costs of the Government of the Northwest Territories is covered by the federal government of Canada. Even in Alaska, where the Northwest Arctic Borough and, especially, the North Slope Borough have been blessed with a capacity to raise public revenue by levying property taxes on industrial installations, the state and federal governments loom large as sources of revenue for local and regional governments. The revenue implications of new patterns of intergovernmental relations in Russia have hardly begun to be addressed. Overall, the recent experience of the Arctic offers a variety of fascinating cases worthy of close examination by those interested in the links between the exercise of political authority and the availability of secure sources of public funding.

The story of devolution in the Arctic is complicated also by concerted efforts to advance the cause of tribal sovereignty in some parts of the region, a movement that, in some ways, runs counter to the conventional pattern of devolution described in the preceding paragraphs. The essential point in this context is that tribal governments are not public governments in the usual sense of the term. They generally operate under the provisions of their own constitutions, possess the authority to decide who is entitled to membership in their political communities, and are not obligated to guarantee a variety of rights that those schooled in Western liberal thinking typically associate with citizenship.[25] What is more, tribal governments are apt to compete with decentralized public governments for the same sources of revenue. Tribal governments are understandably attractive to many northern Natives whose principal concern is the protection of their cultures or distinctive ways of life, but it will come as no surprise that others, including many lifelong residents of the Arctic, view the tribal sovereignty movement with some alarm. The likely outcome of this competition between public governments and tribal governments in the Circumpolar North is anything but clear at this writing. But the unfolding of the resultant drama will be of great interest to all those concerned with the fate of indigenous peoples around the world.

Political devolution has played a key role in calling into question the long-standing pattern of segmentation associated with core/periphery relations in the region and in generating a growing interest in experimenting with various forms of direct North/North interactions. Given the great size of the Arctic, the sparseness of the region's human population, the difficulty of traveling directly from one northern location to another, and the character of northern economies, the opportunities for lucrative industrial or commercial exchanges between northern communities are limited. For the most part, they are confined to transfers of technology, experience, and general know-how likely to prove useful in coping with severe Arctic conditions. Nonetheless, recent years have witnessed a rising tide of other types of direct contact among northern peoples and organizations. Partly, this is a matter of indigenous peoples making contact with their counterparts in other Arctic countries (in some cases, they are related by blood) and seeking to strengthen their hand both domestically and internationally by making common cause among themselves. In part, it involves a diversity of people and organizations who share a common sense of "nordicity" and who wish to interact with their Arctic neighbors concerning matters of culture, education, health, and scientific research.[26]

Among the most interesting recent developments in this realm is the establishment of the Northern Forum. Launched at the Third Northern Regions Conference held in Alaska during September 1990 and given impetus as a result of two transnational meetings during 1991, the forum is an organization of subnational governments (that is, states, provinces, territories, counties, autonomous regions) interested in working together "to improve the quality of decision making and to solve problems" in areas involving commercial opportunities, appropriate technologies for northern conditions, infrastructure, environmental protection, and human resources.[27] Twenty northern leaders— including the heads of five separate regions within Russia, Hokkaido in Japan, and Heilongjiang Province in China, as well as the more familiar northern political units of Alaska, the Yukon, the Northwest Territories, Greenland, and Fennoscandia—joined forces in forming the Northern Forum. No doubt, it would be premature to make assertions about the significance of this fledgling organization. But its development will be of interest to many, not only because it reflects a growing desire to break out of the segmentation associated with core/periphery relations in the Far North but also because it is part of a much broader trend in international society, in which subnational governments are increasingly endeavoring to conduct foreign relations of their own rather than acknowledging the exclusive authority of central governments in the area of international affairs.

A variety of nonstate actors also have contributed to the breakdown of core/periphery relations in the Arctic. Two such groups stand out as objects of attention in this connection: indigenous peoples' organizations and multinational corporations. Though small in number, the indigenous peoples of the Arctic have exhibited a remarkable flair for forging transnational alliances in the interests of promoting their cause in dealings with policymakers located within the various Arctic states. For some years, the Inuit Circumpolar Conference in the North American Arctic and the Nordic Saami Council in Fennoscandia have maintained a high profile in this regard. A striking recent development in this area involves the establishment in 1990 of the Association of the Small Peoples of the Soviet North, an organization representing twenty-six distinct indigenous groups, and the subsequent gathering in 1991 of representatives of the Inuit Circumpolar Conference, the Nordic Saami Council, and the Association of the Small Peoples of the Soviet North to take the first steps toward the creation of a pan-Arctic aboriginal association.[28] Under the best of circumstances, the position of the indigenous peoples of the Arctic, approached in terms of the conventional bases of power (for example, financial resources or political influence), is weak. Yet the growing sophistication of these peoples in articulating their vision of the region coincides to a remarkable degree with the emergence of the Far North as a shared resource region. It is hard to avoid the conclusion that there is some element of causation in this relationship.

A collection of multinational corporations has played an equally significant role in breaking the long-standing pattern of core/periphery relations in the Arctic.[29] Given the economic and political importance of hydrocarbons, as well as the global reach of the oil companies, it is natural to turn first to the actions of players like ARCO, British Petroleum, and Exxon in internationalizing the Arctic. These players already loom large in the political dynamics of the North American Arctic. Over the next few years, students of Arctic politics will have good reason to focus also on the fate of numerous efforts now underway to forge working relations between the multinationals and the government of Russia regarding the development of both onshore and offshore gas reserves in the Russian North. But the oil companies are not alone in encouraging the development of transnational ties affecting the Far North. For example, Cominco, a multinational corporation based in Canada but controlled by investors located in several other countries, has sizable economic stakes in Alaska, northern Canada, and Greenland. Japanese firms have large stakes in the timber and fishing industries in Alaska; they may become major players in opening up the Russian Far East as well. There can be no doubt that it is difficult to maintain the segmentation characteristic of core/periphery relations once a region becomes a focus of attention on the part of multinational corporations, which have no intention of allowing political boundaries to interfere with the formulation and implementation of their industrial and commercial plans.

The passing of colonialism offers no guarantee of the onset of an era of peace and prosperity, whether the colonial system in question is of a conventional character or is more properly construed as a case of internal colonialism. The ethnic conflicts, economic dislocations, and political struggles of many areas formerly under colonial administration are by now well known; there is no reason simply to assume that the Circumpolar North will not be touched by these concerns. Already, tensions between Natives and settlers and the debilitating effects of economic dependence are apparent in many parts of the Arctic. Undoubtedly, the drama now beginning to unfold in the Russian North will prove particularly intriguing in this regard, both because the majority of all Arctic residents live in the northern reaches of Russia and because the Soviet center dominated the northern peripheries of the Soviet Union so effectively during much of the twentieth century. In this context, also, there is much to be said for approaching the political dynamics of the Arctic as a microcosm of more generic issues now claiming our attention. Insights derived from the study of Arctic cases will prove interesting to those concerned with the impact of centrifugal economic and political forces in other parts of the world, just as students of Arctic affairs can look to other regions for ideas relevant to the creation of viable political and economic systems in a postcolonial social environment.

Cold War Paralysis

During much of the postwar era, international relations in the Arctic seemed simple and unambiguous, if not conducive to progress toward the emergence of regional cooperation. On one side stood the Soviet Union, controlling well over 40 percent of the land area and about half of the coastline of the Circumpolar North but interested in the region primarily as a defensive zone and as a base from which to launch naval forces into the North Atlantic in the event of an outbreak of war in central Europe. On the other side stood the United States, Canada, Iceland, Denmark, and Norway, closely allied as members of NATO and concerned, for the most part, with deterring any potential Soviet aggressive moves in Europe. The two neutrals, Finland and Sweden, were simply lost in the shuffle as far as the international relations of the Arctic were concerned. From this viewpoint, the Far North was a peripheral zone, coming into perspective only in connection with ancillary concerns about Europe's northern flank or with the concerns of the 1950s and 1960s about manned bombers flying over the Pole to attack the Soviet Union or North America. Certainly, there was no reason to focus on the Arctic as a political or strategic arena of interest in its own right.[30]

The situation that has emerged in the Circumpolar North in recent years, by contrast, is both less clear-cut and far more interesting. Partly, this is a consequence of the fact that the region emerged in the 1980s as an attractive deployment zone for strategic weapons systems, including nuclear-powered submarines equipped with submarine-launched ballistic missiles and high-endurance manned bombers equipped with air-launched cruise missiles. But far more significant from the point of view of the political dynamics of the Arctic as a distinctive region is the combination of the decline and eventual end of the cold war and the breakup of the Soviet Union, a sequence of events that has stimulated a striking growth of interest in experimenting with various forms of international cooperation in the Arctic.

Though major political shifts always have complex antecedents, the era of peaceful cooperation in the Circumpolar North can be dated, for all practical purposes, from a speech that Mikhail Gorbachev delivered in Murmansk on 1 October 1987. In this landmark statement, Gorbachev not only called for the establishment of an Arctic zone of peace; he also laid out in some detail a six-point program of cooperation encompassing both civil and military initiatives.[31]

The years that have elapsed since the Murmansk speech have witnessed a remarkable series of steps toward international cooperation in a region long dismissed as a sideshow caught in the grip of the cold war. Specific developments have taken the form of initiatives that are regionwide (for example, the Arctic environmental protection agreement), subregional in scope (for example, the Finnish/Norwegian/Soviet cooperative agreement on pollution problems in Fennoscandia), and bilateral in character (for example, the series of Soviet/American agreements relating to the Bering Sea area). They have covered a variety of functional concerns, from scientific research through cultural survival and environmental protection to issues touching on security. They have produced nongovernmental arrangements (for example, the International Arctic Science Committee) and cooperative agreements that are intergovernmental in nature (for example, the Arctic Monitoring and Assessment Program).[32] In some quarters, the Arctic is even seen as a promising arena in which to experiment with innovative forms of international organization (for example, Canada's proposal for an Arctic Council) that would be open to participation on the part of national governments, subnational governments, and nongovernmental entities alike.

All of this activity has transformed the Circumpolar North into a setting for intriguing and potentially important experiments involving a number of issues of great interest to those desiring to foster the growth of institutionalized cooperation in international society.[33] There is, to begin with, the issue of selecting appropriate parties to include in cooperative ventures. Partly, this is a matter of deciding whether to confine participation to the eight Arctic countries or to allow non-Arctic countries to join. In this connection, it will be particularly interesting to follow the progress of the International Arctic Science Committee, which has both a council open to scientists from all countries engaged in significant programs of Arctic research and a regional board limited to representatives of the Arctic Eight. In part, it is a matter of determining how to provide for participation on the part of nonstate actors, such as indigenous peoples organizations and environmental groups, in intergovernmental arrangements (for example, the Arctic Environmental Protection Strategy). What are the relative merits, for instance, of including representatives of these actors in national delegations, in contrast to providing some basis for them to participate as members in their own right, as envisioned in the proposed Arctic Council?[34]

A closely related concern centers on the choice of issues to serve as a focus for the development of cooperative arrangements. The logic of functionalism or neofunctionalism, which pervades much Western thinking about international cooperation, suggests that it is best to start with functionally specific and technically oriented arrangements, leaving the matter of linkages among issue areas to be dealt with as the process of spillover produces de facto connections among specific arrangements. On this account, it is particularly important to separate cooperation regarding civil issues from efforts to deal with military or security concerns on the grounds that efforts to include sensitive military matters will impede or even block progress on the civil issues.[35] Yet at Murmansk, Gorbachev called for a comprehensive program of cooperation, spanning civil and military issues, designed to transform the Arctic into a zone of peace. This attractive vision suggests that it may be worth reexamining the logic of functionalism in the aftermath of the cold war, at least with regard to the creation of cooperative management mechanisms for shared resource regions like the Arctic.

As functionally specific cooperative arrangements accumulate in the Circumpolar North, it becomes increasingly important to ask questions about the connections and possible interactions among them. In some cases, the proper relationship seems easy to identify. It makes good sense, for instance, to treat the Inter-

national Arctic Science Committee as a source of scientific information and advice for those seeking to implement the Arctic
Monitoring and Assessment Program (established under the
terms of the Arctic Environmental Protection Strategy), much as
the Scientific Committee for Antarctic Research serves as an advisory body to the various components of the Antarctic Treaty
System. But beyond this, it is far from obvious how to orchestrate
the suite of cooperative arrangements now coming on-stream in
the Far North in the interests of promoting common goals and
avoiding divisive competition. To those familiar with the recent
history of Antarctica, a comprehensive system analogous to the
Antarctic Treaty System may seem attractive for the Arctic.[36] But
it is surely appropriate to inquire whether an arrangement that
has worked well for a global commons, such as Antarctica, would
prove equally well suited to conditions prevailing in a shared resource region such as the Arctic, where the jurisdictional reach
of regional countries is extensive and where there is no prospect
of freezing relevant jurisdictional claims.

Yet another related matter concerns the form of cooperative
arrangements for the Arctic and the developmental strategy to be
employed by those responsible for fostering cooperation in this
realm. Does it make sense in the Arctic, for example, to rely on
framework conventions of the sort familiar from efforts to deal
with the Mediterranean Sea, long-range transboundary air pollution, and ozone depletion?[37] If so, what are the prospects for
devising strong framework agreements, such as the 1976 Barce-
lona Convention for the Protection of the Mediterranean Sea
Against Pollution and Its Related Protocols, in contrast to weak
framework agreements, such as the 1979 Geneva Convention on
Long-Range Transboundary Air Pollution? To judge from the process that eventuated in the June 1991 agreement among the Arctic
Eight establishing the Arctic Environmental Protection Strategy,
it will not be easy to reach consensus on cooperative arrangements for the Arctic that go beyond weak frameworks. This is not
to depreciate the potential significance of the effort to devise an
environmental protection regime for the Arctic. The 1979 Geneva
Convention, after all, triggered a process that has led in less than
fifteen years to a system for controlling transboundary fluxes of
various airborne pollutants in Europe which is beginning to show

results.[38] Even so, it is legitimate to ask whether the current flurry of cooperative initiatives relating to the Circumpolar North will carry us beyond the stage of window dressing to the emergence of effective institutions.

A final issue in this realm concerns the establishment of one or more organizations intended to administer or manage cooperative arrangements in a shared resource region such as the Arctic. There is widespread confusion regarding the distinction between regimes, or institutions, which are constellations of rules giving rise to social practices, and organizations, which are material entities.[39] Some advocates of international cooperation mistakenly assume that the main issue involves the establishment of organizations in contrast to the formation of effective regimes. But some regimes do not require much administration, and organizations are always costly (in both material and nonmaterial terms) to operate and maintain, a fact that leaves the burden of proof with those who advocate the establishment of new organizations. Even so, this does not license the conclusion that there is no room for new international or transnational organizations focusing on Arctic issues. The most interesting idea currently on the horizon in this realm is the proposed Arctic Council, which would provide an arena (at least in the eyes of its advocates) for consultations among all Arctic constituencies on a wide range of issues.[40] The plan for the council is notable for its innovative approach to issues of participation and operating procedures; it seems particularly well suited to a world in which both states and nonstate actors are expected to play roles of considerable importance. Yet the ability of such a council to manage or even oversee the accumulation of cooperative arrangements now building up in the Circumpolar North is far from clear. There is a danger, that is, that this innovative mechanism could become a mere talk shop, with few links to the administrative or managerial needs now arising in connection with institutionalized cooperation in the Far North.

It is evident from this brief review that the cold war paralysis that gripped the Arctic through much of the postwar period is a thing of the past. The vibrancy and the productivity of the initiatives that have sprung up within a few years to establish new forms of cooperation in the Circumpolar North are remarkable.

Both subregional and regional arrangements are proliferating; they offer clear evidence of the increased willingness in many quarters to conceptualize the Arctic as a shared resource region. To date, there have been fewer advances in the development of mechanisms to link the Arctic region with overarching global processes, though this has become a priority concern for a sizable group of scientists who think about the role of the Arctic or the polar regions in global change. It is possible, therefore, that the Arctic will also become a test case for efforts to devise cooperative arrangements linking international regions with global processes.

Overall, the rise of the Arctic as a region of growing interest to students of international cooperation is extraordinary. Of course, we cannot foresee the future trajectory of this development with certainty. It is far too early to predict the effects of the termination of the cold war and the breakup of the Soviet Union on the strategic significance of the Circumpolar North. And Russia has hardly begun to develop well-defined Arctic policies of its own. Even so, the fact remains that the region has made a transition from being a relatively uninteresting cold war sideshow to an arena for innovative initiatives in the realm of international cooperation in less than a decade.

Conclusion

Although the primary purpose of the preceding discussion is to set the stage for the detailed treatment of various aspects of Arctic politics in the chapters to come, two substantive conclusions stand out at this juncture. The Circumpolar North has begun to acquire an identity of its own in the minds of policymakers and scholars alike. Yet this region cannot be understood properly either as a cockpit or as an arena or global commons. Instead, it belongs to the class of shared resource regions, a category of areas that is acquiring more prominence as the attention of policymakers shifts increasingly to issues involving human/environment relations.

As this observation suggests, moreover, the Arctic is emerging today not only as a region whose political dynamics are of interest in their own right but also as a microcosm in which to study issues of generic interest to students of politics. These issues range across a wide spectrum, from the localized concerns of those seeking to protect the ways of life of indigenous peoples through the regional concerns of those struggling to solve or manage resource conflicts to the international concerns of those endeavoring to form institutional arrangements or regimes to promote common interests in a variety of issue areas.

The chapters that follow explore all of these themes. The chapters of Part One, which center on community studies, seek to illuminate the political concerns of the remote (predominantly Native) communities of the Arctic as they struggle to come to terms with economic problems and health crises and to find new ways to maintain old cultures. Part Two shifts the focus to the regional level, taking up the task of exploring issues that transcend the local level but that are not fundamentally international in character. The specific issues range across efforts to guide the human use of renewable resources, nonrenewable resources, and flow resources, as well as the allocation of proceeds derived from the use of these resources. In Part Three, which broadens the scope to the level of international studies, individual chapters deal both with specific concerns, such as the prospects for Arctic arms control and the international dimensions of sustainable development, and with more general concerns, like the prospects for sustained cooperation in the Arctic treated as a distinctive international region. Throughout the book, the overarching goal remains the same: to establish Arctic politics as a field of study that is both worthy of attention in its own right and interesting to a broader community of students of politics who will recognize opportunities to probe issues of generic interest in connection with the development of this field of study, though their own substantive concerns lie elsewhere.

PART ONE

Community Studies

Prologue

With the exception of Anchorage, Reykjavik, and the larger cities of the Russian North (such as Murmansk, with a population of about 500,000, or Norilsk, with a population of over 200,000), the human settlements of the Arctic are small, widely scattered, and remote. Regional centers (for example, Nuuk in Greenland, Iqaluit in Canada, Barrow or Bethel in Alaska, and Provideniya in the Far Eastern part of Russia) are regarded as large communities, though their populations are generally under ten thousand and, in a number of instances, under five thousand. As one would expect of communities that continue to depend on hunting and gathering activities, distances between Arctic settlements are often great; a separation of several hundred kilometers is not uncommon. Ground transportation linking these settlements is the exception rather than the rule. Typically, those wishing to travel from one Arctic community to another must proceed by sea or by air. In many cases, travelers find it necessary to go south to transportation centers, such as Anchorage or Edmonton, in order to make their way from one northern community to another.

Through much of this century, the fate of the human settlements of the Circumpolar North has been in the hands of governments reflecting different attitudes toward the organization of production and the fulfillment of human needs. At the extremes are the resolutely capitalist perspectives and policies underlying American administration in Alaska and the socialist practices of Soviet administration throughout the northern regions of Russia.

In between are the welfare state systems that the Nordic countries have put in place in Fennoscandia and Greenland and the welfare capitalism of the Canadian administration of the Yukon and the Northwest Territories. There is no doubt that these differences in national policies and practices have left their mark on the human settlements of the Circumpolar North.

Nonetheless, the similarities among these small, remote communities are striking. This is especially true of the common problems they face in coping with an array of contemporary threats to their socioeconomic viability and cultural vitality. They all suffer from their status as subordinate partners in core/periphery or metropole/hinterland relationships. They all face the problem of maintaining cultural integrity in an era in which self-sufficiency based on traditional subsistence practices is no longer a workable proposition. They all confront constraints arising from the ravages of individual pathologies associated with anomic and dependent behavior.

Nor are these parallels confined to the Arctic; analogous problems have arisen in remote and predominantly indigenous communities scattered around the globe. Reports from Amazonia, Central America, and the countries of the South Pacific, for example, bear a striking resemblance to observations made in the Far North. Under the circumstances, there is much to be said for introducing the concept of the "Fourth World," which is now voiced with increasing frequency to describe the circumstances of remote, predominantly indigenous communities locked into overarching societies they can never hope to control. Although it is undoubtedly important not to overlook the unique characteristics of the small communities scattered throughout the Arctic, it is equally important to realize that these communities are members of a larger universe of cases so that findings derived from analyses of individual members of this universe may be of value in illuminating the circumstances of a broader, more encompassing set of cases.

Part One seeks to highlight the problems and prospects of the Arctic's small communities. It begins with a chapter applying the concept of core/periphery relations, or internal colonialism, to the Circumpolar North. Developed initially as a device for interpreting the problems of fringe areas in Europe, such as Wales in relation to England, the idea of internal colonialism is a powerful one when applied to the Far North. The picture it portrays is, in many ways, a harsh one. It not only lays the basis for an indictment of the policies and practices of southern decision makers and administrators who have dealt with northern issues, but it also suggests somewhat pessimistic conclusions about the prospects facing the inhabitants of northern communities during the foreseeable future.

Suggestive as the image of internal colonialism is, there is a sense in which this image is too stark, crowding out or de-emphasizing a number of northern realities as well as attributes of individual communities that deserve attention in any balanced assessment of the circumstances facing northern communities today. The remaining chapters of this part of the book, therefore, seek to flesh out and adjust this picture, not by rejecting the fundamental image of internal colonialism but rather by breaking the problem down and adopting a more pragmatic approach to specific issues.

Chapter 2 deals with the mixed (subsistence and cash) economies that are now in place throughout the Circumpolar North; it examines the relative merits of a number of policy initiatives that might strengthen these economic systems and insulate them, at least in part, from the boom/bust cycles that have predominated throughout the modern history of the Far North. Chapter 3 turns to issues of health and health care delivery in the remote communities of the Circumpolar North. It argues that there is a critical need to allow northerners to play a larger role in operating health care delivery systems and, in the process, take charge of their own health and welfare. Chapter 4 shifts gears and turns to an analysis of the determinants of viability for communities of hunter/gatherers in cases where such communities are embedded in encompassing industrialized societies that hunter/gatherers cannot hope to control. These constitute the norm rather than the exception today. Building on the initial identification of key determinants, the chapter seeks to devise a strategy for hunter/gatherers desiring to protect and maintain the essential features of their way of life.

CHAPTER 1

Internal Colonialism or Self-Sufficiency?
Problems and Prospects in the Circumpolar North

The villages of the Circumpolar North suffer from serious social problems.[1] More often than not, individual communities appear to have lost control of their own destiny; many of them lack both the capability and the will to regain that control. This chapter sets forth a broad diagnosis of this state of affairs, explains how it came to pass, and explores strategies for the future development of these communities that would enable them to overcome their current problems. The chapters that follow present more detailed accounts of particular aspects of this overarching state of affairs.

The Circumpolar North is a homeland for a variety of indigenous cultures: Inuit, Dene, Saami, Chukchi, Komi, Evenki, Nenets, and others. Given this variety, there is a danger of overgeneralization in claiming that a cross-culturally valid pattern of social pathologies can be identified. Nonetheless, it would be

The original version of this chapter, written with John S. Dryzek, appeared in Robert S. Merrill and Dorothy Willner, eds., *Conflict and the Common Good*, Publication no. 24 in Studies in Third World Societies (Williamsburg, Va.: College of William and Mary, 1983), 115–34. The decade elapsing since the preparation of the original version brought a number of developments that have ameliorated the dominance of core/periphery relations in the Circumpolar North and, in the process, blunted the force of internal colonialism as an explanatory device. Nonetheless, the model of internal colonialism remains a critical benchmark against which to measure socioeconomic and political developments in the Arctic and other parts of the fourth world.

hard to deny that something is extremely wrong with many remote communities throughout the Far North; indicators of their unfortunate condition abound. The rate of emigration from northern communities is often high, and many of the emigrants are among the more able and ambitious rather than the more marginal members of these communities. The combined effects of emigration and high birthrates have left many Arctic communities with a population whose median age is eighteen or under. Levels of unemployment and underemployment are high, in some cases affecting the majority of the adult population during certain seasons of the year. The dramatic rise in felt needs experienced in recent years, a development fueled by increased contact with affluent southern societies and exacerbated by the introduction of television, has done much to bring about a decline in traditional authority structures, with an inevitable concurrent rise in intergenerational conflict.

To make matters worse, northern communities are increasingly faced with financial pressures, even the threat of outright insolvency. Rising demands for services (for example, health and education), coupled with a wholly inadequate tax base, have gone far toward making their residents wards of the state. The results of this combination of difficulties are manifested in high rates of individual pathologies, including alcoholism, suicide, homicide, and various forms of mental illness. All of this has given rise to resentment and hostility directed toward outsiders, especially those identified with dominant southern societies. Understandably, these sentiments are particularly pervasive among Natives who have long suffered from attitudes of racial superiority and discrimination.

Despite the weight of this empirical evidence, some will still argue that any talk of "pathologies" is value-laden and culture-bound. Behavior that we in Western society might recognize as symptomatic of alcoholism may be perfectly acceptable in an Inuit community. Whites may prefer to lie drunk in their homes, whereas Inuit will lie drunk in the street. Introducing the idea of pathologies implies some notion as to what constitutes health. But, in the same way that physicians can identify physiological pathologies without being able to define health, there comes a point at which the overwhelming weight of evidence suggests that there is something seriously amiss in these communities. What is more, some of the more eloquent testimony about the extent of their social pathologies comes from members of the affected communities themselves.[2] These observations can hardly by dismissed as the misguided perceptions of outsiders. It would require an extraordinary display of sangfroid to deny that the conditions under consideration have reached crisis proportions in many parts of the Circumpolar North.

The picture, then, is not a pretty one. Moreover, there are few signs of progress toward solutions in most of the communities of the region. How can we explain the emergence of these conditions, and what can be done to alleviate them? This chapter argues that the conditions outlined above and their causes are best understood in the context of the concept of internal colonialism, a phenomenon that has arisen in one form or another in many parts of the world.[3] It follows that solutions will necessarily require the development of means to ameliorate the impacts of internal colonialism.

Internal Colonialism and Economic Dependence

Perhaps the most obvious element in the pattern of internal colonialism is the extraordinary degree of economic dependence that characterizes many of the communities of the Circumpolar North. Of course, few communities in the modern world are completely self-sufficient or independent of outside forces. But interdependence is not the same as dependence. Dependence implies an asymmetrical relationship, as, for example, when a northern community comes to rely on the fur trade for its survival. The fur trade could exist without northern communities; indeed, the world would be affected but little by the disappearance of the fur trade. Yet the community in question will survive or perish according to what happens to the market for furs. In this vein, dependence may be thought of as a situation in which the key decisions affecting the welfare of a community (or other social entity) are under the control of forces external to the community and outside the scope of its influence by virtue of external control of economic resources. In other words, internal colonialism arises from a structural relationship, as opposed to psychological dependence. Even so, a widespread mentality of dependence is one outgrowth of this structural relationship.

In some cases, the sources of dependence can be traced back over several hundred years to early contacts with Europeans. The Aleut villages of the Pribilofs, for example, were originally established and operated by Russian fur traders for their own benefit.[4] More often, however, extreme cases of economic dependence are an outgrowth of social transformations taking place during the twentieth century.[5]

The onset of economic dependence is traceable to sharp changes in the traditional subsistence life-style of northern indigenous peoples.[6] This life-style, though primitive in Western economic terms, provided for the basic needs of life without any reliance at all on outside contacts. In modern times, two striking developments have had profound effects on subsistence as a complex social institution. In the first instance, it is important to recognize the role of European (and, subsequently, Canadian and American) entrepreneurs in stimulating the emergence of an export trade in furs. Although the fur trade arose at different times in various parts of the Circumpolar North, its effects have been remarkably similar throughout the region.[7] This trade diverts attention from subsistence activities as such and inevitably promotes the rise of a cash economy. It leads to the establishment of trading posts, which typically become focal points of permanent settlements and gradually undermine the seminomadic pattern of life common among Native groups in the precontact era. Efforts to maximize the harvest of a cash crop (that is, furs) not only lead to radical changes in orientations toward nature, they also stimulate felt needs for goods available only from outsiders (for example, guns and Western clothing). Above all, the fur trade has generally been both highly volatile and subject to the control of a few large trading companies (for example, the Hudson's Bay Company). Under the circumstances, once the residents of villages in the Circumpolar North get caught up in the fur trade, they quickly become dependent on outside actors who often have the power to determine whether they survive of perish.[8]

Equally important is the capital intensification of subsistence activities. The past several decades have witnessed a marked trend toward reliance on guns, outboard motors, snow machines, and the like in connection with subsistence hunting and gathering.[9] Of course, this enhances the growth of the cash economy. Further, it sets in motion additional sources of economic dependence. Capital intensification permits increased harvests. This, in turn, encourages the depletion of local stocks of animals, making it necessary to go farther afield in order to maintain an adequate harvest. This leads to a demand for even more advanced technologies, hence tighter links with outside suppliers and the cash economy more generally.

Additionally, the growth of the cash economy gives rise to an increasing emphasis on town life, as opposed to bush or country life, and, over time, a gradual attrition of subsistence attitudes and skills. Once underway, this sequence of events rapidly becomes irreversible.[10] Despite some of the nostalgic arguments heard today, it is simply impossible to turn the clock back once social change has produced growing towns, a cash economy, and vocal demands for public services, wage employment, and Western education. The capital intensification of subsistence activities is, then, part of a chain of events undermining the traditional autonomous subsistence life-style but failing to yield any new basis for achieving economic self-sufficiency. Certainly, subsistence as an economic activity remains important in many parts of the Circumpolar North; the point is that the way of life associated with subsistence is no longer viable.

Given these declines in the traditional subsistence life-style, what are the economic alternatives for northern communities? Neither agriculture nor most forms of manufacturing offer much potential. With few exceptions, agriculture is ruled out by the climate of the Circumpolar North. Boreal forest and tundra ecosystems are simply not hospitable to agricultural activities of the sort with which we are familiar in the temperate zones. The restrictions on manufacturing are somewhat more complex but hardly less severe.[11] Local materials are not, in general, plentiful. Large markets are remote, and local markets for most manufactured goods are tiny. Transportation costs are unusually high. Northern communities are ordinarily lacking in many forms of social infrastructure (for example, harbors, road networks, reliable telephone systems) required for manufacturing activities. And the cost of labor is typically high, despite the presence of numerous unemployed workers. All-in-all, therefore, it would be unrealistic to expect agriculture or manufacturing to provide a sound economic base for most of the small communities of the Circumpolar North.[12]

What this leaves for the majority of these communities is an emphasis on the exploitation of natural resources. The Circumpolar North is unusually rich in both renewable and nonrenewable resources.[13] These include, most notably, hydrocarbons, hard minerals, timber, fish, and marine mammals. Moreover, the demand for natural resources in advanced industrial societies is great. Added to this are rising fears concerning resource scarcity, which serve to make the natural resources of the Far North even more attractive to industrialized southern societies. Industrialized countries, such as the United States, Canada, and Russia, also find these resources attractive in geopolitical terms because of the relative ease of securing control over their northern regions. Under the circumstances, it is a safe bet that demands for the natural resources of the Circumpolar North will continue to grow during the foreseeable future. But this holds little promise of an escape from economic dependence for the Arctic's remote communities. On the contrary, there are good reasons to expect the exploitation of natural resources in the region to perpetuate and exacerbate extreme forms of dependence.

To begin with, management authority over these resources typically rests with outsiders, whether governments or private interests, who exhibit no special sensitivity to local concerns in their decision making.[14] The American case is instructive, though hardly unique, in this respect. The federal government controls all of the offshore hydrocarbons and marine mammals adjacent to Alaska, most of the major fisheries of the region, the bulk of the area's hard minerals, and the lion's share of Alaska's timber resources. The remaining natural resources are, more often than not, subject to management by the government of the state of Alaska. Even where title to natural resources has been transferred to Native peoples under the terms of the Alaska Native Claims Settlement Act, the major decisions are apt to be made by officials of regional corporations, who have little contact with the residents of the communities located in areas where the resources themselves lie. What emerges, then, is a pattern in which the small communities of the region are thoroughly dependent on the actions of outsiders with respect to major decisions affecting their economic welfare.[15]

To make matters worse, the exploitation of natural resources in these areas ordinarily requires the development of forms of infrastructure that can be planned and supplied only by outsiders. To illustrate, the village of St. Paul cannot establish a serious bottom fishery in the absence of a boat harbor. But the U.S. Army Corps of Engineers exercises control over the development of facilities of this sort.[16] Similarly, the coal located in Northwestern Alaska will never become commercially valuable unless a transportation network is developed; this can be done only under the aegis of the federal government or the state of Alaska. This is not to suggest that any particular project along these lines is desirable but simply to illustrate another major source of economic dependence for small northern communities, which typically lack the resources to initiate projects of this magnitude.

Adding to these difficulties are capital requirements for natural resource development in the Far North, which are generally far beyond the capabilities of local enterprises. This is obvious in the case of oil and gas development. But it is worth emphasizing that the capital requirements of a modern fishery or timber industry are also large and well in excess of available capital in the communities of the Circumpolar North. Various responses to this difficulty are conceivable. The prospects for joint ventures with outside groups having access to capital may be explored. However, such ventures are apt to produce problems of their own. Outside investors are more likely to be driven by the search for tax advantages than by any concern for community well-being. Such investors are skilled in financial planning and management; hence, they typically seek to dominate decision making in joint ventures. The Native regional corporations in Alaska are large enough to take an interest in natural resource development, but their capital is by no means unlimited, and their managers are often relatively uninterested in the problems of small communities. Certainly, we should not rule out a careful consideration of projects emphasizing appropriate technology and small-scale operations.[17] Nevertheless, the size of the capital requirements for natural resource exploitation in the Far North is another factor contributing to economic dependence. Those in possession of the capital will ordinarily call the shots, and there is little reason to suppose that they will exhibit any special concern for local autonomy or sociocultural integrity.

A further factor contributing to dependence arises from an unexpected quarter: environmental groups. Some of these groups have regularly pushed policies that have heightened the problems of northern communities. A dramatic case in point involves the management of marine mammals. In many areas, a small, well-managed commercial harvest of marine mammals could sustain a local industry without causing any significant depletion of animal stocks.[18] Yet environmentalists have often opposed such practices as a matter of general policy.[19] Similar comments are in order with respect to mining on publicly owned lands, which could be restricted to small operations under the control of local enterprises. From the vantage point of many communities in the Circumpolar North, then, government, big business, and the environmental movement constitute a de facto alliance to perpetuate dependence. All of these groups are made up of distant and alien outsiders with their own interests to pursue and with little regard for the needs of local communities. All are resolutely opposed to transferring management authority over the resources in question to those residing in these communities.

All of these sources of economic dependence are exacerbated by pronounced fluctuations in levels of activity that are characteristic of natural resource exploitation. These fluctuations take the form of boom/bust cycles. In the case of renewable resources, they can result either from the volatility of natural systems or from fluctuations in demand for various products. In earlier times this was a striking feature of the export trade in furs, as many northern communities discovered to their sorrow.[20] Such fluctuations are common today in the timber industry and the fisheries. The demand for wood products is closely tied to fluctuations in national economies. Bad years follow good years in the salmon fisheries. Boom/bust cycles in nonrenewable resource exploitation are both more predictable and more severe.[21] Typically, development commences with a large influx of labor and cash coupled with extensive capital construction. The level of activity falls off as the construction phase is completed and eventually winds down as the resource is exhausted. Jobs simply disappear as pipelines, tank farms, and other projects are completed. This is hardly a recipe for the development of stable and self-sufficient communities; industries based on the exploitation of natural resources are unlikely to offer steady employment or a secure financial base. A more likely result is to add to welfare problems that small communities are ill-equipped to handle.[22]

Some of the problems outlined in the preceding discussion have been offset by the rise of the welfare state during the postwar period. National governments have assumed increasing responsibilities for health, education, and welfare in the communities of the Circumpolar North, just as they have in dependent communities located in metropolitan regions.[23] This development has ameliorated some of the most severe immediate problems afflicting these communities. To illustrate, the incidence of tuberculosis has declined markedly in rural Alaska, and food stamps have found their way even to the most remote settlements. However, welfare and public assistance also accentuate the dependence of northern communities by making them still more subject to the favors and whims of outsiders.[24] Indeed, decision makers in national agencies can exercise extraordinary control over specific communities by threatening to cut off or promising to extend various forms of assistance.

In addition, the extension of public assistance serves to divert attention away from the pursuit of local self-sufficiency. Able individuals in the remote communities may become expert in obtaining grants from government agencies, but they do not acquire any great skill in the development and management of economic activities that would offer hope for the achievement of self-sufficiency. Overall, then, public assistance generates attitudes of dependence, stimulates individual pathologies, and breeds resentments directed with particular force toward outsiders.[25] The result in many settlements is a demoralized and alienated population, thoroughly dependent on the national government but increasingly resentful of its plight. Ironically, this situation is traceable in many cases to the efforts of people genuinely concerned about the problems of disadvantaged peoples.

Local Political Institutions

As a consequence of this economic order, it is exceedingly difficult to foster the development of local political institutions capable of articulating clear conceptions of the community interest and cultivating a strong sense of social solidarity. Consequently, there is a deficiency in political institutions able to enhance the ability of local residents to control their own destiny and to pursue sociopolitical autonomy. The decentralized subsistence life-style of earlier times minimized the need for institutions designed to handle collective or group needs. Subsistence practices traditionally centered on the activities of a small number of (often related) families, so that "few issues of consequence had to be faced or decided upon by the group as a whole."[26] Life was seminomadic; there was no reason for an elaborate division of labor, and self-sufficiency was taken for granted. For the most part, human settlements in the Circumpolar North were small and seldom permanent. The emergence of permanent settlements is traceable largely to the establishment of trading posts and to various concerns projected by dominant southern societies (for example, the need for fixed sites to facilitate the administration of health, education, and welfare). In short, most of the communities of the Circumpolar North lack a history of experience with the creation and operation of local institutions of the sort required to promote sociopolitical autonomy under contemporary conditions.[27]

Equally important, however, is the fact that dominant southern societies have done little to encourage the development of effective local institutions. On the contrary, they have frequently contributed to cynicism by paying lip service to the promotion of local autonomy or home rule while systematically withholding the authority or the resources that real progress toward this goal would require. To illustrate, consider the case of St. Paul, Alaska, a village that is better off than others in the Circumpolar North in many ways.[28] The U.S. Fur Seal Act of 1966 (as amended in 1983) lays down the pursuit of local autonomy as an explicit goal of public policy, and some steps have been taken under the terms of this mandate to turn over responsibility for various services to the municipality of St. Paul. But what are the real prospects for

St. Paul? The U.S. federal government has not only exercised control over the community's traditional industry, the commercial harvest of fur seals, but it also acted to terminate this harvest in the 1980s irrespective of local concerns.[29] The leading public issue in St. Paul recently centered on the idea of installing a boat harbor, but the fact that decisions in this area are in the hands of the U.S. Army Corps of Engineers truncated local debate concerning the issue. Oil and gas development in the St. George Basin or the Navarin Basin could have far-reaching impacts on St. Paul in the 1990s, but the basic policy choices in this realm will be made by officials in Washington, D.C., who are poorly informed about St. Paul and have little interest in the fate of the community. St. Paul is incorporated as a city under the laws of the state of Alaska, but it has no significant tax base and is subject to severe restrictions on its taxing powers in any case. The federal government has turned over functions such as the maintenance of roads and the airport to local officials, but these are carried out under contracts with the federal government, which provides the necessary funds and could, of course, cut off funding as a result of dissatisfaction with the performance of local officials. The federal government also retains direct control over the most critical community services, such as the generation and distribution of electrical power.[30] This is hardly the record of an outside agency anxious to promote the development of effective local institutions or a sound basis for economic self-sufficiency. It should come as no surprise, therefore, that the most able members of the community typically do not focus their attention on the municipal council and that some of them have chosen to pursue careers requiring that they leave St. Paul altogether.

Another problem characteristic of the communities of the Circumpolar North is the fragmentation of authority among competing groups. For the most part, this problem has arisen through the overlay of new authority patterns on the preexisting authority structures of traditional society. Under the decentralized arrangements characteristic of the subsistence life-style, elders (or religious leaders) and leading hunters shared authority in a relatively unambiguous fashion.[31] With the rise of permanent settlements, village councils or local governments have come into existence all over the region. But this has not led to the elimination of traditional authority structures, a fact that has produced both confusion and a good deal of conflict. More recently, additional sources of fragmentation have arisen; again, the Alaskan case is illustrative. Village corporations have been established throughout Alaska under the terms of the Alaska Native Claims Settlement Act. Though these corporations are private, for-profit enterprises in legal terms, they have taken on the role of competing repositories of authority in many villages. There are several reasons for this development.[32] All of the members of the individual villages (at least those born prior to 18 December 1971) are shareholders in these corporations. For the moment, the corporations have access to greater resources than do village councils. The more energetic members of many villages have chosen to devote their time to running the village corporation rather than the village council. The upshot is another layer of authority operating concurrently with existing layers.

This fragmentation has promoted rising levels of confusion. There are cases in which a particularly powerful individual has attempted to solidify control over his constituency by dominating the village council and the village corporation simultaneously. More often, however, competing leaders (including members of the same family in certain notable cases) use these several institutions as power bases in a fashion that precludes the emergence of consensus concerning conceptions of the public interest or the common good. And there are communities where traditional leaders (for example, whaling captains) are still capable of exercising authority effectively. Under the circumstances, there is little movement toward the articulation of new ideas on which to base a drive toward community integration. Conditions of this sort hardly constitute a sound basis for overcoming the extreme forms of economic dependence discussed in the preceding section.

Equally disturbing is the fact that this lack of effective local institutions contributes to what might best be described as a mentality of dependence, especially among Native peoples.[33] Many individuals, faced with the erosion of traditional authority structures, together with an inability to control their own destiny, make psychological adjustments to what they perceive as an unalterable environment. In subtle ways, such adjustments are reg-

ularly encouraged by members of dominant groups, for whom
this process is an efficient method of maintaining control over
subordinate people. Extreme examples of this phenomenon are
well known in connection with slavery. But somewhat milder versions are common when specific groups of people remain highly
dependent on superordinate groups over long periods of time.
The resultant mentality of dependence does not disappear overnight in the wake of formal changes in relationships between
these groups. Vestiges of the mentality often linger for a long
time, especially in a social environment characterized by substantial elements of de facto control on the part of outsiders and
by the fragmentation of local authority structures.³⁴ This serves
as an impediment to the acquisition of the self-esteem and new
skills needed to develop both local institutions and a sound basis
for economic self-sufficiency.

To close the circle, the conditions under consideration here are
frequently exacerbated by problems of alienation and emigration.
In many communities there are deep splits between (usually
younger) individuals who have been educated outside, have urban tastes, aspire to assimilation, and are willing to sacrifice traditional ways of life to achieve this goal and (usually older)
individuals who would like to reestablish local autonomy and cultural integrity on the basis of traditional practices. This is often a
recipe for confrontation.³⁵ The younger modernizers, who are seldom accepted without reservation by members of the dominant
southern societies, often succeed in alienating many members of
their own communities as they attempt to instigate major changes
upon their return from several years of education outside. Ultimately, they are apt to fall between two stools, with the result
that either they emigrate permanently, taking their talents with
them, or they remain in the community, only to become increasingly bitter and resentful with the passage of time.

For their part, the older traditionalists are engaged in a battle
they cannot win. Social transformation has gone too far in most
villages of the Circumpolar North to permit a return to older ways
and the traditional subsistence life-style. Further, the traditionalists are not skilled in dealing with government agencies and
corporate structures, activities that cannot be avoided today. The
results of these confrontations are not only destructive to indi-

viduals, but they also serve to produce a severe loss of energy and direction for communities. It is as though many communities have reached an internal stalemate that makes it impossible for them to move forward or backward in the development of coherent local initiatives, even though they are often severely buffeted by forces of change generated outside. Understandably, this combination of circumstances exacerbates the social and individual pathologies referred to at the beginning of this chapter.[36] What it has not done so far is to engender any movement of a sort that would permit these communities to break the grip of internal colonialism.

Crisis and Response

The conditions described in the preceding sections are severe and debilitating. Although the total population of the region is relatively small (only a fraction of 1 percent of the Earth's population is resident in the Circumpolar North), the human tragedy embedded in these conditions is profound. Perhaps the most troublesome feature of this situation is the extent to which it exhibits the characteristics of a vicious circle. Extreme forms of economic dependence constitute a major source of the inability to develop autonomous and effective local institutions; the underdeveloped and fragmented state of these institutions serves, in turn, to perpetuate economic dependence. The result is a self-reinforcing cycle of problems that often seems virtually impossible to break. Sometimes, the efforts of those who are strongly motivated to break this cycle only make matters worse. It is this vicious circle, rather than its component elements, that is the real core of internal colonialism.

Many individuals in the dominant southern societies exhibit well-meaning (though often ill-informed) attitudes toward the communities of the Far North and would happily go along with efforts to alleviate the problems of these communities. Despite this, internal colonialism remains a predictable consequence of the contact between affluent industrialized societies with a largely uncontrollable need for raw materials and small communities in a region that is sparsely populated but unusually rich in natural resources. The dominant southern societies, whether

capitalist or socialist, cannot control their appetite for natural resources, and the northern communities cannot acquire an effective voice in policy-making processes. If we add to this an element
of racism arising from the fact that a large proportion of the population of the Far North consists of indigenous peoples, it is
hardly surprising that internal colonialism flourishes.[37]

The social and individual pathologies outlined in this chapter
have reached crisis proportions in many communities of the Circumpolar North.[38] What steps might be taken, then, to alleviate
the vicious circle of internal colonialism? Given the argument of
the preceding paragraph, the resultant problem is a peculiarly
puzzling one, even for those with a genuine desire to help. As a
way of exploring the dimensions of this problem, it may help to
comment briefly on the reasons that the most common responses
of southern societies to the difficulties of northern communities
leave a lot to be desired.

These responses fall into four categories. There is, to begin
with, the policy of encouraging assimilation on the part of northern peoples. In the case of indigenous peoples, this means making individual Natives into good whites through education or
exposure to white attitudes and values. For others, it means inducing individuals to adopt the approved life-style of affluent
southern societies. Policies of this type have generally yielded unfortunate results.[39] Above all, they have produced individuals
who are neither fish nor fowl in the sense that they never really
achieve a southern life-style even though they are no longer capable of living comfortably in the small communities of the Far
North. Additionally, assimilationist policies are based on radical
misconceptions of both the natural environment and the socioeconomic conditions prevailing in the region. These circumstances are simply not compatible with efforts to reproduce the
affluent urban life-style of southern societies on a small scale. It
should come as no surprise, therefore, that policies of this sort
have exacerbated rather than ameliorated the problems of small
communities in the Far North.

Equally unfortunate results have attended policies characterized by the provision of welfare coupled with a broader posture
of benign neglect. This approach has enjoyed considerable currency in the United States, but the results have been no better in

the small communities of Alaska than they have been in the urban ghettos of the lower forty-eight. Such policies do nothing to overcome extreme forms of economic dependence, and they often produce drastic consequences in terms of the loss of individual self-esteem, disruption of family units, and the growth of hostility directed toward outsiders.[40] These reactions are accentuated by the fact that dominant southern societies are not content to isolate these communities and ignore them. Rather, there are powerful pressures to exploit the natural resources of the region, even while maintaining a posture of benign neglect toward the indigenous peoples. It is too much to expect local residents to refrain from drawing unflattering inferences about the intentions of dominant southern societies from this combination of circumstances.

Somewhat more enlightened policies toward the communities of the Far North feature efforts to promote political autonomy through the establishment of home rule arrangements. But such policies become shams when they are not accompanied by serious efforts to provide a reasonable basis for economic self-sufficiency and when home rule is coupled with arrangements that ensure a continuation of de facto economic dependence. The results are even worse when the idea of promoting political autonomy is combined with continuing outside control over the principal resources of communities. Under these conditions, the more energetic members of these communities cannot fail to experience rising levels of frustration, and many of them will be afflicted by a growing sense of failure as they witness the continuing deterioration of their communities despite the appearance of local autonomy. Developments along these lines make it hard for local leaders to explain their failures by pointing to political as well as economic dependence on outsiders. The Danish policy of promoting home rule in Greenland should certainly be carefully assessed from the point of view of the concerns articulated in this paragraph. For example, although Denmark has turned over many functions to the Greenland Home Rule, the continuing dependence of this government on sizable transfer payments from Denmark is surely a source of concern.

A particularly complex set of difficulties can be traced to policies of land claims settlements, as exemplified by the Alaska

Native Claims Settlement Act of 1971 and the James Bay and Northern Quebec Agreement of 1975.[41] On the surface, at least, the Alaska settlement appears to constitute a reasonable response to the claims of Native peoples and to go some way toward providing them with the resources necessary to achieve economic self-sufficiency. Yet it is increasingly apparent that this response, too, has contributed to the problems of village Alaska.[42] The bulk of the resources flowing from the settlement end up in the hands of the regional corporations, large for-profit ventures that have failed to exhibit much sensitivity to the problems of small communities. There are restrictions on the funds going to both regional and village corporations that make it hard to use them in dealing with problems of health, welfare, and social infrastructure. The creation of the regional corporations initiated a brain drain from small communities, further impoverishing them in terms of human resources. As already indicated, the establishment of corporations has contributed to the fragmentation of authority structures in many communities. Far from ensuring the financial solvency of their communities, many of the village corporations failed to obtain sufficient financial resources to capitalize their own continued operation, with the result that a number of them have become moribund or have had to file for bankruptcy during the years since their creation in 1972.[43] But above all, the Alaska settlement contains provisions that exert pressure on indigenous people to embrace the capitalist system of contemporary America. Though some individual Natives have adjusted to this mold with considerable success, it has proved a source of new problems in many communities.[44] There is a sense, therefore, in which this settlement has promoted assimilation with a vengeance. Predictably, the consequences in many communities are beginning to look like exaggerated forms of the results of more traditional assimilationist policies.

Given the failure of these four categories of policies, is it possible to come up with a better response to the crisis conditions facing many northern communities? Though there is no magic formula, the following paragraphs outline the elements of what may be a realistic approach. Any successful response must rest on the following postulates. There is no going back to the traditional subsistence life-style of earlier times. The Circumpolar

North as an anthropological museum is both infeasible and un-attractive. Any real progress must involve a large element of self-help. Even with the best will in the world, outsiders cannot substitute for the emergence of local political and entrepreneurial skills. Outside intervention will be predisposed to failure precisely because it is from the outside, hence insensitive to local circumstances. By the same token, however, the pathologies of these communities can never be overcome so long as outsiders continue to control most of the important decisions affecting individual communities and refuse to turn over effective control to them.

The results of sharing or even devolving authority in this realm might prove painful to influential groups in the dominant southern societies. The people of Kaktovik might reject offshore oil and gas development in their immediate vicinity, regardless of its commercial potential. The residents of Gambell or Wainwright might develop ideas about the management of marine mammals that conflict with those of biologists as well as of environmentalists. The affected communities in southern Greenland might exhibit little interest in exploiting uranium deposits, even if this development seems critical to Danes and others worried about fossil fuel shortages. Nevertheless, the only alternative to local control is to perpetuate conditions in which northern peoples are wards of the state, with all of the moral as well as economic burdens associated with such a policy. Though there are reasons to doubt the willingness of southern societies to provide northern communities with a fair opportunity to escape the bonds of internal colonialism, the prospects for these communities will continue to be bleak in the absence of some such opportunity.

Assuming such an opportunity does arrive, however, the key to solving the problems of these communities lies in the pursuit of economic self-sufficiency. Self-sufficiency does not mean the capacity of a community to survive in isolation from the rest of the world. Of course, subsistence economies, in which there was practically no trade with outsiders, were self-sufficient. And there are advocates of autarky for northern peoples today: some of the proponents of an autonomous "Dene Nation" in Canada's Northwest Territories in the 1970s and 1980s suggested just this.[45] But, as already indicated, there is simply no returning to the traditional subsistence life-style that autarky would necessitate. Economic self-sufficiency should therefore be conceived of as a situation in which a community is capable of satisfying the basic needs of its members through a combination of local production for local use and imports financed by exports. Self-sufficiency in this sense eliminates the need to depend on transfer payments, in such forms as welfare, from outsiders and reduces the control of remote actors over key decisions affecting the community and its members.

More specifically, self-sufficiency would require the development of small-scale industries, relying on appropriate technologies and using local materials wherever possible.[46] Renewable resource development, as advocated by Canada's Berger Commission and others, could contribute to a strategy for the attainment of self-sufficiency for some communities. But it is not obvious that embracing this as a central postulate makes sense.[47] It is remarkably easy to deplete renewable resources, especially given the slow rate of recovery of many natural systems in the Far North and the widespread availability of efficient harvesting technologies.

The critical tests to apply to any economic activity contemplated should be, first, that it is capable of being carried out under local control and, second, that it can become viable at a small scale of operations. Given these constraints, cottage industries, some uses of renewable resources, subsistence hunting and fishing, agriculture, and even some types of nonrenewable resource development could contribute to the strategy. Diversification of economic activities would cushion communities against the effects of boom/bust cycles affecting any one activity. The preferred mix of activities would be expected to vary according to local conditions and potential. Beyond this, investments in social infrastructure geared to small-scale industries and the creation of local markets would be desirable. The guiding principle should be to import only what cannot be produced locally; this would reduce dependence on outside decision makers.

Along with the promotion of economic self-sufficiency, the renewal of local cultures possessing genuine integrity is critical. Policies of assimilation do not constitute a viable option. At the same time, however, cultural disintegration combined with the rise of individual pathologies could well undermine efforts to achieve self-sufficiency, even if an opportunity to escape the bonds of internal colonialism should arise.[48] What is needed, then, is a cultural renaissance that stresses traditional values but that is forward-looking rather than constituting a form of nostalgia for a past that cannot be recaptured. As the authors of *Letters to Howard* put it: "We don't want to become better white men or beat them at their own game. We just want a chance to develop our traditional values into a satisfying way of life that we can understand."[49] To the extent that some such cultural renaissance can be coupled with a drive toward economic self-sufficiency, the vicious circle of internal colonialism can be reversed. As is the case with individual development, community development commonly takes the form of a self-reinforcing spiral: economic self-sufficiency and cultural renewal can progress together and reinforce one another. Additionally, each of these achievements would contribute substantially to the emergence of local institutions capable of articulating clear conceptions of the public interest and enhancing prospects for success in the promotion of sociopolitical autonomy.

CHAPTER 2

The Mixed Economies of Village Alaska:
Crisis and Response

A creeping economic crisis is threatening the welfare of many of Alaska's remote (predominantly Native) communities. Transfers of fishing permits to nonresidents have resulted in a loss of income from commercial fishing in some communities; depressed timber markets have undermined economic well-being in others. Sharp reductions in expenditures by the energy industry on efforts to locate and develop new oil fields have eliminated some local employment opportunities and curtailed the demand for locally supplied support services. A majority of the village corporations created under the terms of the Alaska Native Claims Settlement Act (ANCSA) of 1971, faced with inadequate liquid assets as well as a lack of appropriate investment opportunities, are moribund or facing bankruptcy. State assistance, in direct forms like the Municipal Assistance Program, as well as in indirect forms like state-funded capital construction programs, is declining. Both state and federal regulators have added complications by imposing more burdensome restrictions on subsistence hunting and gathering in rural Alaska.

This chapter originated as a paper prepared for presentation at a meeting of the Society for Applied Anthropology in Oaxaca, Mexico, 5–8 April 1987. Some of the factual material in the chapter reflects conditions as they were in the mid-1980s. World market prices for oil, for instance, have recovered somewhat from the low levels resulting from the crash of 1985–1986. Yet the basic issues concerning the problems of mixed economies in the small communities scattered throughout the Circumpolar North are just as pressing today as they were in 1987.

It should come as no surprise, given these conditions, that residents of the communities of village Alaska are turning to a variety of desperate measures to solve their economic problems. An illegal trade in raw walrus ivory flourishes in western Alaska. People in places like St. Lawrence Island are pillaging archaeological sites in a search for salable artifacts. Village corporations in some communities are selling or developing land that could otherwise be used for hunting and gathering in the hope of staving off bankruptcy. The governments of the North Slope Borough and of nearby communities, such as Kaktovik, support hydrocarbon development in the Arctic National Wildlife Refuge, despite the fact that such development may prove disruptive to subsistence activities in the area. And these are not isolated occurrences. They merely illustrate the range of reactions on the part of communities in village Alaska struggling to maintain economic viability in a hostile socioeconomic and political environment.

What can be done to set these communities on a firmer footing in economic terms? Any effort to answer this question must be rooted in an understanding of the dynamics of the mixed economies that have emerged in village Alaska over the past several decades. Such an understanding will make it clear why many conventional propositions about subsistence economies are no longer helpful in thinking about the economic problems besetting Alaska's remote communities. It will also provide a basis for identifying and evaluating the options that are available to those seeking to alleviate the economic plight of these communities.

Mixed Economies in Village Alaska

Though the details vary from village to village, the fundamental pattern of economic life that prevails today in the remote communities of Alaska is unambiguous. The economies of these communities are *not* subsistence economies; they are mixed economies, encompassing large public or government sectors and sizable commercial sectors as well as ongoing subsistence sectors.

To say this is not to imply that domestic production (including subsistence activities like noncommercial hunting, fishing, and gathering) has declined or lost its significance in these commu-

nities. Far from it. Numerous studies have confirmed that subsistence continues to play a vital role throughout the Far North,
especially as a source of country food.[1] There is ample evidence
to suggest that community residents who take jobs in the public
and commercial sectors remain active in the subsistence sector at
the same time. Although we do not have the data to measure such
things precisely, it is probable that domestic production of one
sort or another accounts for a quarter to a half of the total income
stream of the residents of remote Alaskan communities.[2]

As this proposition implies, however, half or more of the income that the residents of these communities receive stems from
the commercial sector (mainly in the forms of wage labor and
commodity exchanges) or from the public sector (mainly in the
forms of salaries, services, and transfer payments provided by
governments). Moreover, subsistence itself is no longer a self-
contained practice, giving rise to a largely independent or self-
sufficient life-style. Despite its undeniable importance as a source
of country food, subsistence is now tightly linked to the other
sectors of the mixed economies that prevail in village Alaska.[3]
Partly, this is attributable to the capital intensification of subsistence activities, a development that makes it necessary for subsistence harvesters to participate, at least part-time, in the cash
sectors of the economy or to form alliances with others (for example, family members or members of extended kinship groups)
who participate full-time in the cash economy.[4] In part, it stems
from the coupling of traditional lifeways with a rising demand
throughout village Alaska for goods and services (from modern
homes and television sets to modern education and sewage systems) that can be obtained only with cash, a trend that reinforces
the need for a division of labor in these communities between
domestic production and other types of productive activities.

It follows that any effort to grapple with the economic problems currently facing village Alaska must rest on an understanding of the interactions among the principal sectors of the mixed
economies that operate in these communities and include an
analysis of the conditions necessary to achieve a stable balance
in these interactions.[5] Without exception, studies adopting this
perspective highlight the importance of securing adequate flows
of cash into the mixed economies that now prevail in village

Alaska.[6] Of course, a sizable and predictable flow of cash is integral to the functioning of the commercial and public sectors of these local economies. But subsistence practices have also evolved in such a way as to make regular injections of cash necessary to the successful pursuit of domestic production in these communities. It should come as no surprise, therefore, that the economic problems of village Alaska revolve around impediments to the maintenance of a flow of cash that is adequate to support the operation of mixed economies without, at the same time, disrupting the ecosystems that are critical to domestic production or eroding the cultural practices of those residents of northern communities who remain closely tied to subsistence activities.[7]

Distressed by the implications of this line of analysis, some local residents and sympathetic outsiders have taken to advocating an economic transformation under which the residents of village Alaska would abandon the mixed economies that exist today in favor of the pure subsistence economies that once flourished (or are believed to have flourished) in the remote areas of Alaska. For most of the communities of village Alaska, however, this is simply not a live option.[8] It has been a long time since anything resembling pure subsistence economies prevailed in this part of the world. In some cases, such as the Aleut communities of St. Paul and St. George, there is no history of pure subsistence economies at all.[9] More important, any serious effort to reestablish pure subsistence economies in village Alaska would require a drastic restructuring of the fixed or year-round settlements that presently characterize the remote areas of the state, along with the life-styles associated with these communities. As long as subsistence harvesters are based in fixed communities, making periodic forays to hunting or fishing grounds, subsistence will remain tightly linked to the other sectors of the mixed economy. This is so because this type of subsistence requires harvesters to travel long distances (often in short periods of time) and to make frequent trips to their homes in the settlements, rather than leading a seminomadic existence on the land.[10] This, in turn, produces an inevitable demand for technologies whose purchase and maintenance require a regular flow of cash. Depending upon the local circumstances, these technologies include snow machines, all-terrain vehicles, pickup trucks, boats with gasoline engines, air transport, and high-powered rifles, along with the fuel and ammunition required to keep these systems in operation.[11] Additionally, fixed settlements cannot survive in the absence of regular expenditures on goods and services, including heating oil, electricity, communications systems, health care facilities, organized schools, and waste disposal systems. These are precisely the sorts of things that individuals and groups normally secure through the operation of a cash economy, even in remote communities where domestic production accounts for a substantial proportion of total income.

It is unlikely, moreover, that the residents of village Alaska would voluntarily agree to give up the life-style associated with fixed settlements, even if it were feasible for them to do so. We have witnessed throughout the Far North in recent times an accelerating demand for goods whose acquisition requires cash. Whereas northern Natives once entered into monetized exchanges primarily to obtain modest supplies of tea and tobacco, along with ammunition for their rifles, the residents of northern communities today want to enjoy the benefits of computers, VCRs, washing machines, automobiles, and (in more and more cases) outside vacations. And who is to say there is anything wrong with this? What is more, the solidification of fixed settlements in the North during the twentieth century is (justifiably) associated in the minds of many with striking improvements in important services, such as decent health care and organized education. Although it is conceivable that delivery systems for these services could be adapted to the conditions that would arise in connection with a return to pure subsistence economies, there are good reasons to believe that such a drastic transformation would entail unacceptable social and economic losses.

Threats to Economic Stability

It is reasonable to conclude, therefore, that the mixed economies of village Alaska are here to stay. But it is equally important to recognize that these mixed economies are presently under severe pressure from a number of quarters. In essence, this is a consequence of the fact that these economies exhibit high levels of exposure to outside forces.[12] When conditions in the outside world change rapidly, the mixed economies of the remote communities of Alaska are subjected to extreme fluctuations over which they have little or no control. A brief discussion will make it clear that each of the sectors of these economies is presently under siege as a consequence of such external changes.

Despite the size of the public sector in the economies of village Alaska, the ability of these communities to raise revenue through local taxation is minimal. As a result, most of the funds flowing through the public sector in these communities come from programs established and controlled by the state of Alaska or the U.S. government.[13] State revenue sharing and municipal assistance accounts for a large share (more than half in many cases) of local government budgets in the remote communities of Alaska. Federal revenue sharing has provided another significant component of these budgets. The state and federal governments supply the funds to pay for many of the key services. The state of Alaska covers most of the costs of public education throughout much of village Alaska. The federal government picks up most of the costs associated with health care through programs of the Public Health Service available to Alaska Natives. Special programs, such as the state's Power Cost Equalization Program and various job training programs, further enhance the public sector in the remote communities of Alaska. Additionally, many individuals in these communities benefit directly from an array of state and federal transfer payments going to individuals in such forms as unemployment compensation, medicaid, Aid to Families with Dependent Children (AFDC), food stamps, and so forth.

Under the circumstances, it is not surprising that recent efforts to cope with massive budget shortfalls or deficits afflicting both the state of Alaska and the federal government have produced severe impacts in the remote communities of Alaska. Social programs of all sorts are among the major targets of those seeking to reduce federal deficits. For its part, the state responded to revenue shortfalls in the 1980s by proposing 20 percent cuts in its revenue sharing and municipal assistance programs, not to mention reductions in a wide variety of more specific programs benefiting village Alaska. As a result, those responsible for administering the public sector in the remote communities of Alaska have faced the unenviable task of adjusting to substantial cuts in revenues flowing from Juneau and Washington while preparing for the prospect of additional cuts during the foreseeable future.

A somewhat similar picture emerges from an examination of the commercial sector in the remote communities of Alaska. Many employment opportunities in these communities are linked to enterprises that produce commodities for export and that are controlled by decision makers in distant boardrooms. The energy industry, of course, constitutes the paradigmatic case. Thus, the collapse of the world market price for oil in the mid-1980s led to dramatic cutbacks in exploration and construction activities in Alaska, a development that reduced the demand for local employees, the need for local businesses to provide support services, and, in some cases, the local tax liability of major corporations.[14] But other industries are hardly immune from these fluctuations. Oversupplies of timber in world markets have led to reductions in employment opportunities in this industry in south central and southeast Alaska as well as to losses of net worth for a number of Native corporations. The collapse of the world market for seal skins in the 1980s played a key role in the decline of the Pribilof sealing industry. It remains to be seen whether Cominco's Red Dog lead/zinc mine in northwest Alaska can be consistently profitable in the face of volatile world market prices for nonfuel minerals.

Another major source of wage employment in village Alaska in recent times has been the capital construction programs funded by the North Slope Borough, the state of Alaska, and the federal government. Accordingly, the marked erosion of these programs constitutes yet another threat to the commercial sector of the mixed economies of village Alaska. The North Slope Borough's Capital Improvement Program is largely complete, and in any case, the borough has experienced a decline in tax revenues needed to sustain a capital budget as a result of the slump in the oil and gas industry. Although the state and federal governments cannot eliminate their capital budgets for the remote communities of Alaska overnight (some projects are already underway and others are fully committed), these budgets are obvious targets for those seeking to control large public deficits and will certainly shrink during the near future. It follows that there is no basis for expecting any significant growth in the commercial sector to take up the slack created by recent and anticipated reductions in the public sector in the mixed economies of village Alaska. Even the subsistence sector of the economies of these communities is currently under siege from a number of quarters. Partly, this is a matter of the growth of restrictive public regulations governing subsistence activities. Systems of licensing, open/closed seasons, and bag limits, devised originally to control sport and recreational hunting in the lower forty-eight states, have been imposed on subsistence harvesters, often with little appreciation of the complexities of subsistence practices in the remote areas of Alaska.[15] Public land managers have become more vocal in opposing the use of certain modes of transportation, such as all-terrain vehicles, widely used by subsistence harvesters. And there have been continual controversies surrounding efforts to distinguish true subsistence harvesters from others who claim subsistence rights.[16]

In part, the problems stem from threats to the markets for the salable by-products of subsistence harvesting activities.[17] It has been illegal for some time to sell raw walrus ivory or raw baleen from bowhead whales taken for subsistence purposes. But the new threat on the horizon today arises from the antiharvesting and antitrapping movements, which seek to impose more or less severe restrictions that would impede efforts to produce an income from the sale of animal skins and pelts.[18] Underlying all of these concerns is the fact that contemporary subsistence practices require regular injections of cash to purchase equipment as well as to obtain fuel and ammunition.[19] Far from being an invitation to expand subsistence activities, therefore, recent declines in the public and commercial sectors of the mixed economies of village Alaska constitute a threat to the subsistence sector because they make cash harder to obtain. Under the circumstances, income derived from domestic production is more likely to decline than to increase as a consequence of growing problems facing the public and commercial sectors.[20]

Options for the Future

Overall, it seems fair to conclude that the problems besetting the mixed economies of many remote Alaskan communities are now reaching crisis proportions. These problems are hardly likely to subside on their own accord. A simple rededication to more traditional subsistence practices does not offer a way out of the present difficulties. What, then, are the options available to these communities as they seek to (1) secure an adequate flow of cash to sustain their economies, (2) reduce their exposure to outside forces, and (3) protect the integrity of their cultures and the viability of the ecosystems upon which they depend? The remainder of this chapter surveys the principal options and offers some preliminary comments on their relative merits, judged in terms of these three criteria.

Economic Returns and Rents

Many observers have noted that few of the proceeds derived from the exploitation of northern natural resources remain in the Far North.[21] With a few exceptions (for example, the Red Dog mine), effective title to these resources or management authority over them resides with the state government or the federal government.[22] Accordingly, the economic returns accruing to the owners or managers of the resources typically flow into the state and federal treasuries in the forms of bonus bids, royalty payments, income from sales, and so forth. Similarly, local communities have little ability to capture the economic rents (that is, profits in excess of a normal rate of return) associated with the exploitation of northern natural resources.[23] It is true that the North Slope Borough has captured some of the rents derived from oil production on the North Slope by winning the authority to levy property taxes on the Prudhoe Bay facilities. The prospect of similar arrangements applying to the Red Dog mine undoubtedly had much to do with the creation of the Northwest Arctic Borough in the NANA (originally "Northwest Native Alaska Association") region in 1986. In most cases, however, the economic rents flow to distant governments (in the forms of severance taxes and corporate income taxes) or to those who own/control the oil companies and other relevant corporations (in the form of excess profits).[24] No doubt, the economic returns and rents flowing from hydrocarbon development constitute the most dramatic illustration of this problem. But this case is not unique. Few observers now remember, for example, that the Pribilof fur seal harvest generated a sizable annual return to the U.S. Treasury (and later to the state of Alaska) for decades before revenues fell below the cost of administering the Pribilof Islands Program during the 1970s.[25]

The obvious implication of these observations is that we could restructure existing arrangements to grant the remote communities of Alaska a share of the economic returns and rents associated with the exploitation of northern natural resources. Arranging for local (municipal or tribal) governments or village corporations to acquire title to the resources themselves would, of course, be one way to achieve this goal. In most cases, however, this option is not likely to prove politically or economically feasible.[26] Perhaps the most realistic method of addressing this problem would be to remit to these communities a specified share of the bonus bids, royalties, and so forth accruing to state and federal governments and to accord them the authority to levy taxes on natural resource operations occurring within their jurisdictions (which should include adjacent marine areas as well as nearby terrestrial areas). Undoubtedly, the major drawback to this suggestion arises from the fact that it would be difficult to persuade the state and federal governments to accept it. But such arrangements are not unheard of (as the taxing authority of the North Slope Borough attests), and any such mechanism could be justified as a kind of exchange in which individual communities would agree to accept resource development (under suitable regulations) in return for a fair share of the economic returns and rents arising from such activities.[27]

Other players are apt to be concerned that any such arrangement would give the residents of village Alaska enhanced incentives to support the exploitation of nonrenewable resources, even in cases where such projects might interfere with certain subsistence activities. This concern is undeniably real. Under the circumstances, it would fall to the leaders of these communities to strike a proper balance between subsistence activities and other activities (for example, hydrocarbon development) that would produce a flow of needed cash into the communities.[28] But there is no reason to doubt the capacity of leadership at the community level to arrive at appropriate decisions in dealing with such matters.

Enclave Development

A second option is to encourage the introduction of capital-intensive projects that can be physically segregated from existing settlements while still offering jobs and business opportunities to the residents of remote Alaskan communities. The Kuparuk Industrial Complex (KIC) on the North Slope exemplifies this option. The leaders of NANA and the Northwest Arctic Borough have followed a similar strategy in encouraging the development of the Red Dog mine. Those residents of the North Slope Borough who favor the opening of the coastal plain of the Arctic National Wildlife Refuge for hydrocarbon development have a similar idea in mind. The pattern of development that occurred at Dutch Harbor/Unalaska in connection with commercial fishing and that seems likely to accompany gold dredging on the Nome waterfront, by contrast, does not fit into this mold because there is no way to prevent the type of development occurring in these cases from intruding deeply into the day-to-day activities of the nearby settlements.[29]

The attractions of enclave development are easy enough to identify. Such projects may offer wage employment for local residents (the Red Dog mine is expected to create four hundred jobs, many of which are to be filled by residents of the NANA region). They frequently generate opportunities for the establishment of small businesses to provide various support services (many of the subsidiaries of the regional corporations created under the provisions of ANCSA provide support services for the oil and gas industry). They may even produce a tax base of critical importance to local governments otherwise dependent on state and federal revenues (the Northwest Arctic Borough was established in large part in order to levy property taxes on the Red Dog mining operation).

Yet it is important not to lose track of the pitfalls associated with enclave development as an economic option for remote Alaskan communities. Whenever such operations rely on nonrenewable resources, they can offer only a temporary solution (often no more than ten to twenty years) to the needs of these communities for a secure cash flow. The jobs they create do not always go to local residents, frequently require protracted separations of workers from their families, and often are difficult to integrate with the continuation of domestic production.[30] Because their products are typically exported to world markets, enclave operations are subject to sharp and sometimes unexpected fluctuations as world market prices change; the 1986 collapse of the world market price for oil is merely the most recent case in point. And operations of this type can cause severe disruptions to important ecosystems, even when they are segregated and confined to limited areas. Although the attractions of enclave development are considerable for the cash-starved, mixed economies of village Alaska, therefore, the costs of embracing this option may prove steep over the long run.

Commercialization of Renewable Resources

There is nothing new about the idea of relying on commercial sales of renewable resources as a means of securing an adequate flow of cash into the mixed economies of village Alaska.[31] The commercial harvest of fur seals on the Pribilof Islands has a long history. Trapping for commercial markets is a well-established practice in interior Alaska, as is the commercial harvest of timber in south central and southeast Alaska. And, of course, commercial fishing, which sometimes occurs side by side with subsistence fishing, is an important component of the commercial sector in many Alaskan communities.[32] Nonetheless, there is considerable scope for expanding commercial harvests of renewable resources in some parts of Alaska. There is room for growth in the commercial fisheries, especially for those interested in the bottom fisheries now managed in such a way as to favor American harvesters under the terms of the Fishery Conservation and Management Act of 1976.[33] Similarly, entrepreneurs located in remote communities could develop or, in some cases, expand reindeer herds for commercial exploitation, or they might even explore ideas for marketing the meat of wild animals, like caribou, moose, and walrus. What is more, there are interesting possibilities for establishing markets for by-products derived from animals taken for subsistence purposes. An obvious example is the controlled sale of raw walrus ivory, but careful analysis might well turn up other interesting options along these lines.

The attractions of deriving cash from the harvest of renewable resources are clear-cut and substantial. Given proper management, such harvests can continue indefinitely without causing any serious harm to the relevant ecosystems. Practices of this sort are also relatively easy to combine with various forms of domestic production (in some cases the actual mode of production is the same), and they are less threatening in cultural terms than many of the other options for generating cash income.

Yet the commercialization of renewable resources is not without drawbacks as a solution to the economic problems of village Alaska. Such activities are typically oriented toward exporting products to outside markets, which tend to fluctuate rapidly in response to factors that the remote communities of Alaska have little ability to control.[34] Sometimes the fluctuations arise from the antiharvesting campaigns of animal protectionist groups, as in the case of the recent collapse of the fur seal industry. In other cases, the problem stems from the natural volatility of markets resulting from dramatic fluctuations in supply (because of swings in the availability of the resources) or rapid shifts in demand (because of the effects of fashion on the consumption of what are frequently superior or luxury goods). Beyond this, state and federal policies, which are always difficult for the remote communities of Alaska to control, are major determinants of the role of industries based on renewable resources in the mixed economies of village Alaska. Under the Alaska limited-entry system for commercial fishing, for example, rural locals, especially Natives, have lost a considerable number of the fishing permits originally issued to them.[35] The limited entry system is hard to integrate into the social practices of remote communities in any case. Similarly, any effort to commercialize by-products, such as raw walrus ivory or raw baleen, would require significant changes in prevailing federal statutes, which would undoubtedly be opposed by a sizable segment of the environmental community, not to mention the animal protectionist movement.[36] As a result, the commercialization of renewable resources cannot be counted on to reduce the exposure of remote communities to outside forces, and it may not result in a secure cash flow.

Domestic Production
Domestic production, particularly in the form of subsistence hunting and gathering, is already far more important in village

Alaska than it is anywhere in the lower forty-eight. Yet some observers have come to believe that other types of informal economic activity hold great potential for remote northern communities. These include the establishment of various types of collectives, cooperatives, skills exchanges, and community enterprises.[37] In fact, serious efforts have been made to pursue this option in the Far North. Some communities have fishing cooperatives, which usually handle the marketing and even the processing of locally harvested fish.[38] The village store is run as a community enterprise in many communities (usually as an arm of the local ANCSA corporation). Skills exchanges are widespread in remote Alaskan communities, though they are usually conducted in a highly informal manner. As well, there is considerable interest among Alaskans in experience arising from the cooperative movement that has spread through the Canadian North over the past several decades.[39] Even so, there are undoubtedly possibilities for expanding the role of these informal arrangements, perhaps turning to them as a means to foster intraregional trading networks linking some of the individual communities of village Alaska.

The attractions of this option are easy to grasp.[40] Informal economic arrangements can operate on a small scale so that there is some chance that they will remain under local control. Similarly, it is far easier to operate such productive activities on the basis of social accounting principles than it is to sensitize large oil companies or mining companies to the local concerns of remote Alaskan communities. With all due respect to the attractions of this option, however, informal economic activities hardly constitute a panacea for the remote communities of Alaska. To the extent that cooperatives and community enterprises do not concentrate on products that can be sold in outside markets, they tend to be perpetually undercapitalized and to contribute little toward solving the need of these communities for a secure flow of cash. When they do specialize in products for export (for example, fish, works of art, artifacts, qiviut), by contrast, they become vulnerable to the fluctuations of the relevant markets, a problem that is especially severe because such enterprises typically do not have the resources or the diversified operations needed to ride out slumps in key markets. Additionally, many northern cooperatives and community enterprises have experienced serious management problems. Although informal economic activities are undoubtedly worth encouraging, therefore, it is not likely that we can rely on them to solve the fundamental economic problems of village Alaska.

Income Security Programs

Yet another option for the remote communities of Alaska is to explore the establishment of income security programs adapted to the specific needs of village Alaska. In a general way, such programs would resemble the negative income tax schemes that many analysts (including an array of conservatives) advocate to solve the problems of the working poor who engage in productive activities on a regular basis but who are unable to secure an adequate cash flow.[41] There are many variations on this theme, and it is perfectly possible to design income security programs with the particular circumstances of specific groups in mind. Nevertheless, all such programs share a common core. In contrast to conventional welfare schemes, they feature transfer payments from state or federal governments linked to the actual efforts of those whose productive activities fail to generate an adequate cash flow. Interestingly, this option has already been introduced with some success in the Canadian North. The leading example is undoubtedly the Income Security Program for Cree Hunters and Trappers set up under the provisions of Section 30 of the James Bay and Northern Quebec Agreement of 1975.[42] More generally, many observers have begun to think in terms of programs of this sort as a means of saving family farming or small-scale commercial fishing throughout the United States.

Like every alternative, this option is not without its pitfalls as a response to the economic problems of village Alaska. Because they involve transfer payments, income security programs can never be insulated completely from the vagaries of the policy-making process. To the extent that such programs are administered by bureaucratic organizations, they may become rigid or inflexible, a development that could cause serious problems in the characteristically fluid economies of remote Alaskan communities. And of course, it may be politically difficult to establish programs of this sort in the first place. Nonetheless, there is no reason to treat such problems as insuperable obstacles. Insofar as income security programs can be portrayed as a device to compensate people for relinquishing aboriginal rights or as a means to stabilize a way of life (such as family farming or small-scale commercial fishing) that society as a whole wishes to preserve, it may not be so difficult to sell such programs to the Alaska state legislature or to the United States Congress. As well, it would be perfectly possible to design elements of flexibility into such programs by putting representatives from village Alaska on the relevant administrative boards and requiring that applicable rules and regulations be negotiated with members of the recipient groups.[43]

Conclusion

Little by little, the mixed economies of village Alaska have been sliding toward a condition of crisis. If nothing is done to address this problem in a coherent and concerted fashion, it is probable that the residents of these communities will experience severe erosions in their welfare over the next decade or two. Yet there are options available that could help to stabilize the mixed economies of village Alaska and to provide the residents of these communities with some control over their own destinies as well as a sense of economic security. An appropriate economic support program for these communities should include a number of elements.

Projects involving the extraction of nonrenewable resources should be designed to minimize disruption to subsistence practices, and the remote communities of village Alaska should receive a sizable share of the economic returns and rents associated with such projects. Steps should be taken to commercialize renewable resources under regimes designed to protect local users as well as the renewable resources themselves. Such regimes should operate both to secure continued participation on the part of local residents in existing commercial enterprises (for example, commercial fishing) and to encourage the controlled development of new commercial enterprises based on renewable resources (for example, raw walrus ivory). Income security programs sufficiently entrenched in legislative terms to withstand the vagaries of state and federal budgetary cycles should be established to backstop the efforts of those who choose to operate as subsistence hunters and gatherers in the remote communities of Alaska. Without doubt, the adoption and administration of such a multifaceted economic support program would require a significant exercise of political will (not to mention coordination) on the part of the state government and the federal government. In the final analysis, however, some such program would not only serve the needs of the residents of village Alaska themselves, but it should also prove more appealing to the state and federal governments than a series of ad hoc welfare programs that leave a costly trail of human wreckage in their wake.

CHAPTER 3

The Politics of Pathology:
The Problem of Health in Village Alaska

It is no exaggeration to say that the remote (predominantly Native) communities of village Alaska are currently in the midst of a health crisis and that this crisis may well deepen in the years to come. An array of individual pathologies runs rampant among the residents of these communities.[1] The death rate from accidents is currently almost five times the national average; accidents constitute the leading cause of death among Alaska Natives. Suicides occur among Alaska Natives at a rate in excess of three times the national average. Together, accidents and suicides account for the majority of years of potential life lost among Alaska Natives.[2] Violence directed toward other persons is widespread in the remote communities of Alaska. A 1977 study found rates of murder, rape, and other violent crimes in village Alaska "two and three times the state average and many times those of the nation";[3] most knowledgeable observers believe that this situation has worsened over the past decade. Though the data are less satisfactory, no one doubts that many forms of mental illness are also pervasive in Alaska's remote communities.

All of these pathologies are closely associated with alcohol

This chapter is based on a paper presented at the Western Regional Science Association Meetings in Napa, California, 24–28 February 1988. Although the chapter focuses on conditions in village Alaska, similar conditions prevail throughout the Circumpolar North. If anything, the resultant threats to social and cultural integrity have intensified over the past several years.

abuse and drug abuse, both of which are widespread throughout much of village Alaska. It is understandable, therefore, that the Alaska state legislature has responded to the health crisis of village Alaska by granting individual communities the authority to take strong measures to combat alcoholism and drug addiction. Many of these communities have responded vigorously under the terms of these programs, especially in the area of alcohol abuse.[4] But these efforts have not reduced the incidence of individual pathologies in village Alaska. In fact, the overall picture with regard to individual pathologies has gotten worse rather than better in recent years, a trend suggesting that alcohol and drug abuse are symptoms of deeper problems rather than ultimate causes of accidental deaths, suicides, and violence directed toward others. It should come as no surprise, under the circumstances, that efforts to curb alcohol and drug abuse often stimulate criminal behavior among addicts while doing little to reduce the incidence of various individual pathologies.[5]

The Problem of Health

Today no one denies either the incidence of the pathologies referred to in the preceding paragraphs or the linkages between these dysfunctional forms of behavior and alcohol and drug abuse. Yet little has been done to explore or come to terms with the root causes of the resultant health crisis in a serious manner. Overwhelmed by a welter of confusing developments and the constant struggle to maintain a way of life that is under siege, the residents of village Alaska are poorly situated to think through this crisis in a systematic fashion.[6] For their part, outside observers commonly approach the emerging health crisis as a conventional public health problem, much like the problem of combating tuberculosis in village Alaska a generation ago or dealing with tooth decay today.[7] In effect, they assume that the problem of controlling individual pathologies can be isolated from economic, political, and social issues and addressed through the establishment of health care programs managed by outside professionals able to bring modern medical knowledge and technology to bear on the problem. But this approach misses much that is critical to any serious effort to come to grips with the problem of health in the remote communities of village Alaska. There can be no doubt about the existence of powerful links between the socioeconomic and political conditions now prevailing in these communities and the individual pathologies currently afflicting their members.[8] To ignore these links would be like trying to understand changes in ecosystems while ignoring the impact of human actions on these systems.

More specifically, we must turn to an analysis of anomie and dependence in any attempt to get to the bottom of the problem of health in village Alaska. Anomie is a condition in which socially defined norms or rules of proper conduct lose their hold on the behavior of individuals.[9] Anomie is a common concomitant of social settings characterized by rapid and disruptive change of the sort that has been occurring in the remote communities of Alaska for some time. Most of these communities have experienced extraordinary rates of change affecting virtually every aspect of their material culture. Many current residents have witnessed in the course of their own lives transitions to fixed settlements, mixed economies; modern modes of housing, communication, and transportation; Western-style school systems, and the like. Yet the nonmaterial aspects of culture, such as child-rearing practices, authority patterns, collective choice processes, and responses to social conflict, seldom change at a comparable pace.

As a result, most of the middle-aged and older residents of the remote communities of Alaska were socialized into modes of conduct ill-suited to the realities of the present material culture. Many of the younger members of these communities, by contrast, have not been effectively socialized at all because their parents and extended families lack an appropriate cluster of social practices to transmit to them.[10] The predictable result is a widespread sense of disorientation, individual feelings of isolation, and anxiety. These are precisely the sorts of conditions that give rise to individual pathologies like mental illness (particularly among the older members of the communities) and suicide or violence directed toward others (especially among the younger members of the communities). In these terms, alcohol and drug abuse emerge as intermediate conditions or proximate causes rather than as root causes of pathological behavior. Although alcohol or drug

abuse can certainly serve to trigger accidents, suicides, or violence directed toward others, these abuses typically arise from
efforts to escape the anomie resulting from prolonged periods of
disruptive social change in the remote communities of Alaska.
Any programs designed to treat or control alcohol and drug abuse
that do not recognize this fact will fail to yield anything more than
marginal improvements, and they may well stimulate other types
of pathological behavior.

Dependence, on the other hand, is a condition that arises
when people possessing a long tradition of self-sufficiency and
pride in their ability to adapt to a wide range of environmental
conditions find themselves unable to control their own destiny
and forced to adjust to drastic changes that are largely imposed
from outside. By now, of course, this is a familiar story in many
of the remote communities of Alaska.[11] The mixed economies that
prevail in village Alaska today are, for the most part, products of
outside influences, and they continue to experience a heavy impact from an array of exogenous forces. The labyrinth of local political organizations that has emerged over the past two decades
is largely the result of state and federal initiatives. Even traditional modes of production, such as subsistence hunting and
gathering, are increasingly governed by elaborate sets of regulations that are ill-suited to the social conditions prevailing in village Alaska and that, as often as not, are administered by officials
who would rather impose their own preferences in a paternalistic
manner than endeavor to interact with the residents of the remote
communities of Alaska on a basis of equality or mutual respect.[12]

The efforts of well-intentioned outsiders to ameliorate the
ravages of dependence, moreover, often have perverse consequences. As the experiences of the inner cities and the Indian
reservations of the lower forty-eight states, as well as the remote
communities of village Alaska, attest, welfare programs can and
frequently do have the effect of undermining the residual authority of local leaders, eroding family ties, sapping the ability of
individuals to take the initiative on their own behalf, and generally deepening the mentality of dependence that is one of the
root causes of the problems under consideration here. Highly
publicized efforts to avoid these consequences of welfare programs, ranging from housing initiatives like the Model Cities Pro-

gram to a variety of job training programs, have generally failed
to overcome or circumvent these problems. Under the circumstances, the fact that alcohol and drug abuse, along with various
crimes associated with substance abuse, have risen sharply in the
inner cities and on the reservations over the past several decades
should come as no surprise.

Given these conditions, it is understandable that many residents of village Alaska feel helpless or severely frustrated and
that Alaska Natives, like many Native Americans living on or
around reservations in the lower forty-eight, find it difficult or
impossible to hang onto the central values, beliefs, and practices
necessary to ensure the integrity of their cultures.[13] The result is
a loss of self-esteem, which produces carelessness in some individuals and outbreaks of uncontrollable anger in others. These
conditions, in turn, are closely associated with the occurrence of
serious accidents, suicides, and violence directed toward others.
Any public health approach that fails to come to terms with the
role of dependence in the etiology of many of the pathologies now
rampant in village Alaska is doomed to failure from the start. As
the most thoughtful and observant health care professionals
themselves have noted, the pathologies under consideration here
will not finally subside until northern communities are given effective control over their own destinies, including the right to
veto projects involving the development of natural resources
which they believe would be unduly disruptive to their way of
life. Efforts to address the problem of health in village Alaska that
do not acknowledge this basic fact can only be regarded as hypo-
critical.

What Is to Be Done?

What can we do to alleviate the root causes of the individual
pathologies rampant in the remote communities of Alaska? Overall, it is hard to dispute Peter Sarsfield's conclusion, articulated
in a discussion of the Canadian North but equally relevant to village Alaska:

If it is accepted that the main obstacles to the health of rural and remote
communities are in fact social and political and not medical, then it becomes obvious that what is needed is social and political change. Spe-

cifically, communities must be given control of local budgets, as well as the right to hire and fire all employees, management of all local facilities and institutions, ownership of regional traditional-use lands, control of sub-surface resources, and the setting of policy in such areas as wildlife management and education. The right of control in all these areas is vital to community health, and if constitutional change is required to extend such rights to communities then this must be done.[14]

To this I would add only that the communities of village Alaska must be assured adequate financial resources to make such a grant of rights a meaningful transfer of authority rather than a hollow gesture.

Attractive as this prescription sounds, however, it would require changes that are too sweeping to be politically feasible during the near future. Accordingly, there is a need to focus on more specific responses available to those desiring to take steps toward solving the health crisis in village Alaska, even as we continue to think through the relative merits of longer-term solutions.

Coping with Anomie

Turning first to the problem of anomie, there is much to be said for programs designed to stimulate cultural and spiritual renewal among Natives residing in remote Alaskan communities. The "Inupiat Ilitqusiat" campaign of the NANA region exemplifies this approach.[15] The point of this campaign is not to roll back various elements of modernization or to reinstitute some sort of pure subsistence life-style in place of the mixed economies that prevail today. Rather, the effort focuses on the maintenance of the Inupiat "cultural spirit" and the transmission of key Inupiat values, such as knowledge of language, sharing, humor, respect for nature, and responsibility to tribe. The campaign concentrates on young people, through the operation of a "spirit camp," on the theory that it is critical to provide each succeeding generation with culturally grounded rules of conduct as an antidote to anomie. Of course, cultural and spiritual renewal does not offer a solution to all of the problems of the remote communities of Alaska. But it can provide a coherent vision of the future featuring a middle ground between the resumption of a pure subsistence life-style, which is neither feasible nor widely desired, and the acceptance of assimilation, which is a recipe for perpetuating the ravages of anomie. In short, this approach offers a means of adapting and strengthening the central cultural norms and myths that are so important to the maintenance of adequate levels of self-esteem among the residents of village Alaska.[16]

More broadly, education can become an important means of combating the ravages of anomie in the remote communities of Alaska. At present, unfortunately, the schools operating in these communities are more often a part of the problem than a means of coping with the problem. This is so because the schools are controlled, in fact if not in principle, by outsiders who espouse, tacitly if not explicitly, an assimilationist approach to the education of Native northerners.[17] The results are reflected in the lack of emphasis on Native languages (especially in the lower grades), the structure of the curriculum, and the teaching materials commonly used in the schools.

What is needed in this connection is a fundamental restructuring of local education. Perhaps the most interesting exemplars of this approach among Native peoples in the North American Arctic today are the programs run by the Kativik Regional School Board and the Cree School Board (entities established under the James Bay and Northern Quebec Agreement of 1975) in the largely Native communities of northern Quebec.[18] Kativik, for example, has made no effort to abandon classroom instruction in a vain attempt to revive the processes of transmitting knowledge directly from parents to children characteristic of more traditional social practices.[19] Rather, the school board has taken steps to transform classroom instruction into an effective vehicle for cultural survival. Thus, Kativik has devised a program under which Inuktitutt is employed as the primary language of instruction in the early grades; instructional materials developed entirely by Inuit educators are used, and, above all, Inuit teachers (trained under the supervision of Kativik) have become the principal instructors in local schools rather than serving in such obviously subordinate roles as teachers' aides. Not only does this program have the effect of producing young people who exhibit a comparatively high level of cognitive integration, but it also promotes feelings of pride and self-respect among local residents, who see that there is an alternative to being treated as objects by outside educators who come and go without ever becoming full-fledged members of their communities. The Kativik program thus facili-

tates the transmission of traditional Inuit values by passing on
language skills and helps to provide rules of proper conduct
rooted in the Inuit culture. Naturally, similar educational programs for village Alaska would have to be adapted to the circumstances prevailing in various parts of Alaska. But the basic point
is clear enough: locally controlled education can play a significant
role in coping with the individual pathologies currently rampant
in the remote communities of Alaska.

Combating Dependence
    Turn now to a consideration of some practical responses to the
debilitating effects of anger and loss of self-esteem arising from
dependence. For starters, it is important to provide the residents
of village Alaska with some means of support that does not breed
the well-known emotional and social problems associated with
conventional welfare programs. Without doubt, the most interesting experiment along these lines in the North American Arctic
today is the Income Security Program for Cree Hunters and Trappers, which was established under the provisions of Section 30
of the James Bay and Northern Quebec Agreement and which
resembles the negative income tax schemes advocated by some
policy analysts to assist the working poor in more mainstream
social settings.[20] In contrast to conventional welfare schemes, this
program provides payments to hunters and trappers in proportion to the amount of time and energy they devote to productive
activities. It does not, therefore, have the perverse effects on
incentives that we associate with most conventional welfare
schemes. Since the program does involve transfer payments, it
cannot be insulated entirely from the political process, and it does
engender a need for administration on the part of a bureaucratic
organization. No doubt, these features of the program could
cause problems at some future time. So far, however, the Income
Security Program has played a significant role in stabilizing the
economies of the Cree communities of northern Quebec. And it
has done so in a manner that avoids some of the most debilitating psychological effects associated with conventional welfare
schemes.[21]
    Any strategy designed to combat dependence in village Alaska
must also include mechanisms to draw the residents of these

communities into the management of their own affairs in such a way as to give them a sense of control over their own destiny. Perhaps the most interesting recent initiatives in this realm involve the establishment of co-management regimes for wildlife harvesting under which local user groups play a significant role in making decisions regarding the wildlife in question.[22] For the most part, wildlife management in Alaska and the adjacent marine areas has been monopolized by officials of the federal Fish and Wildlife Service and National Marine Fisheries Service or the Alaska Department of Fish and Game, who have treated user groups as subjects expected to comply with decisions emanating from those agencies. Such an approach reinforces the mentality of dependence by treating the residents of village Alaska in a paternalistic fashion. Additionally, it yields poor results with regard to wildlife management as such because users, lacking any sense of ownership of the decisions made, regularly fail to comply with decisions promulgated by wildlife managers. Recognizing the futility of this approach, a number of key players have begun to espouse co-management arrangements under which officials collaborate with user groups in managing wildlife rather than attempting to impose solutions from above.

Without doubt, the collaboration that has grown up in recent years between the National Marine Fisheries Service and the Alaska Eskimo Whaling Commission has helped to defuse the controversy surrounding the bowhead whale.[23] The Yukon-Kuskokwin Delta Goose Management Plan involves a similar effort to foster collaboration between the Fish and Wildlife Service and various user groups in the interests of affording effective protection to several endangered species of geese.[24] There are indications that comparable collaborative arrangements are now emerging with respect to walrus. These co-management schemes cannot, of course, be expected to work well in the absence of a continuing willingness on the part of all participants to engage in joint problem solving. But they do offer a way out of the fundamental problems associated with the traditional approach to wildlife management. Even more to the point, in the context of this discussion, they serve to ameliorate rather than to exacerbate the problem of dependence by transforming the residents of village Alaska from passive subjects into active partners capable of exercising some real control over their own destinies.

Efforts to solve the problem of dependence in village Alaska must also address the debilitating effects of the political fragmentation that pervades these communities today. As is true of many Indian communities in the lower forty-eight, there are deep splits among the residents of Alaska's remote communities between modernizers and traditionalists.[25] In Alaska, however, a welter of new organizational forms have served to deepen and complicate such splits.[26] The modernizers have seized on the Alaska Native Claims Settlement Act (ANCSA) corporations to promote their vision of the future (becoming corporate Natives in the process), and the traditionalists struggle to enhance the power of various tribal entities (such as traditional tribal councils or Indian Reorganization Act councils) by seeking to assert control over Native lands that could be accepted as "Indian country" in Alaska.[27] For their part, the various municipal and borough governments operative in the remote communities of Alaska are beset by internal frictions involving the interests of those who support nonrenewable resource development as a means of expanding employment opportunities in the cash economy and the concerns of those who fear the effects of such a strategy on traditional subsistence practices.

The net result of this political fragmentation is a sense of inefficacy that merely heightens feelings of dependence among the residents of village Alaska. There are good reasons to fear that the situation will get worse as the impact of the state's economic problems hits the remote communities of Alaska harder, creating a situation in which local leaders will have to cope with severe budget cuts in an environment already charged with political tensions.[28] To be sure, it will not be easy to transcend differences, such as those currently reflected in the deep and disturbing division between the Alaska Federation of Natives and the Alaska Native Coalition regarding organizational arrangements for the future in village Alaska.[29] But the inefficacy and bitterness resulting from a failure to come to terms with such issues would inevitably serve to reinforce the mentality of dependence that is a root cause of many individual pathologies in the remote communities of Alaska today.

Circles—Vicious and Virtuous

It is apparent from this discussion that there are powerful linkages between the problem of health and the problems of economic viability and political integration in village Alaska. Existing economic conditions, which push individuals toward the ranks of the unemployed, the recipients of welfare, or the migrants hoping to find a better life in the cities, obviously cut people off from their cultural roots and exacerbate feelings of anomie. Similarly, the political fragmentation so prevalent in village Alaska today heightens the mentality of dependence by producing feelings of inefficacy and contributes to the problem of anomie by accentuating the gap between older social practices and the requirements of the emerging organizational environment.

No doubt, a sharp reduction in the incidence of individual pathologies would make it easier to address the economic and political problems of village Alaska in a constructive fashion. But it is equally important to observe that progress toward solving the economic and political problems afflicting the remote communities of Alaska would help to alleviate the problem of health. This is certainly a key feature of the complex of problems facing village Alaska today. Viewed from one perspective, it is easy to conclude that these communities are caught in a vicious circle. Efforts to deal with each of their major problems seem to depend on the achievement of progress with regard to the others. Approached from another vantage point, however, the linkages among these problems may prove advantageous. Improvements on any front are apt to produce gains in connection with the other problems as well. It follows that what may seem like a vicious circle on the way down can emerge as a process featuring positive feedback loops and reinforcement when conditions are improving.

Conclusion

Individual pathologies, including accidental deaths, suicides, and violence directed toward others, are rampant in the remote (predominantly Native) communities of Alaska. But the resultant health crisis is fundamentally a socioeconomic and political problem rather than a conventional problem of public health. The roots of the pathological behavior in question lie in feelings of anomie and dependence arising from the abrupt social transformations and loss of self-sufficiency that have befallen village Alaska in modern times. This does not mean, of course, that there is no role for sophisticated medical care in treating the victims or the survivors of pathological behavior in the remote communities of Alaska. Still, it does suggest that responses directed toward proximate causes, such as alcohol and drug abuse, can do little to solve the underlying problem of health in village Alaska. Similarly, it helps us to understand why approaches to the crisis that conceptualize it as a conventional public health problem are doomed to failure from the start.

Ultimately, we must face up to the politics of pathology and take steps to ameliorate the root causes of pathological behavior in these communities. This will almost certainly entail a drastic restructuring of education in village Alaska. It may well require the establishment of income security programs and co-management schemes to alleviate the mentality of dependence that pervades village Alaska today. None of these changes will be easy to accomplish. Above all, the active participation of local residents is necessary to bring about such changes, a fact that implies that outsiders—even well-intentioned outsiders—can do no more than provide opportunities, encouragement, and material support for constructive changes focused at the community level. The resultant approach to the problem of health in the remote communities of Alaska does not offer the attractions of a quick fix; it may take years or decades to implement. Nonetheless, it does offer the satisfaction of grappling with the root causes of the problem rather than simply offering another palliative.

Hunter/Gatherers in Advanced Industrial Societies: Determinants of Cultural Survival

> And Isaac . . . said unto [Esau], Behold, thy dwelling shall
> be the fatness of the earth, and the dew of heaven from
> above.—Genesis 27:39

C an communities of hunter/gatherers or subsistence harvest- ers locked into advanced industrial societies they cannot hope to control survive intact during the foreseeable future? Or to use an evocative metaphor Finn Lynge has proposed, can Esau find a secure niche in a social setting dominated by Jacob?[1] In this chapter, I seek answers to these questions. In doing so, I draw heavily on the experience of the American Arctic as a source of illustrations. But the underlying issue is generic, arising not only throughout the Circumpolar North but also in other parts of the world where hunter/gatherers find themselves embedded in advanced industrial societies.

My thesis is that subsistence harvesters face long, though not necessarily insuperable, odds. As it turns out, however, the fundamental threats to the survival of hunter/gatherer communities do not arise from conscious policies adopted and implemented by governments or agencies of the state. Rather, the source of the most serious threats lies deeper in a cluster of societal dynamics that serve to structure relations between dominant societies and remote (predominantly Native) communities located in outlying

This chapter is a substantially revised version of a paper presented at the Second Arctic Policy Conference at McGill University in Montreal, 1–3 December 1988. Although the text focuses on survival strategies for hunter/gatherers operating in the Far North, the argument applies with equal force to the problems communities of hunter/gatherers face throughout the world.

areas. This proposition has profound implications for the development of a strategy to enhance prospects for cultural survival, a theme to which I return in the final section of the chapter.

American Arctic Policies

The Arctic policies of the United States, including those applicable to the Circumpolar North as a whole as well as those directed more specifically toward the indigenous peoples of the American Arctic, are best described as vague and volatile.[2] The most recent attempt to spell out a comprehensive American Arctic policy is contained in National Security Decision Directive (NSDD) No. 90 of 14 April 1983. This policy statement begins with a declaration that the "United States has unique and critical interests in the Arctic region," a proposition that leads to the conclusion that the region "warrants priority attention by the United States." It then proceeds to define the principal elements of American policy for the Arctic as (1) "protecting essential security interests in the Arctic region," (2) "supporting sound and rational development in the Arctic region," (3) "promoting scientific research in fields contributing to knowledge of the Arctic environment," and (4) "promoting mutually beneficial international cooperation in the Arctic." NSDD 90 also specifies that the Interagency Arctic Policy Group (IAPG), a coordinating body chaired by the representative of the Department of State and reporting directly to the National Security Council, "will be responsible for reviewing and coordinating implementation of this policy."[3]

It does not require any sophisticated exercise in policy analysis to realize that this statement of policy has little behavioral content. What, for example, are the essential American security interests in the Arctic? Do they require the adoption of a forward maritime strategy, or do they mandate a serious effort to devise arms control arrangements, such as submarine sanctuaries, for the Arctic? What forms of development are sound and rational under the conditions prevailing in the Arctic today? Would large-scale hydrocarbon development in the Arctic National Wildlife Refuge or tanker traffic in the Northwest Passage be compatible with this policy? How can we determine when opportunities for mutually beneficial international cooperation arise in the Arctic? What does this policy statement tell us, for instance, about the position the United States should adopt with regard to the Canadian proposal for an international Arctic Council? Nor can we confidently assume that the IAPG will act to determine the operational meaning of this Arctic policy. The IAPG's mandate is limited (for example, it is not to concern itself with "purely domestic matters"), and a number of agencies with line responsibilities have either refused to participate in the group in a meaningful way or have expressed their displeasure with an arrangement under which the representative of the State Department serves as chair. Under the circumstances, it will come as no surprise that the IAPG has seldom become a significant player in molding the actions of the U.S. federal government regarding Arctic issues.

A somewhat different picture emerges from an examination of the policies of the United States toward the indigenous peoples of the American Arctic. Despite several landmark Supreme Court decisions alluding to the sovereignty of Indian tribes treated as "dependent nations," Congress early on assumed plenary power over relations between Native Americans and the United States. Because they are not represented directly in Congress, this has ensured that Native Americans must strive to promote or protect their interests in the arena of congressional politics by operating as a pressure group or lobby. With regard to matters of little importance to other groups in American society, the interests of Native peoples have often fared well in this process. But when their interests come into conflict with those of other organized groups, the disadvantages of Native Americans as players in the arena of congressional politics are regularly exposed.

The outcomes conform, for the most part, to the erratic pattern that students of politics describe as pluralism, a pattern that bears little resemblance to the ideal of clear-cut policies applied consistently to move society over time in identifiable directions. Two other factors, one quite general and the other more specific, add to the resultant volatility of American policy regarding the permanent residents of the Arctic. Because Congress mirrors the shifting attitudes of the voting public, the policies embedded in the statutes Congress enacts fluctuate, sometimes abruptly, with changes in public attitudes. It is no cause for surprise, for example, that the late-nineteenth-century attitudes of assimilationism reflected in the General Allotment Act of 1887 gradually gave way to more sympathetic attitudes toward indigenous communities, exemplified by the Indian Reorganization Act of 1934 (and its extension to Alaska in 1936), which were superseded, in turn, by the terminationist attitudes of the 1950s.[4]

Because the indigenous peoples of Alaska constitute a distinctive minority within the larger category of Native Americans, the actions of Congress affecting these peoples have been particularly erratic. Sometimes this results in the adoption of policies whose implications are difficult to determine under the conditions prevailing in Alaska (for example, those pertaining to the authority of federally recognized tribes in "Indian country"). In other cases, it yields legislation enacted to deal with issues that are uniquely relevant to the indigenous peoples of Alaska (for example, the land settlement of the Alaska Native Claims Settlement Act of 1971 or the subsistence provisions set forth in Title VIII of the Alaska National Interest Lands Conservation Act of 1980).

The conclusion to be drawn from this brief overview, in my judgment, is that the Arctic policies of the United States do not constitute a critical determinant of the circumstances facing communities of hunter/gatherers in the American Arctic today. These policies are either too vague to have any identifiable impact on the chances of subsistence harvesters or too volatile to move events in well-defined directions over time. It is correct, of course, to observe that the United States has not acted to enhance the viability of hunter/gatherer communities by adopting conscious policies to achieve this goal. But it also seems fair to conclude that the principal threats to the survival of hunter/gatherer communities embedded in American society do not arise from the Arctic policies of the United States.

Societal Dynamics

Far more troublesome, from the point of view of hunter/gatherers concerned with cultural survival, is a cluster of societal dynamics at work in every advanced industrial society. The forces unleashed by these dynamics are not products of conscious policies; they are better understood as unplanned and generally unforeseen side effects of the day-to-day operation of highly modernized social systems. Social forces of this sort are peculiarly difficult to combat for those seeking to protect distinctive ways of life precisely because they are unintended consequences of actions motivated by other considerations rather than results of deliberate policies articulated and implemented by organs of the state. To lend substance to this proposition, consider again the conditions prevailing in the American Arctic.

The Terms of Social Intercourse

Whenever and wherever hunter/gatherers in the American Arctic come into contact with representatives of the advanced industrial society in which they are embedded, it is taken for granted that the terms of the resultant social intercourse will be those of the dominant society. The Arctic's permanent residents are expected to function comfortably and effectively in English; it seldom even occurs to members of the dominant society to make an effort to communicate with indigenous peoples in their own languages. Hunter/gatherers who enter into economic relationships with members of the dominant society find it necessary to adapt to the standard practices of industrial societies regarding wage labor and the role of corporations in economic transactions. The remote communities of the American Arctic experience constant pressure to organize politically along Western lines to interact effectively with state and federal agencies. And when disputes arise between hunter/gatherers and representatives of the surrounding society (for example, conflicts over rights to use the sea ice or to harvest marine mammals), they are turned over for resolution to the courts of the dominant society, which routinely employ Western laws and legal procedures in rendering their judgments.[5]

Many individual Natives have exhibited an impressive capacity to adapt to these terms of social intercourse, becoming successful corporate executives, effective members of the state legislature, and articulate spokesmen for indigenous causes in international forums. From the perspective of hunter/gatherers as a social group, however, there is a high price to be paid for these individual achievements. Successful Natives often lose contact with their cultural roots, becoming, to use a phrase popular in Alaska, "Brooks Brothers Natives." Others, frustrated by the difficulties they encounter in their efforts to adapt to the practices of the dominant society, resort to destructive forms of behavior, such as alcoholism. In both cases, the distinctive social practices of hunter/gatherer communities suffer as the energies of individual Natives are diverted from the activities required to secure a distinctive way of life.

The Erosion of the Resource Base

By definition, hunter/gatherer communities depend for their survival on uninterrupted access to a secure base of renewable resources. Yet the day-to-day operation of an advanced industrial society poses serious threats to the resource base. Industrial development, both in the Arctic itself (for example, the Prudhoe Bay oil field) and in distant areas frequented by Arctic wildlife in the course of their annual migrations (for example, the agricultural districts of northern California), degrades the northern resource base by destroying important habitats. Side effects of the commercial harvest of renewable resources (for instance, the depletion of marine mammal stocks arising from entanglement with lost or discarded fishing nets) erode important components of the resource base. Pollution caused by industrial wastes (in such forms as Arctic haze) contaminates Arctic wildlife and may well prove disruptive to northern ecosystems in more general terms. Decisions to include northern lands in national parks, refuges, and wilderness areas lead to the imposition of alien and cumbersome regulations on subsistence practices and sometimes make it difficult to manage whole ecosystems on a coordinated basis. And social movements based in the urban centers of the dominant society (for example, antiharvesting campaigns) severely affect hunter/gatherer communities by undermining markets for the by-products of subsistence harvests, such as seal skins, or by leading to outright prohibitions on important subsistence practices.[6]

These threats to the resource base are not, for the most part, intended consequences of state or federal policies. Rather, they are side effects of the operations of an advanced industrial society. It follows that the settlement of Native land claims offers no guarantee of a secure resource base for indigenous peoples. Nor do policies granting a preference to subsistence users suffice to protect hunter/gatherers from the impacts of agricultural production in California, tall smokestacks in Europe or western Siberia, or animal protectionist campaigns based in southern urban centers.

The Externalities of Service Delivery
The rise of the advanced industrial society has been accompanied by a striking growth in the role government agencies play in the delivery of social services to individual citizens. In the United States, both the federal government and the government of the state of Alaska have included the indigenous peoples of the American Arctic within the scope of the resultant public programs. The Indian Health Service, for instance, has done much to combat diseases such as tuberculosis in village Alaska. Every Alaskan community of any size now has a local high school funded, for the most part, by the state government. Welfare programs, such as Aid to Families with Dependent Children (AFDC) and food stamps, are available as a matter of course in the American Arctic.

These programs have produced obvious benefits for many individual residents of village Alaska. But they have also taken an unintended toll of the viability of hunter/gatherer communities. Pressures to deliver social services in a cost-effective manner played a critical role in the transition to fixed, year-round settlements in many parts of the North. Coupled with the capital intensification of subsistence practices, this development has served to lock hunter/gatherers more and more tightly into the economic and political structures of the dominant society. Additionally, the introduction of comprehensive social services has given rise to the several forms of dependency that are widespread in the American Arctic today. In collective terms, this development has produced a growing dependence on transfer payments to local governments from the state and federal governments. At the individual level, it breeds the mentality of welfarism that commentators have associated with the expansion of social programs in a wide range of settings. These developments are externalities in the sense that they are unintended and often unforeseen by-products of the delivery of social services. But this does nothing to mitigate their corrosive effect on the ability of hunter/gatherer communities to maintain a way of life that differs significantly from that of the dominant society.

The Inroads of Popular Culture

The popular culture of modern America has become a universal phenomenon. Many Arctic residents have become regular consumers of fast foods. The golden arches of McDonald's rise today in Barrow, just as they do in Tokyo and Moscow. Rock music and television sitcoms, complete with the full panoply of English slang, are prominent features of village life throughout the Far North. Casual American clothing has, for the most part, replaced traditional garments fashioned from the skins of animals. Some of the more destructive concomitants of this pervasive popular culture, like the widespread use of drugs, are much in evidence in the American Arctic today.

Popular culture entered the American Arctic abruptly during the past two or three decades, borne initially by satellite television hookups and shortly thereafter by the advent of inexpensive video equipment. As some sympathetic observers have pointed out, these technologies can and sometimes do play a role in efforts to sustain the way of life of hunter/gatherer communities by helping to disseminate traditional knowledge (including the cultural practices embedded in Native languages) and assisting hunter/gatherers separated by long distances to form effective coalitions in defense of their unique way of life.[7] No doubt, there is much to be said for this proposition. Yet the relentless homogenizing force of American popular culture is undeniable. Faced with the demoralizing effects of a growing dependence on transfer payments, coupled with the insidious attractions of popular culture, those committed to protecting the alternative way of life associated with hunter/gatherer communities must often experience acute frustration regarding the terms of the struggle in which they are engaged.

Variable Vulnerability

It would be a mistake, however, to infer from this that all hunter/gatherer communities are equally vulnerable to the disruptive impact of the societal dynamics at work in advanced industrial societies. In fact, we can pinpoint a number of factors that serve to help or hinder the efforts of those seeking to protect the way of life of the hunter/gatherer in the face of the assimilationist forces at work in highly modernized social systems. None of these factors by itself is sufficient to ensure the success of these efforts. Yet several of them may well constitute necessary conditions for cultural survival; combinations of them may prove sufficient. Taken together, these factors also license the prediction that we should expect to encounter considerable variation in the success of individual communities of hunter/gatherers in their struggle to resist the homogenizing forces at work in advanced industrial societies.

Geographical separation, so long as it is not achieved in an arbitrary or artificial manner, generally serves to reduce the vulnerability of hunter/gatherer communities. In the Arctic, the most dramatic case in point is Greenland, a self-contained area that is far removed from Denmark and that supports a population that is approximately 80 percent Greenlandic. A somewhat similar situation could arise in the Canadian Arctic, with the emergence of Nunavut as a distinct and separate political entity. On the other hand, the achievement of geographical separation through socially and ecologically artificial arrangements, as exemplified by the Indian reservations of the American lower forty-eight, generally gives rise only to demoralizing backwaters rather than promoting the well-being of hunter/gatherer communities. Given the demographic as well as the geographic realities of the American Arctic today, it seems doubtful whether geographical separation can play an important role in protecting the hunter/gatherer communities of this region.

Another factor affecting the prospects of hunter/gatherers is the vitality of Native languages within communities of subsistence harvesters. Those who approach this subject from a sociolinguistic perspective invariably reach the conclusion that language plays a critical role in transmitting both culturally distinctive visions of reality and key social practices. Additionally, a shared language contributes to productive intergenerational relations and constitutes a defense against the feelings of disorientation or anomie that so often accompany acculturation. In this sense, the hunter/gatherer communities of the eastern Canadian

Arctic, where the Inuktitutt language remains a vital force, are better off than the communities of Alaska's North Slope, where few members of the younger generations are fluent in Inupiaq. The role of language in cultural survival also goes a long way toward providing a compelling rationale for educational programs, such as those of the Kativik Regional School Board in northern Quebec, under which all instruction in the early years of school is conducted in the Native language by Native instructors. Although the maintenance of Native languages may not in itself suffice to ensure the survival of the hunter/gatherer way of life, there is much to be said for the proposition that this way of life cannot survive the loss of indigenous languages.

Majority status within a well-defined and widely recognized political unit certainly strengthens the hand of hunter/gatherers. In these terms, the communities located within the North Slope Borough and the Northwest Arctic Borough are better off than those of southwestern Alaska; much the same can be said of the indigenous peoples of the Northwest Territories in contrast to those of the Yukon, or of the Native peoples of Greenland in contrast to those of Fennoscandia. This is not to say that indigenous peoples must induce the dominant society to accept their sovereignty by acknowledging the role of tribal governments possessing substantial power and authority. The North Slope Borough, the Government of the Northwest Territories, and the Home Rule in Greenland are all public governments rather than tribal governments. What matters to indigenous peoples in this context is effective control of governments able to exercise power over matters affecting the survival of hunter/gatherer communities.[8]

Economic independence, in the communal rather than the individual sense, clearly facilitates the efforts of hunter/gatherers to protect their distinctive way of life. It is undeniable, for example, that the substantial tax base the North Slope Borough has enjoyed as a result of oil development in northern Alaska has helped the Native peoples of the region to protect their way of life (despite some problems attributable to unfortunate borough fiscal policies). In these terms, there is a striking contrast between the North Slope Borough on the one hand and, on the other, the Greenlandic Home Rule, which depends on Denmark for about half of its public revenues, or the Government of the Northwest

Territories, which receives about two-thirds of its operating budget from the Canadian federal government. Economic independence translates regularly into political strength, whether the problem is one of bringing pressure to bear on the decision-making processes of outside governments or of resisting the inroads of outside forces on the home front. Economic independence also plays a critical role in warding off the corrosive effects that inevitably arise from a long-term dependence on transfer payments at the communal level as well as at the individual level.

Finally, the prospects of hunter/gatherers depend, in part, on their political skills. Because hunter/gatherer communities are small, not represented directly in the political institutions of the dominant society, and located in areas of substantial geopolitical significance, they must seek to build effective coalitions with other groups whose interests, at least with regard to issues that are critical to indigenous peoples, are compatible with their own. Without doubt, the most promising coalition partners for hunter/gatherers in the American Arctic are the conservation groups and the moderate environmental groups (as opposed to radical groups, such as Sea Shepherd, or animal protectionist groups, such as Friends of Animals or Defenders of Wildlife). In this regard, it is interesting to observe the efforts now underway to forge alliances between indigenous groups (for example, the Inuit Circumpolar Conference, Indigenous Survival International) and environmental groups (for example, the International Union for the Conservation of Nature and Natural Resources, the World Wildlife Fund) in connection with the sustainable-development movement and the campaign to formulate a revised version of the World Conservation Strategy. At a minimum, such alliances may prove helpful in blocking forces like the antiharvesting movement that threaten the resource base on which hunter/gatherers depend.[9]

A Strategy for Hunter/Gatherers

What are the implications of the argument I have sketched out for the strategy hunter/gatherers should adopt to carve out a secure niche for themselves in a social setting dominated by advanced industrial societies? Because the resources available to hunter/gatherers are severely limited, especially by comparison with those available to groups promoting the concerns of the dominant society, it is essential for hunter/gatherers to establish priorities and to concentrate on a few key areas, avoiding the trap of spreading themselves so thin that they are unable to protect their core values. More specifically, I suggest the following guidelines for those seeking to secure a future for hunter/gatherer communities in the American Arctic.

1. *Place strict limits on the expenditure of scarce resources to influence the policies of state and federal governments.* The Arctic policies of the United States are vague and volatile; they do not constitute the critical threats to the survival of hunter/gatherer communities in today's world. As the case of the Alaska Native Claims Settlement Act demonstrates, moreover, even policies initially supported by the Native community itself can, in practice, turn out to be disruptive to hunter/gatherer communities. What is more, the opportunity costs associated with efforts to influence public policies are high, in the sense that such efforts consume large quantities of resources that are consequently unavailable for other activities. In exceptional cases (for example, the subsistence provisions set forth in Title VIII of the Alaska National Interests Lands Conservation Act of 1980), it is probably important for hunter/gatherers to make a concerted effort to influence the substantive provisions of public policies. But under normal circumstances, they would be well advised to place sharp limits on the resources devoted to attempts to influence the terms of federal and state policies.

2. *Attach highest priority to initiatives aimed at ensuring the vitality of Native languages in hunter/gatherer communities.* There is little prospect of resurrecting the traditional practice of educating children in the home or in the field rather than in the schools. It is therefore critical to make use of the schools to sustain the hunter/gatherer way of life rather than allowing the schools to become homogenizing agents of the dominant society. This suggests that the approach to education developed by groups like the Kativik Regional School Board offers the best hope for the future.

3. *Take full advantage of all arrangements capable of preventing the erosion of the resource base or minimizing the imposition of restrictions on access to the resource base.* The land bank provisions of the 1987 amendments to the Alaska Native Claims Settlement Act should be exploited fully in this regard.[10] But this initiative by itself cannot solve the problem because much of the resource base that hunter/gatherers depend on is owned by others (as in the case of land-based resources), subject to the exclusive management authority of others (as in the case of marine resources), or vulnerable to the unintended side effects of the activities of distant actors. It is therefore imperative for hunter/gatherers to pursue vigorously options like the co-management arrangements that have emerged in recent years for bowhead whales in northern Alaska and the goose populations of the Yukon/Kuskokwim Delta area.[11]

4. *Explore every opportunity to reduce economic dependence through measures featuring sustainable development, income security programs, and arrangements intended to capture a fair share of economic returns or rents.* Mixed economies are a fact of life in the American Arctic. No one believes it is possible (or even desirable) to recreate pure subsistence economies—if they ever existed—in the communities of village Alaska. But a concerted effort is needed to decouple the economies of village Alaska from the economy of the dominant society, thereby reducing the exposure of these local economies to the fluctuations of world markets and the volatility of state and federal policies.

5. *Forge effective alliances among hunter/gatherers themselves and between hunter/gatherers and other groups possessing compatible interests.* Frictions between Indian and Inuit peoples, splits between remote communities and the regional corporations in Alaska, and disagreements over issues like tribal sovereignty serve only to weaken the effectiveness of an interest group whose resources are, at best, severely limited by comparison with those of other interest groups. It is therefore imperative to overcome these frictions and create an effective indigenous coalition in the process. At the same time, the forging of a united front between Native interests and the concerns of moderate environmental groups

holds considerable promise for advancing the agenda of hunter/
gatherers.

6. *Launch direct, grass-roots campaigns to appeal to the residual
hunter/gatherer instincts present in the urbanized populations of dominant societies.* Finn Lynge may well be right in arguing that the
triumph of cultural coding in highly modernized societies has led
to a systematic neglect of the instinctive tendencies embedded in
Western man's genetic endowment.[12] But these instinctive tendencies have not disappeared altogether. The resultant vision is
often based on crude stereotypes and couched in highly romanticized terms, but the fact remains that many members of the
dominant society exhibit a continuing fascination with "Eskimos" and their hunter/gatherer way of life. What is required is
some means of unleashing this fascination by demonstrating to
members of the dominant society, in an emotionally comprehen-
sible way, that their actions may have the unintended consequences of destroying a way of life they not only find intriguing
but whose survival may also make a significant contribution to
the protection of ecosystems threatened by industrial development. The struggle to free the gray whales trapped off Barrow in
1988 did wonders for the cause of whales more generally, as millions of viewers followed their plight on nightly television news
broadcasts. What can Esau do to attract the same sort of emotional support for the survival of the hunter/gatherer way of life?

PART TWO

Regional Studies

Prologue

Some Arctic issues are regional in scope by virtue of the fact that
they extend far beyond the concerns of individual communities
yet do not, for the most part, center on interactions at the international level. Included here are a range of matters involving the
governance of northern states, territories, or autonomous regions; intergovernmental relations (both state and local and state
and national); and the impact of events originating outside the
region (for example, the sustainable-development movement) on
Arctic areas. Typically, these issues have a high political content.
Sometimes they raise questions about the extent to which national governments are capable of devising coherent Arctic policies and about the consequences flowing from efforts at various
levels to implement such policies. In many cases, they engender
conflicts over the allocation of authority or power among different
levels of government (for example, federal, state, and borough
governments in Alaska) or between public governments on the
one hand and indigenous political organizations (for example, tribal governments) on the other. Here, too, the Arctic is not unique;
it offers numerous opportunities to examine empirically a variety
of issues that recur in one form or another throughout much of
the world.

One of the most attractive features of the regional perspective
on Arctic politics is the chance it affords for the conduct of systematic comparative studies. A few examples will suffice to
illustrate this potential. Those interested in intergovernmental

relations and constitutional development will find it interesting to compare and contrast the Home Rule government established in Greenland in 1979, the North Slope Borough and the Northwest Arctic Borough governments now in place in northern Alaska, and the complex of governing arrangements resulting from the gradual devolution of the federal government's authority in the Canadian Arctic. The relationships between these public governments and regional arrangements whose membership is restricted to indigenous peoples (for example, the Inupiat Community of the Arctic Slope or some of the proposed versions of Nunavut in northern Canada) constitute a related topic of considerable importance.

Similar comments are in order regarding comparative studies of Arctic institutions or regimes governing the exploitation of natural resources and, more broadly, human/environment relations. There are significant differences in the resource regimes that have grown up to guide the efforts of public and private actors concerned with the use of both renewable and nonrenewable resources in various parts of the Arctic. Yet throughout the region there is a growing interest in the potential of co-management arrangements as mechanisms for building constructive relations between public agencies (for instance, the U.S. Fish and Wildlife Service or the Canadian Wildlife Service) possessing the authority to manage natural resources and groups of users who often possess valuable knowledge concerning the relevant resources and who are expected to comply with the directives of public agencies, even when the agencies have little capacity to enforce the rules they promulgate.

The disintegration of the Soviet Union and the opening up of Russia (which encompasses well over 40 percent of the land area of the Arctic) has added an exciting new dimension to comparative analyses of Arctic issues. Partly, this is due to the fact that Soviet policies and administrative practices in the North have differed significantly from their Western counterparts for a long time, though the physical and biological systems of the two halves of the Circumpolar North are broadly similar. These circumstances afford extremely attractive opportunities for field studies focusing on the impact of social institutions. In part, the interest in the Russian North arises from the facts that the practices developed over time by Soviet administrative agencies are now undergoing rapid change and that many Russian analysts and policymakers are eager to learn from Western practices in this realm. The resultant desire to compare and contrast experiences concerning such matters as constitutional arrangements, intergovernmental relations, safeguarding indigenous rights and cultures, exploitation of natural resources, and protection of natural areas is striking.

This part of the book begins with a chapter that presents an overview of Arctic resource conflicts. Drawing primarily on American experience in this realm, the chapter canvasses the range of resource conflicts currently arising throughout the Far North, assesses the severity of these conflicts, and classifies them in terms of several illuminating analytic distinctions. This sets the stage for an examination of the efficacy of a variety of techniques for handling conflict and of the value of developing a tool kit of substantive approaches to the conflicts now arising in the Arctic. The chapter suggests that there is much to be said for the idea of establishing an Arctic Resources Council, which could provide a neutral forum for regular exchanges of ideas both about specific conflicts in the Far North and about the dynamics of Arctic resource conflicts more generally.

The chapters that follow deal with prominent Arctic issues approached, for the most part, in regional terms. Chapter 6 focuses on a constellation of increasingly intense clashes pitting preservationists against consumptive users with regard to the management of wildlife in the North. There is every reason to expect that this will become an increasingly confrontational issue area in the years to come. Chapter 7 employs the concept of social traps to illuminate the problems that can befall public governments in northern areas when they experience sudden but not necessarily lasting increases in public revenues resulting from the exploitation of nonrenewable resources like oil and gas. Chapter 8 turns to flow resources, comparing and contrasting Soviet efforts to establish the Northeast Passage as a commercial artery through the development of the infrastructure and administrative apparatus of the Northern Sea Route and the far less energetic efforts of Canadians and, to a lesser extent, Americans to encourage commercial shipping in the Northwest Passage.

CHAPTER 5

Arctic Resource Conflicts:
Sources and Solutions

U ntil World War II, the Far North was a remote and isolated
area of interest only to a handful of explorers, fur traders,
missionaries, and scientists and to a sparse population of indigenous peoples who had managed to adapt to the harsh natural
environments of the region over several millennia. The war
changed all of that, initiating a series of far-reaching developments that have accelerated rapidly during the past generation.
Major battles were fought in the Aleutian Islands and around the
North Cape of Europe during the war. Both Alaska and the Kola
Peninsula emerged as key links in the transit route for American
lend-lease materials bound for the Soviet Union. Following the
war, the Far North attained prominence as the most direct route
for bombers and missiles to fly between the United States and the
Soviet Union. Consequently, the region became an important site
for military installations, such as Distant Early Warning (DEW)
Line radar sites and strategic airbases.

This chapter, co-authored with Gail Osherenko, originated as a presentation to a conference, "U.S. Arctic Interests," held at the Woods
Hole Oceanographic Institution in 1983. An earlier version of the chapter, also entitled "Arctic Resource Conflicts: Sources and Solutions," appeared in William E. Westermeyer and Kurt M. Shusterich, eds., *U.S.
Arctic Interests: The 1980s and 1990s* (New York: Springer-Verlag, 1984),
199–218. The events of the intervening years have merely confirmed the
importance of Arctic resource conflicts and the need to devise imagi-
native procedures for handling them.

Even more important, field exploration has revealed that the Far North contains vast reserves of oil, natural gas, coal, and hydroelectric power. The estimated recoverable reserves of oil north of 60°N run as high as 300 billion barrels. The largest oil strike in American history resulted in the development of the Prudhoe Bay and Kuparuk fields in Alaska, yielding 1.5 to 2 million barrels of oil per day, or approximately 25 percent of American daily production. The coal reserves of Alaska alone have been calculated at between 1.9 and 5 trillion short tons, about the same as the combined reserves of the lower forty-eight states. The extraordinary hydroelectric potential of the region has already given rise to megaprojects in Siberia and the Canadian North such as the Churchill Falls project in Labrador and the James Bay project in Quebec.

Conflicts of Use

The growth of interest in exploring and exploiting the natural resources of the Far North has generated an array of more or less severe resource conflicts. These are situations in which the efforts of one party (individual or group) to obtain benefits by using a given natural resource harm or threaten to harm the interests of other parties, regardless of the benefits accruing to the initial user(s).[1] Such resource conflicts become interesting to students of social conflict when they lead to conflicts of interest between more or less well-organized and influential human groups capable of advancing and defending their interests in economic, legal, and political arenas.

Today, several powerful interest groups, each representing deeply held and legitimate concerns, are locked in a profound struggle over the content of northern resource policies, both in the United States and in the other circumpolar nations. Industries endeavoring to meet the demands of affluent populations in the temperate zones for energy and raw materials see the Circumpolar North as a resource frontier that can be developed in an atmosphere of relative political certainty and security. At the same time, the region contains many of the largest and most dramatic unspoiled natural environments on the planet, a fact that has led environmentalists to place top priority on the struggle to protect vast areas of the Far North. What is more, we are presently witnessing a sharp rise in the consciousness and political sophistication of the indigenous peoples of the Far North, a development producing a surging tide of well-directed claims concerning the rights of these peoples to land and sociocultural autonomy.

The Extent of Arctic Resource Conflicts

What is the incidence of resource conflicts in the Far North? Are such conflicts pervasive, or are they merely episodic occurrences of no more than passing concern? To answer this question, it will help to group Arctic resource conflicts into several broad categories rather than simply listing them one after another.

In some cases, the pursuit of material or tangible interests in the Arctic can be expected to harm the material interests of others. Offshore oil developments may prove destructive to populations of fish, marine mammals, or birds on which local residents depend for subsistence purposes. Drilling or mining operations may produce severe physical disturbances in areas of tundra underlain with permafrost. Similarly, oil or gas operations may generate forms of water or air pollution that are physically harmful to local residents. In a sense, these material conflicts are the easiest resource conflicts to come to terms with in an orderly fashion. Though relevant data may be unavailable or controversial, it is possible, at least in principle, to measure the physical impacts that engender such conflicts. Moreover, it is sometimes feasible to resolve conflicts of this type through technical measures (for example, introducing construction techniques suitable for building in permafrost).

In other cases, the pursuit of material interests results in injuries to the intangible interests of others. To illustrate, large-scale development involving oil or hydroelectric power in the Far North may severely disturb or distort important social institutions or central elements of the preexisting indigenous way of life (for example, subsistence economies, cultural norms of sharing, traditional authority structures). By the same token, construction projects associated with the development of northern resources may produce severe stresses on delivery systems for health, education, and welfare even in larger modern settlements (for example, Fairbanks during the construction of the Trans-Alaska Pipeline in the 1970s).[2] Conflicts of this type are hard to come to grips with systematically, both because it is difficult to measure the relevant injuries or negative impacts with precision and because there is no straightforward methodology for comparing these injuries with the benefits accruing to the developers (and their clients).

In still other cases, the pursuit of intangible interests damages the intangible interests of others. For example, the vision of developing the natural resources of the Far North through the use of modern, high-technology operations may prove fundamentally incompatible with the ideal of preserving a network of more traditional subsistence-oriented, self-sufficient communities in the North.[3] Despite the optimism of thoughtful observers like Thomas Berger, it seems doubtful that two such radically different visions of socioeconomic organization can coexist comfortably in the Far North for any length of time.[4] This is so whether or not the introduction of modern high-technology operations damages the material interests of those desiring to maintain a more traditional way of life. These clashes of ideals (or ideational conflicts) are particularly hard to resolve, both because they are fundamental in nature and because it is difficult to devise any neutral currency in terms of which to calculate their severity.

The Severity of Arctic Resource Conflicts

The preceding discussion suggests that Arctic resource conflicts will be common, perhaps even pervasive, during the foreseeable future. It seems inevitable that industry interests will clash regularly with Native interests as well as with the interests of environmental groups in the Far North. But how severe or intense are these conflicts apt to become? Is there any reason to expect them to go beyond the array of routine or normal frictions that attend virtually all human endeavors?

Conflicts are severe to the extent that they (1) involve high stakes for the parties concerned, (2) give rise to sharply divergent preferences among the parties with regard to alternative outcomes, and (3) cannot be resolved through the application of simple and widely accepted solution procedures. Several problems plague efforts to assess the severity of Arctic resource conflicts in these terms.

• Many of the concerns underlying Arctic resource conflicts involve injuries expected to occur in the future rather than injuries that are already occurring. Depending upon the assumptions chosen, it is relatively easy to magnify or diminish the significance of prospective injuries.

• Arctic resource conflicts often focus on events that are probabilistic in nature (for example, the occurrence of oil spills under unfavorable weather conditions or during whale migrations). This makes attitudes toward risk an important consideration in evaluating the severity of these resource conflicts. Moreover, since there is seldom any objective basis for assigning probabilities to the relevant events, subjective probability estimates become major determinants of calculations concerning the intensity of conflicts.[5]

• Most Arctic resource conflicts involve complex ecosystems and their interactions with equally complex social systems. In such contexts, it is often difficult to isolate the causal significance of individual actions or proposed actions that figure prominently in conflicts among human interest groups.[6] The fact that it is ordinarily impossible to conduct systematic field experiments, much less controlled laboratory experiments, on the affected systems only exacerbates this problem.

• There is no suitable metric for measuring the full range of values at stake in Arctic resource conflicts. The limitations of utilitarian procedures such as benefit/cost analysis are apparent in this connection.[7]

• If anything, the problems of making intergroup comparisons (that is, devising a common metric in terms of which to make meaningful comparisons of gains and losses accruing to different groups) in analyzing Arctic resource conflicts are greater than the well-known problems of making interpersonal comparisons discussed in numerous mainstream analyses of social or collective choice.[8]

Accordingly, there are no simple answers to questions regarding the severity or intensity of Arctic resource conflicts. In fact, efforts to arrive at generally acceptable answers to such questions sometimes generate disputes or conflicts themselves. The best we can do at this stage is to identify some indicators of the importance attached to these conflicts by the principal interest groups involved. All of the interested parties have continually allocated substantial resources to the protection and promotion of their interests in the Far North (consider, for example, the resources expended by British Petroleum, the North Slope Borough, or the Alaska Coalition). Arctic resource conflicts have been publicized heavily and on a continuing basis in the media. The central issues raised by plans for the development of northern resources have provoked a sizable volume of litigation. What is more, the interested parties have often proved unwilling to accept the initial outcomes of litigation, appealing adverse decisions handed down by the lower courts (for example, North Slope Borough v. Andrus) or initiating new litigation raising the same fundamental questions (for example, the continuing series of lawsuits pertaining to offshore oil and gas development in waters adjacent to Alaska).[9] Despite the methodological problems outlined in the preceding paragraphs, therefore, it seems safe to conclude that many Arctic resource conflicts are regarded as severe or intense by the parties involved.

As the basis for an examination of alternative methods for resolving Arctic resource conflicts, it will help to focus on the following questions:

1. How can we handle these conflicts in a fashion that satisfies the legitimate concerns of the parties affected?

2. Are there ways to avoid perpetuating in the Arctic a situation in which certain concerns or values are so heavily favored by prevailing institutional arrangements that some interests consistently dominate or triumph over others in the treatment of Arctic resource conflicts?[10]

3. Will any of the resultant procedures yield outcomes that promote the broader public interest or the common good in addition to satisfying the concerns of the parties directly affected?

Standard Procedures for Handling Resource Conflicts

The prevailing approaches to conflict resolution in the United States include both private sector procedures (market mechanisms and private bargaining) and public sector procedures (litigation and related adversarial activities and legislation). Recent experience suggests that all of these standard procedural approaches to conflict resolution leave much to be desired in the search for solutions to Arctic resource conflicts, though each offers a possible response to certain types of conflict in the Arctic.

Market Solutions

It is tempting to argue that market mechanisms, which are widely used in Western capitalist systems to arrive at collective choices in the face of divergent interests, can be relied upon to resolve many Arctic resource conflicts.[11] Yet the operation of any market mechanism requires the presence of several conditions that seldom obtain in the Arctic. There is no structure of private property rights (or other transferable rights) associated with most Arctic resources, a necessary condition for inducing parties to enter into market-oriented exchange relationships. This is partly attributable to the prevalence of public ownership (or exclusive management authority) throughout the Far North. Even the changes brought about by the Alaska Native Claims Settlement Act of 1971 have left the overwhelming majority of natural resources in the Arctic in some form of public ownership or management.[12] In part, this is because of the inherent difficulties confronting any effort to impose a system of transferable rights on these resources. Additionally, many of the values involved in Arctic resource conflicts are difficult or impossible to represent in the utilitarian terms required to give them exchange value in market transactions. Thus, it is hard to compute the value of biological diversity or of subsistence practices to indigenous communities in terms of money or some convenient surrogate for money. None of this means that deliberate efforts to create markets or quasi-markets (for example, markets in harvesting permits for marine mammals) will never constitute a suitable response to Arctic resource conflicts.[13] Nonetheless, market solutions can hardly be expected to constitute a simple means for coming to grips with this entire class of conflicts.

Private Bargaining
    Even in the absence of functioning markets, it is sometimes possible to rely on private exchanges to resolve conflicts of the type under consideration here. Such processes focus on private bargaining, in which the parties to resource conflicts negotiate mutually acceptable agreements in the absence of any involvement on the part of a public authority.[14] Depending on the content of the prevailing system of liability rules, this may force parties expecting to be injured by resource development to pay the developers to alter their plans, or it may require the developers to offer the affected parties some form of compensation in exchange for their consent to proposed development activities. Whatever the merits of private bargaining in terms of efficiency, this approach raises serious questions with regard to equity as well as the larger public interest or the common good.[15] For the most part, the parties expecting to be injured by resource development will be weaker in terms of bargaining strength than the prospective developers. In many cases, those injured by resource development constitute large, poorly organized groups; it is often unclear who can or should represent these groups in negotiation. As a result, problems may arise with regard to identifying and including all of the interested parties in the negotiations and final agreements. The transaction costs associated with this response to Arctic resource conflicts are apt to be high because the resultant negotiations will ordinarily be protracted and cumbersome. Further, unless the prevailing liability rules are well defined and widely accepted, private bargaining can be expected to give rise to disputes over the content of liability rules that serve to divert attention from the substantive issues at stake in the initial resource conflicts. These observations are not meant to disparage the potential for private initiative in handling Arctic resource conflicts; private actions have some obvious attractions that should not be overlooked. Yet there is no basis for expecting private bargaining to provide a simple solution for most Arctic resource conflicts.

Litigation
    A recognition of the limitations of private procedures for resolving Arctic resource conflicts suggests a shift of focus to look

at some standard procedures involving legitimate and properly constituted public authorities (judicial systems or legislatures) coupled with an agreement to accept outcomes arrived at through the operation of these procedures as both binding and socially desirable. Consider first adversary processes, including the courts and quasi-judicial administrative bodies. Some years ago, Derek Bok, then president of Harvard University, called for fundamental reforms in the American legal system, which he attacked as imposing excessive costs, causing frustrating delays, and not providing equal access to all economic classes.[16] In doing so, he joined a growing group of thoughtful observers who have noted the inefficiencies and inequalities of litigation as a mode of conflict resolution. Adversary processes place a premium on strategic behavior in contrast to problem-solving activities or integrative behavior. They compel the parties to think in terms of winning or losing rather than seeking solutions accommodating several legitimate concerns at the same time. Adversary processes also encourage players to explore opportunities for gaining advantages through the manipulation of complex procedures rather than searching for creative solutions to substantive problems. As a result, it is frequently difficult to obtain a clear understanding of the substantive issues underlying a conflict from a reading of the record produced by litigation. What is more, the remedies available to courts are typically confining. To illustrate, awards involving monetary compensation for damages may be of little value in redressing the injuries sustained by indigenous peoples or environmental groups. Under the circumstances, it should come as no surprise that the judgments of courts seldom resolve Arctic resource conflicts in a decisive fashion and that the relevant interest groups clash over and over again in a stream of repetitive and costly lawsuits.[17]

Legislation
    Although legislatures provide appropriate forums for resolving certain types of conflict, existing legislative bodies are not likely to achieve satisfactory results in handling most Arctic resource conflicts. Legislatures are not only slow to act in handling conflicts; they also typically produce statutes that are internally

inconsistent or too general to provide solutions to specific conflicts. The efforts of administrative agencies to implement ambiguous or vague laws usually lead to ongoing conflicts rather than to any resolution of disputes.[18] In many cases, moreover, there are no institutions that all of the relevant interest groups can accept as legitimate and appropriate to deal with Arctic resource conflicts. Why should the Inupiat communities of the North Slope accept the authority of the United States Congress, a body in which they are largely unrepresented and that operates on the basis of alien procedures? How should jurisdictional authority over these conflicts be allocated among the United States Congress, the Alaska state legislature, and the Assembly of the North Slope Borough? Even in cases where the relevant interest groups are willing to pursue their interests within the same institutional arena, it takes no profound insight to recognize that these groups are anything but equal with regard to the access and influence at their disposal.[19] It is difficult to see how Native interests can ever constitute a powerful force in the legislative bargaining that occurs within the Congress. Despite the popular appeal of certain environmental groups, they too can rarely hope to match the political resources at the disposal of associations representing industry interests. Consequently, the theoretical attractions of public procedural solutions are seldom likely to be realized in practice in the realm of Arctic resource conflicts.

Substantive Solutions for Arctic Resource Conflicts

The preceding discussion of the limits of various procedural approaches to conflict resolution suggests that it may prove helpful to consider a range of possible substantive responses to Arctic resource conflicts. None offers a simple solution for all of the conflicts, and the analysis presented here identifies some of the limitations associated with particular responses.[20] Taken together, however, this range of substantive responses constitutes a valuable collection of tools for dealing with the complexities of Arctic resource conflicts. The following section addresses the issue of devising a mechanism to match these substantive responses to specific conflicts in the Arctic.

Minimizing Conflict

An obvious initial response to conflicts arising from actual or proposed natural resource developments is for public authorities to undertake, or at least to fund, a search for ways to eliminate or substantially ameliorate the relevant conflicts without imposing excessive costs on anyone.[21] Such conflict-minimizing efforts can take at least three forms:

• Research may reveal new technologies (for example, safer drill rigs, less toxic drilling muds) or practices capable of mitigating prospective injuries.

• Careful planning and coordination may make it possible to avoid injuring the interests of others without significantly slowing down resource development (for example, confining construction activities on Alaska's North Slope to winter months or avoiding offshore activities during whale migrations).

• Reasonable restrictions (for example, public regulations establishing seasonal limits on drilling) may help to protect ecosystems or social systems without imposing excessive costs on resource developers.

Conflict-minimizing techniques are extremely useful in handling Arctic resource conflicts as well as many other types of conflict. These techniques are often more economical (in both monetary and nonmonetary terms) than other approaches to conflict resolution, and they are likely to arouse less public controversy in specific cases. It follows that they should be explored routinely as a first line of attack in dealing with specific conflicts.

At the same time, this approach has severe limitations as a response to the most pressing Arctic resource conflicts. Both ecosystems and social systems are so complex that it is difficult to foresee, much less to control, many of the impacts produced by large-scale resource development. The issues underlying Arctic resource conflicts often involve an irreducible core of divergent values that cannot be avoided through research or planning. Further, research and planning are seldom neutral processes; they typically pose the following dilemma with regard to resource conflicts. On the one hand, a precautionary principle suggests that developmental activities be suspended or slowed down while research or planning takes place, in which case the interests of industry (and its clients) will suffer. Alternatively, developmental activities can be allowed to proceed during the phase of research and planning, in which case the interests of indigenous peoples and environmentalists will suffer. Moreover, there are often opportunities for powerful interest groups to manipulate research and planning efforts to promote their own ends. A search for technical measures designed to mitigate conflicts will frequently seem attractive to a dominant interest group anxious to make a public display of concern about the interests of others but equally determined to avoid raising deeper value questions embedded in resource conflicts (for example, do subsistence users have primary rights; is the preservation of biological diversity of transcendent importance?).

Optimal Mixes
   When trade-offs involving divergent values are unavoidable (that is, when conflict-minimizing measures fail to eliminate conflicts of interest), public authorities may attempt to maximize social welfare or net social gains by choosing some optimal mix of uses for the resources in question. Two approaches to the choice of optimal mixes are in common use. One is the multiple-use criterion set forth in the organic acts of the Forest Service and the Bureau of Land Management.[22] The other is the proper-balance standard incorporated in the revised federal regime for offshore oil and gas development.[23] These approaches have achieved the status of primary guidelines, at least in federal efforts to resolve resource conflicts. In general terms, moreover, they are significant in the sense that they put pressure on policymakers not to favor the concerns of one interest group to the exclusion of others when values conflict. The problem with relying on these approaches to yield clear-cut solutions for specific Arctic resource conflicts is that they must either make use of utilitarian procedures such as benefit/cost analysis or degenerate into subjective processes vulnerable to manipulation by those wielding political influence.[24] As the preceding discussion indicates, it is difficult to capture many of the values at stake in Arctic resource conflicts (for example, the preservation of the Inupiat whaling complex or the protection of the ecosystems of the Arctic National Wildlife

Refuge) in any quantitative, much less monetary, form. None of
this vitiates the general approach to conflict resolution underlying the idea of optimal mixes. But these limitations do restrict the
usefulness of concepts like multiple use, and they suggest the
importance of being aware of the possibilities for these seemingly
objective procedures to be used in a manipulative fashion.

Lexicographic Orderings
   Alternatively, conflicts of use can be resolved by ranking the
relevant values or uses hierarchically and then proclaiming that
the highest value must prevail whenever a conflict of use arises.
Some such perspective underlies all proposals for single or dominant uses of natural resources. Ironically, this approach has been
followed both for hard-rock mining on the public domain and for
wilderness preservation, though the standard is regarded by
many as an undesirable anachronism in the case of hard-rock
mining and as an inappropriate innovation in the case of wilderness preservation.[25] Although this procedure is naturally attractive to those endeavoring to protect core or fundamental values,
it is subject to significant limitations as applied to Arctic resource
conflicts. As soon as we move beyond the realm of straightforward utilitarian calculations, there is no simple or obvious way
to rank conflicting uses or values. Is energy independence more
or less important than preserving biological diversity by protecting endangered or threatened species (for example, the bowhead
whale) or safeguarding cultural diversity by protecting the subsistence cultures of indigenous peoples? According priority to a
dominant use or value makes it difficult to engage in meaningful,
comprehensive land-use or resource-use planning for a region.
Moreover, lexicographic orderings always produce some risk that
large sacrifices in terms of other values will be sanctioned for the
sake of achieving marginal gains with respect to the preferred or
dominant value.

Zonal Systems
   The problems outlined in the preceding paragraphs with regard to optimal mixes and lexicographic orderings have often
given rise to proposals for zonal arrangements. The essential idea
here is to divide a region spatially into two or more distinct zones,

managing each of the zones in a different fashion with respect to resource development. The withdrawal provisions incorporated into modern federal land management practices have had the effect of creating a de facto zonal system regarding activities such as hard-rock mining, timber harvesting, and hydrocarbon development in contrast to habitat protection and wilderness preservation. What is more, zonal concepts are already being employed in the Arctic as a means of handling resource conflicts. To illustrate, the siting of installations such as the Kuparuk Industrial Complex (KIC) in a highly compact configuration is intended to produce a sharp differentiation between an intensive-use industrial zone and a series of other zones that are not open to industrial use.

Nonetheless, zonal systems have limited application as a mode of handling Arctic resource conflicts. There is no simple and acceptable way of designating certain areas as sacrifice zones where human values (such as preserving cultural integrity or a cherished way of life) are concerned. Northern ecosystems are typically large systems featuring relatively small numbers of species that are highly migratory, so it is difficult to demarcate separated zones to protect wildlife in the region.[26] The problems raised by conflicts involving intangible and, especially, ideational concerns are not likely to be alleviated by the establishment of spatially defined zones in any case. If modern high-technology development proves fundamentally incompatible with the continuation of traditional life-styles in the Far North, for example, confining development activities to certain spatially demarcated sites will not resolve the central conflict.

Primacy of Rights
Articulate observers perturbed by the consequences of applying utilitarian procedures such as benefit/cost analysis to resource conflicts have repeatedly advocated a shift to a nonutilitarian perspective emphasizing the inviolability of primary rights. The fundamental idea here is to recognize the existence of certain priority rights (Native subsistence rights, rights of species to survival?) and then to declare that no gains calculated in utilitarian terms can be large enough to justify violating these primary rights. The attraction of this approach is that it shifts attention away from

tortuous efforts to quantify values such as the protection of cultural integrity or the preservation of biological diversity. As might be expected, moreover, a focus on rights appeals to lawyers, who are accustomed to resolving conflicts among claims advanced by the bearers of rights, in the same way that an emphasis on benefit/cost calculations appeals to economists, whose entire analytic apparatus rests on utilitarian premises. But the idea of employing "rights as trumps," as Dworkin has put it,[27] also has limitations as a means of resolving Arctic resource conflicts. It is not always easy to establish which rights are valid on any terms, much less deserving to be called primary rights. Are Inupiat rights to landfast ice or certain rights accorded to bowhead whales (either individually or as a species) suitable for inclusion in this category? Frequently, Arctic resource conflicts involve controversies between interest groups, each of which asserts claims based on rights, rather than disputes in which only one side asserts such claims. Consider, by way of illustration, the Canadian Baker Lake case, in which the Inuit based their position on rights stemming from aboriginal use and occupancy while the opposing mining companies asserted rights deriving from leases and permits granted by the federal government of Canada.[28] Beyond this, espousing the primacy of established rights as a means of resolving resource conflicts introduces a significant conservative or status quo bias. Just as utilitarian calculations are apt to bias decisions toward the interests of certain groups, an approach emphasizing the primacy of established rights can be expected to bias outcomes toward the interests of other groups.

Proposal for an Arctic Resources Council

The preceding sections have identified and evaluated several common procedures as well as a range of substantive solutions as responses to Arctic resource conflicts. But there exists no sensitive mechanism for assigning specific conflicts to appropriate forums for resolution or for determining which response or combination of responses is most likely to yield generally acceptable and equitable outcomes in particular cases. The task of matching specific conflicts with appropriate responses is a poorly understood and often neglected area in dealing with the whole range of social conflicts, including Arctic resource conflicts. To handle this task in the realm of Arctic resource conflicts, it would help to establish an Arctic Resources Council. Such a council would function neither as a legislative body enacting lawlike decisions nor as a court handing down binding judgments in the wake of adversarial confrontations. Instead, it would be a deliberative forum, reflecting the concerns of all legitimate stakeholders in the Arctic and operating in a problem-solving mode.

The term "problem-solving" refers both to a general orientation toward conflict resolution and to a collection of techniques designed to assist parties in reconciling specific conflicts of interest.[29] Problem solving rests on the proposition that it is important to deemphasize strategic behavior, a mode of operation that encourages individual parties to social conflicts to bend every effort toward maximizing their own gains, on the assumptions that others will approach conflict in the same terms and that conflict resolution generally produces winners and losers.[30] Problem solving stresses the likelihood of mutual losses arising from interactive decision making and promotes processes through which parties reconceptualize their conflicts as common or joint problems requiring efforts to accommodate two or more legitimate interests.

Those involved in problem solving typically take a lively interest in the development and application of specific techniques for redirecting attention from strategic maneuvering to the accommodation of legitimate interests. Such techniques range from mediation and controlled communication to simulation exercises and future imaging. Under the circumstances, the principal concerns of the Arctic Resources Council would be to contribute toward conceptualizing Arctic resource conflicts as common problems, suggesting appropriate procedural or substantive responses to these problems and devising techniques to assist the parties in reconciling their legitimate concerns in specific cases.

Jurisdiction
The Arctic Resources Council would be authorized to play an active role in dealing with the whole range of conflicts over the use of natural resources in the Arctic. Yet it would not operate like a court, either in the sense of being able to exercise compul-

sory jurisdiction or in the sense of possessing the authority to hand down binding judgments. In essence, the council would seek to enter conflicts at an early stage, attempting to weigh the relative merits of different approaches to their resolution and helping the parties to devise responses capable of accommodating several sets of interests at once.

To get the Arctic Resources Council underway, it would probably make sense to focus initially on resource conflicts arising within the jurisdictional reach of the United States. This arrangement would greatly improve the chances of getting the council up and running effectively. Many Arctic resource conflicts, however, involve interests that extend beyond the jurisdictional boundaries of individual states or call into question some of the principles underlying the concept of sovereignty on which jurisdictional boundaries are based. Consider, for example, the conflicts over pollution control in the High Arctic, navigation in the Northwest Passage, and the use of landfast ice by Native peoples.

Accordingly, it would be desirable to encourage an expansion of the council's jurisdictional scope to include other parts of the Circumpolar North at the earliest opportunity. The addition of Canadian representatives alone would be a major step in the right direction. Ideally, the council would eventually come to include representatives of interest groups and stakeholders located in each of the circumpolar nations. Given the problems of creating supranational organizations, however, it would be a mistake to put off establishing the Arctic Resources Council until the problems of international cooperation in this realm can be fully solved.

Composition

Fundamentally, the Arctic Resources Council would be a representative body composed of individuals capable of voicing the concerns of all of the interest groups possessing deeply held and legitimate points of view regarding the use of Arctic resources. Without doubt, the council would encompass representatives of industries operating in the Arctic, Native residents of the Arctic, and environmental groups interested in the ecosystems of the Arctic. It might well come to include individuals associated with additional interest groups, such as the academic or research community and recreational users. At the same time, the council would encompass representatives of various public authorities or governments with sizable stakes in the Arctic. This would include the federal government of the United States, the state of Alaska, and regional public governments, like the North Slope Borough. It might even extend to the village governments of some of the smaller, remote communities of the Arctic, such as Kaktovik or Point Hope, and to recognized tribal governments, such as the Inupiat Community of the Arctic Slope. Because the council would be a deliberative body rather than a voting body, it would not be important to devise elaborate formulas governing the number of members to be included. The main objective would be to ensure that representatives of all legitimate stakeholders in the Arctic be granted a voice in the council's deliberations. Under the circumstances, it would be desirable to allow each interest group to select representatives to participate in the deliberations of the council in its own fashion. This would allow Native peoples, industries, environmental groups, and public agencies to make use of different procedures in selecting representatives. Once again, the key to success with a mechanism such as the council would be the representativeness of its membership rather than the uniformity of the procedures through which individual members are chosen.

Mode of Operation
    As already suggested, the Arctic Resources Council would function neither as a court nor as a legislative body. Rather, its role would center on efforts to encourage the emergence of a problem-solving atmosphere regarding Arctic resource conflicts. In this connection, the emphasis would be on the development of creative ways to accommodate diverse interests rather than on the exercise of strategic skills to maximize the chances of achieving victory in adversarial encounters. More specifically, the council would concentrate on efforts to assess the applicability of the various responses to conflict (set forth in the preceding sections of this chapter) to specific Arctic resource conflicts. In cases where private initiative is deemed appropriate, the role of the council would be confined to encouraging the parties to interact with each other on this basis. In other cases, however, the council might undertake additional steps, supervising relevant research,

analyzing proposals for zonal arrangements in the Arctic, or assessing the validity of claims regarding the existence of established rights in the Far North.

In all probability, the council would eventually want to create a series of commissions to assist it in undertaking tasks of this sort. For example, it is easy to foresee uses for a commission on Arctic research and planning, a commission concerned with rights-based claims to land in the Arctic, and a commission dealing with the design of institutional arrangements, such as quasi-markets. These commissions would be composed of individuals chosen for their expertise in the relevant subject matter, and they would be limited to functioning as advisory bodies to the council as a whole.

Organizational Arrangements

The discussion in the preceding paragraphs indicates that the Arctic Resources Council would require at least a modest administrative apparatus. The council should have a permanent secretary general, who would supervise small professional and clerical staffs providing support for the council itself as well as for the various commissions. The council would not require a large in-house research program but would need to have a staff of its own capable of assembling relevant information and supplying competent assessments of analyses undertaken by others. This, of course, implies that the council would have to be furnished with both a headquarters facility and a regular budget. It seems important that the council's headquarters be located in the Arctic proper. This would serve to separate the council from the pressures that pervade all of the political capitals, and it would provide the council with an atmosphere of legitimacy as an authentic Arctic body. Any disadvantages arising from remoteness could be alleviated substantially through appropriate uses of modern communications and transportation technologies.

Turning to the council's budget, it would seem wise to ask each interest group and public authority participating in the work of the council to bear an equal share of the costs of its operations. The council would not require a large operating budget ($500,000 per year would probably be adequate at the outset). The proposal for equal assessments would not create severe problems for any of the participants, and it would have the effect of encouraging the development of an atmosphere of equality and mutual respect among those involved in the work of the council. The maintenance of a high degree of informality in the operations of the Arctic Resources Council would be desirable. The essential idea underlying the council emphasizes the importance of promoting creative problem solving in an institutional environment that is not restricted by the procedural rules characteristic of either courts or legislative bodies. Without doubt, any initiatives leading to the bureaucratization of the council's administrative apparatus would be detrimental to the maintenance of a suitable institutional environment.

Pitfalls
The proposal under consideration here reflects a more general argument concerning the virtues of procedural or nonconsequentialist methods of handling social conflicts. The strength of this argument arises from the proposition that interest groups are more likely to accept outcomes produced by a legitimate procedural mechanism they have had a hand in creating than they are to subscribe in advance to substantive responses to conflict of the sort outlined in the preceding section.[31] Nonetheless, the idea of establishing an Arctic Resources Council is not without pitfalls of its own. The proposed council is distinctly unconventional in the context of American social and political thought. It would be a forum in which membership is determined in terms of legitimate interests in the subject at hand rather than a more conventional forum in which membership is based on geographic or demographic criteria. Furthermore, the council would emphasize problem-solving techniques designed to give all interested parties a stake in any solutions worked out for specific conflicts. All of this is somewhat alien to the American experience with legislative bodies, courts, and administrative agencies. To gain acceptance for the council, it would be necessary to convince the relevant interest groups that they would be able to participate in the activities of the council on an equal footing, while overcoming the reluctance of public authorities to operate in an arena of this sort on the basis of mere equality with a collection of interest groups.
Even if the council could be initiated successfully, it might well

encounter problems in its ongoing operations. The council would lack both the authority and the power to impose solutions on unwilling parties. To operate successfully, therefore, it would have to develop and maintain an atmosphere of trust and participation in a common enterprise so that its members would acquire a sense of ownership regarding council recommendations. Substitution of cooperative and trusting attitudes for the adversarial attitudes that pervade many Arctic resource conflicts today will not be easy.

Farther down the road, the council could easily become a victim of its own success. There is a natural tendency to expect any successful institution to assume additional functions whenever the need arises. Yet this can easily lead to severe problems of overload, jeopardizing the handling of initial functions while failing to satisfy the demands of the additional functions. Accordingly, it would be important for the Arctic Resources Council not to stray from its basic role of providing a forum in which parties involved in Arctic resource conflicts could seek mutually satisfactory accommodations of their interests in an atmosphere characterized by equality and procedural informality.

Conclusion

Arctic resource conflicts will become increasingly pervasive and severe during the foreseeable future as industries experience a growing interest in exploiting the region's natural resources, environmental groups continue to gain influence in Western societies, and indigenous peoples become both better organized and more sophisticated in articulating their claims. Yet both the legislative and the adversarial processes traditionally employed to resolve conflicts in American society are severely limited as methods of resolving Arctic resource conflicts. The relevant interest groups are anything but equal with regard to access to and influence in legislative arenas, and adversary processes regularly bog down in streams of repetitious and costly lawsuits that fail to settle the underlying issues at stake. This chapter seeks to find a way out of this growing dilemma. It outlines a range of responses to Arctic resource conflicts with the idea that collectively they constitute a valuable tool kit for coming to grips with the complexities of these conflicts.

However, there is nothing automatic about the process of matching these responses to specific conflicts and supervising their application to the unique circumstances prevailing in individual cases. To handle these tasks, this chapter proposes the creation of an Arctic Resources Council, a representative body that would emphasize problem-solving activities in contrast to voting or judicial decision making. Although the council would undoubtedly face limitations of its own, the development of some such mechanism could play an important role in moving toward the accommodation of legitimate concerns in the Arctic and avoiding a continuing dominance of strategic perspectives that are likely to make everyone a loser and no one a winner in dealing with Arctic resource conflicts.

The Politics of Animal Rights:
Preservationists versus Consumptive Users
in the Circumpolar North

The past twenty years have witnessed a surge of opposition to the killing of wild animals, based in part on concerns about inhumane killing techniques and the preservation of species but rooted, ultimately, in ethical objections to the killing of wild animals to serve human purposes.[1] Nowhere has this development given rise to sharper conflicts than in the Circumpolar North, where the consumptive use of wild animals is not only critical as a source of cash income but also integral to subsistence economies and cultures.[2] A striking feature of this set of conflicts is the variation in the outcomes that have occurred. Preservationists have succeeded in putting a stop to the killing of some wild animals (for example, newborn harp seals in eastern Canada), but consumptive users have rallied to protect their practices with regard to other wild animals (for example, bowhead whales in northern Alaska). Drawing on a selection of prominent northern cases, this chapter seeks to identify the principal factors that determine the outcomes of these conflicts over the killing of wild animals. The chapter takes no stand on the ethical issues associated with the conflicts; its purpose is simply to explain differences in the outcomes of major conflicts pitting preservationists

This chapter came into existence as a presentation to the Fifth Inuit Studies Conference held at McGill University in Montreal, 6–9 November 1986. A slightly different version appeared in *Etudes/Inuit/Studies* 13(1) (1989): 43–59.

and consumptive users against each other in the Circumpolar
North.

The Cases

To set the stage for this inquiry into factors determining the
outcomes of conflicts over the killing of wild animals, a brief introduction to the cases to be considered is in order.

Harp Seals
The modern commercial harvest of harp seals (especially
newborn seal pups, or whitecoats), which began in the late eigh-
teenth century in the Gulf of St. Lawrence and on the Newfoundland "Front," assumed its contemporary configuration in the
1940s.[3] Two distinct groups have participated in this hunt: lands-
men relying heavily on shore-based operations and Canadian or
Norwegian corporations using larger vessels operating at sea.
Starting in the 1960s, organized opposition to the harp seal harvest emerged, initiated by the New Brunswick Society for the Prevention of Cruelty to Animals and subsequently spearheaded by
the International Fund for Animal Welfare (IFAW) and Greenpeace.[4] The resulting conflict pitted the sealers and processors,
represented ultimately (that is, after 1982) by the Canadian Sealers Association (CSA), against an array of preservationist groups
that found the antisealing campaign both ethically satisfying and
lucrative as a source of income to support many of their causes.
The Canadian federal government, operating largely through
the Department of Fisheries and Oceans (DFO), assumed an ambivalent posture toward this conflict, playing the dual role of
somewhat reluctant advocate for the sealing industry and chief
regulator of the harvest, responsible for articulating and enforc-
ing regulations governing the hunt.[5]

Through the 1970s, the preservationists focused on media
events, arousing worldwide public opinion with lurid images of
the hunt but failing to put a stop to the commercial harvest. The
1980s, however, brought a dramatic change in the course of this
conflict. In 1983, opponents of the harvest succeeded in per-
suading the Council of Ministers of the European Economic Community (EEC), backed by the European Parliament, to ban the

import of the skins of harp and hooded seal pups.⁶ They followed
up in 1984 by organizing a boycott of Canadian fish products in
American and British markets. The result was dramatic, touching
off a collapse in the world market for seal skins. By 1985, the commercial harvest of harp seals in eastern Canada was essentially
over, brought to an end by the evaporation of the market for seal
skins.⁷ Additionally, the campaign against the harp seal harvest
produced striking side effects, undermining the market for ringed
seal skins harvested by Inuit in the Canadian Arctic and interfering with the market for northern fur seal skins harvested in
Alaska.⁸

Bowhead Whales
    Reacting to reports that the harvest of bowhead whales on the
part of Alaskan Eskimos was increasing rapidly, while the western Arctic stock of bowheads might contain no more than six hundred whales, the International Whaling Commission (IWC) acted
at its 1977 annual meeting to impose a ban on the hunting of bowhead whales for the 1978 season.⁹ This action triggered a sharp
conflict, pitting the Eskimos of northern Alaska, represented by
the Alaska Eskimo Whaling Commission (AEWC) and backed by
the resources of the government of the North Slope Borough
(NSB), against the international conservation community, represented by the Scientific Committee of the IWC and supported
vigorously by preservationist groups such as Greenpeace and the
American Cetacean Society. The U.S. federal government found
itself severely divided over this issue, with some elements desiring to protect the rights or interests of the Eskimos and other elements worried about compromising the role of the United States
as a leader in the struggle to put an end to commercial whaling
worldwide.
    The ensuing conflict played itself out over a number of years,
both in the annual meetings of the IWC and in a series of complex
negotiations between the AEWC and the National Oceanic and
Atmospheric Administration (NOAA) acting on behalf of the U.S.
federal government.¹⁰ The outcome has been agreement to (1)
mount an extensive program of biological research on the bowhead whale and (2) accept a joint AEWC/NOAA management system governing Alaskan Eskimo harvesting of bowheads. The

research program has now established, among other things, that the western Arctic bowhead population numbers over four thousand.[11] The management regime has provided a framework for working out annual quotas for the bowhead hunt[12] coupled with mutually agreed upon measures covering the monitoring of the hunt, the enforcement of regulations pertaining to the conduct of the hunt, and the organization of ongoing biological research.[13] Although the IWC retains jurisdiction over the issue and regularly exerts pressure to keep the annual bowhead quotas low, it has approved the basic operation of the AEWC/NOAA management regime at each of its recent annual meetings. For the foreseeable future at least, the annual bowhead whale hunt on the part of the Eskimos of northern Alaska will continue.

Northern Fur Seals

For many years, the U.S. federal government conducted a commercial harvest of fur seals on the Pribilof Islands under the terms of an international regime embodying the conservationist goal of providing "the greatest harvest year after year."[14] With the onset of the 1980s, this harvest came under increasing attack from an array of preservationist groups led by Defenders of Wildlife, the Fund for Animals, Friends of Animals, Greenpeace, and the Humane Society of the United States. This precipitated a sharp conflict, pitting the Aleut residents of the Pribilof Islands, deeply attached to the harvest in both cultural and economic terms,[15] against a collection of preservationist groups that opposed the harvest on biological as well as ethical grounds.[16] On this issue also, the U.S. federal government was deeply divided. The Reagan administration, acting through the National Marine Fisheries Service (NMFS), supported a continuation of the harvest, but opposition grew rapidly in congressional circles.

Undeterred by their failure to block the ratification of a 1980 protocol extending the international regime for an additional four years, the preservationists intensified their campaign to terminate the harvest. Under the terms of the Fur Seal Act Amendments of 1983 (PL 98–129), the federal government withdrew as the actual harvester of fur seals, contracting with Tanadgusix, Inc. (the village corporation for the Pribilof Community of St. Paul) to carry out the 1984 harvest.[17] This set the stage for a bruis-

ing battle over the ratification of a 1984 protocol extending the
international regime for another four years. Although the administration recommended ratification, a stalemate arose when opposing forces in the Senate Foreign Relations Committee proved
unable to reach a mutually acceptable compromise. The resultant
impasse brought about radical changes in the management of Pribilof fur seals.[18] The international regime lapsed as a consequence
of the Senate's unwillingness to ratify the 1984 protocol; management of the Pribilof fur seals has come under the purview of
the Marine Mammal Protection Act (MMPA), and the commercial
(as opposed to subsistence) harvest of these seals has ceased. Nor
is this situation likely to change in the foreseeable future. Biological constraints (the fur seal population has experienced serious
declines in recent years) and economic constraints (the future of
the world market for all seal skins and seal products is bleak) will
see to this.[19]

Fur Trapping

Buoyed by the success of the antisealing campaigns, animal
welfare and animal rights groups have turned their attention increasingly to fur trapping, especially in the Canadian North. The
resultant antiharvest campaign has touched off a conflict that
promises to become even more explosive than the conflicts over
sealing.[20] Not only is fur trapping economically important, but it
is also the basis of an established way of life in many parts of the
North.[21] Additionally, trapping is a key link in a sizable and influential international fur industry. Yet the preservationists have
demonstrated clearly that they are a force to be reckoned with,
and they have momentum derived from the striking successes of
the antisealing campaigns.

The circumstances surrounding the antiharvest campaign differ in some significant ways from those prevailing in the other
cases under consideration. The consumptive users are better organized. The Aboriginal Trappers Federation of Canada (ATFC)
and Indigenous Survival International (ISI), a transnational organization representing the interests of consumptive users in
Greenland and Alaska as well as in Canada, have joined the fight.
None of the animal populations of interest to the trappers is endangered or threatened. Mainstream conservation groups, such

as the World Wildlife Fund (WWF) and the International Union for the Conservation of Nature and Natural Resources (IUCN), have distanced themselves from the leaders of the antiharvest campaign, such as the World Society for the Protection of Animals (WSPA), I Kare International Wildlife Coalition, ARK II, the Association for the Protection of Fur-Bearing Animals, and Beauty without Cruelty. Even Greenpeace International is having second thoughts about the antiharvest campaign.[22] Though the Canadian federal government remains reluctant to raise the profile of an issue like this in international circles, it has taken meaningful steps to protect the fur trade through the activities of the Fur Institute of Canada and the Interdepartmental Steering Committee on Humane Trapping (ISCHT). The consequences of these differences with regard to the outcome of the conflict, however, remain to be seen. Over the past several years, the preservationist lobby has mounted a vigorous effort to persuade the European Parliament to pass a resolution banning sales of fur products in EEC nations and to induce parties to the Convention on International Trade in Endangered Species (CITES) to adopt a resolution banning international trade in furs caught in leg-hold traps. These initiatives have not yet succeeded, but the animal rights groups seem fully prepared to make trapping a priority issue during the 1990s. The conflict over fur trapping will almost certainly grow in intensity over the next few years.

Determinants of Outcomes

Turn now to a consideration of the factors determining the outcomes of these conflicts over the consumptive use of wild animals. It is tempting to single out economic factors, such as market power, as principal determinants of the outcomes of these conflicts. Without doubt, the evaporation of the market played a key role in putting a stop to the harp seal harvest in eastern Canada. It was common among those opposed to the continuation of the commercial harvest of fur seals on the Pribilofs, moreover, to emphasize the uncertainties surrounding the market for seal skins.[23] Understandably, supporters of fur trapping are particularly anxious about the efforts of those involved in the antiharvest campaign to undermine the European market for furs. By contrast, it is certainly an advantage to Alaskan Eskimo whalers that they are not engaged in a commercial hunt linked to a world market in whale products.

Yet it is easy to exaggerate the significance of these economic factors as determinants of the outcomes of conflicts over the killing of wild animals. Natural or unmanipulated markets for seal skins, furs, and other animal products are highly volatile. For the most part, these products are luxury items or superior goods, whose sales decline disproportionately during economic downturns, and many of them are subject to unpredictable swings in fashions or styles. The trade in Canadian furs, for example, virtually collapsed with the onset of the Great Depression in the 1930s.[24] Similarly, the commercial harvest of harp seals declined sharply during World War II, coming to a virtual halt in 1943.[25] But these dramatic market fluctuations failed to put an end to the trade in wild furs or seal skins. When economic conditions improved, those involved in the commercial harvests resumed their activities. This may be a tribute to the lack of other opportunities to generate cash income in the remote communities of the Circumpolar North. But it surely means that we should be careful to avoid mistaking temporary suspensions for permanent terminations of commercial harvests of wild animals.[26]

Note also that some market fluctuations are unintended side effects of initiatives launched in other conflicts rather than consequences of intended market interventions. The recent collapse of the market for ringed seal skins harvested in the Canadian Arctic and in Greenland, for instance, is simply a by-product of the campaign against the harvest of harp seals in eastern Canada.[27] It is probable that fluctuations in the market for Alaskan fur seal skins are attributable to the same cause. In such cases, economic factors certainly play a role in influencing the course of specific conflicts. But it is important to emphasize that these economic factors are part of the general environment of the conflicts; they are not decision variables subject to conscious manipulation on the part of those who are parties to the conflicts.

Beyond this, it is apparent that governments in contemporary societies often come to the assistance of industries that run into trouble due to declines or swings in relevant markets. Even in the United States, a staunch supporter of private enterprise in ideological terms, government agencies provide loans to ailing automobile manufacturers, build roads for timber harvesters, and subsidize passenger train services. The government also routinely offers substantial tax breaks (for example, depletion allowances) to enterprises exploiting nonrenewable natural resources. It is hardly surprising, therefore, that many observers now refer to the prevailing system as a form of state capitalism in contrast to a classic free enterprise system.

Perhaps even more relevant to this discussion of the commercial harvest of wild animals are the massive government programs designed to shore up agricultural production in the face of volatile markets. Faced with imbalances between supply and demand for various agricultural products, governments have resorted repeatedly to programs of price supports, government purchases of surplus production, and land bank arrangements to keep farm communities economically alive. Additionally, governments are vigorous supporters of commercial fishing, offering subsidized loans to fishers, devising marketing schemes, and mounting elaborate management systems for common property resources, with no expectation of reaping any returns on the resource. More often than not, an influential rationale underlying such programs focuses on the value to society of maintaining a cherished way of life, regardless of the ability of individual farmers or fishers to turn a profit in conventional economic terms. What is more, there are precedents for similar programs in industries involving the commercial harvest of wild animals. The Income Security Programme for Cree Hunters and Trappers in eastern Canada is a case in point.[28] So are the efforts of several countries to create marketing boards designed to explore and promote new markets for animal products.[29]

Even where market intervention has played a key role in conflicts over the killing of wild animals, efforts to influence markets have typically taken the form of political action rather than initiatives aimed at influencing supply or demand in more straightforward economic terms. Those desiring to attack the market for harp seal skins carried their case to the Council of Ministers of the EEC. The objective of the fish boycott was to stimulate Canadian fishers and fish processors to bring pressure to bear on the DFO to drop any advocacy activities on behalf of the sealing industry. Similarly, those in charge of the antiharvest campaign with regard to fur trapping have pinned their hopes on the European Parliament and on the meetings of the parties to the CITES. Even in the case of the Pribilof fur seal harvest, the battle came to focus on the actions of the Senate Foreign Relations Committee; it was not simply a matter of influencing supply or demand without reference to political action. What all of this suggests is that there is no simple line of demarcation between economic initiatives and political action when it comes to manipulating the markets for the products of wild animals. Although attacking these markets has proved to be a powerful strategy, the most effective way to attack them is typically through political action.

Given the importance of political action in connection with these conflicts over the killing of wild animals, it is appropriate to turn at this point to an analysis of the political influence of the parties to these conflicts. Such an examination reveals a clear and predictable pattern.

Consumptive users in the North have intense interests, but they are small groups bound to experience difficulty in mustering influence within those legislative arenas possessing jurisdiction over the relevant issues. Whether we turn to Alaska, Canada, or Greenland, northern communities have little representation in federal legislatures, and their official representatives (for example, the members of the Alaskan congressional delegation) sometimes have interests that conflict with those of subsistence or commercial hunters and gatherers.[30] The best bet for those who depend on the killing of wild animals, under the circumstances, is to seek support within the administrative agencies responsible for the day-to-day operations of governments. The NOAA, for example, has offered considerable support for the Eskimo whalers of northern Alaska in their battles with the preservationist lobby within the arena of the IWC. For the most part, the NMFS worked hard to protect the commercial harvest of fur seals on the Pribilof Islands. Even the DFO made an effort to defend the harp seal harvest in eastern Canada, though it is true that it was unable to overcome the reluctance of the Ministry of External Affairs to raise the profile of this issue in international circles.

The preservationist lobby, by contrast, frequently runs into problems in dealing with the administrative agencies. The ethical and often absolutist tone of the preservationist stance does not appeal to many administrators, who think of themselves as professional managers endeavoring to handle resource issues in a scientific manner.[31] On the other hand, the preservationists have been remarkably successful in legislative arenas (especially at the federal and supranational levels) heavily populated with representatives who are able to please their constituents by taking public stands in defense of animals while incurring few if any political costs in the process. It is no accident that those orchestrating the antisealing and antiharvest campaigns have carried their cases to the European Parliament and to the biennial meetings of the CITES parties. Nor is it surprising that opponents of the fur seal harvest had more success within the Senate Foreign Relations Committee than in the relevant administrative agencies.

The implications of this pattern are clear-cut. Unless consumptive users are well organized and vigilant, their cause will be drowned in a wave of popular sentiment expressed in legislative arenas. Consumptive users have a reasonable chance of appealing to professional administrators in line agencies. They may well be able to form long-standing, mutually supportive relationships with administrators who are responsible for regulating harvests (for example, the NOAA in the case of bowhead whales) and who sometimes even take on responsibility for the conduct of harvests (for example, the NMFS in the case of the fur seal harvest prior to 1984). But consumptive users are likely to fare poorly in legislative arenas populated with legislators who have little comprehension of the industries or cultural complexes in question and who must face constituencies easily aroused by the imagery and media campaigns of the preservationists.

A key factor in the ability of both groups to exert influence in all of these political arenas is their success in organizing themselves effectively and in forming alliances with like-minded interest groups. Some concrete examples will serve to emphasize the significance of this point. Those engaged in the harp seal harvest were extremely slow to organize—the CSA did not come into existence until 1982. By contrast, the protesters, spearheaded by the IFAW, were well organized and well funded by the mid-1970s, a fact that gave them a distinct advantage in putting a stop to the harp seal harvest. A strikingly different pattern emerges with regard to the bowhead hunt. The Alaskan Eskimos organized early and effectively, forming the AEWC under the able leadership of Eben Hopson and with the financial backing of the NSB. The AEWC has maximized its influence at the annual meetings of the IWC by forging a strong working relationship with the NOAA. For its part, the preservationist lobby failed to establish a powerful coalition in this case, relying primarily on the data pertaining to the bowhead population generated by the IWC's Scientific Committee. As a result, the bowhead hunt continues under a joint AEWC/NOAA management regime.

The fur seal case reveals yet another pattern. The Aleut communities of the Pribilofs were severely fragmented in political terms, and the role of the NMFS as an advocate for the harvest was muted as a consequence of the dismantlement of the Pribilof Islands Program under the terms of the Fur Seal Act Amendments of 1983. At the same time, however, a number of the major environmental groups (for example, the National Wildlife Federation, the National Audubon Society, the Alaska Conservation Society) distanced themselves from the preservationist position on this issue, a fact that added to the stridency and detracted from the credibility of the preservationist position. It is hardly surprising, therefore, that the outcome of this conflict hung in the balance for some time, with the eventual outcome shaped as much by fortuitous factors (for example, the decline of the Pribilof fur seal stocks and the erosion of the world market for seal skins resulting from the harp seal controversy) as by the organized efforts of the preservationists themselves.

In the case of fur trapping, the consumptive users have moved vigorously to create effective organizations, such as ISI, and to forge alliances with important conservation groups, such as the WWF and the IUCN. There is also some evidence that the federal Department of Indian Affairs and Northern Development (DIAND) has taken steps to rally governmental support behind the cause of the fur trappers.[32] For its part, the preservationist lobby seems less effectively organized on this issue. Nonetheless, it may prove able to maximize its impact by taking steps to split the fur trappers and the fur farmers/ranchers who together make up the fur industry, thereby crippling the fur lobby in legislative arenas like the European Parliament.

Do any significant generalizations or indications of secular trends emerge from this discussion of the role of organization and tactical alliances as bases of success in political action? There is some indication that the consumptive users are improving their ability to organize and work with other interest groups, especially in cases where the harvesters are largely groups of indigenous peoples. The high profile of groups of consumptive users, such as ISI and the Inuit Circumpolar Conference (ICC), and the rapid emergence of the fourth world as an international political force are surely significant in this context.[33] Additionally, the preservationists may find their base of support narrowing somewhat as the movement comes to focus more and more on ethical stances involving animal rights in contrast to arguments regarding animal welfare or the biological status of animal populations. Thus, the fact that those promoting the way of thinking embedded in the World Conservation Strategy, such as the IUCN and WWF, have sought explicitly to differentiate themselves from the program of the preservationists is certainly worth emphasizing in this analysis of the politics of animal rights.[34] But it would be easy to overdo these propositions. The circumstances surrounding individual cases vary greatly with respect to the development of effective organizations and the forging of alliances. Above all, it is important not to overlook the role of leadership in this context. It seems undeniable, for example, that the dogged determination of Brian Davies as director of IFAW in the harp seal case and the inspired guidance of Eben Hopson as mayor of the NSB in the bowhead whale case were important factors in assembling winning coalitions capable of putting a stop to the harp seal harvest and of defending the bowhead whale hunt.

The cases make it clear, in addition, that biological factors and the analysis of these factors can play a significant role in conflicts over the consumptive use of wild animals. There is no doubt that perceived threats to the survival of animal stocks or populations are sufficient to stimulate powerful opposition to the killing of wild animals.[35] The observation that the western Arctic bowhead stock had (apparently) declined (600–2,000 whales, as compared with an original population of 15,000–20,000) was obviously important in touching off the bowhead whale conflict in 1977. Similarly, the realization that the stock now numbers over four thousand and that the original western Arctic population may well have been divided into two stocks has greatly strengthened the position of the Alaskan Eskimos in this conflict.[36] To take another illustration, the fact that the stocks of northern fur seals breeding on the Pribilof Islands have declined in recent years, at a rate as high as 5 to 8 percent per year, became a powerful argument in the case for terminating the commercial harvest of fur seals. Interestingly, this is so despite the fact that there was no scientific evidence linking the commercial harvest with the declines in the fur seal stocks.[37]

Notice, however, that perceived threats to the survival of animal stocks or populations are not necessary to touch off or propel sharp conflicts over the consumptive use of wild animals. The antisealing movement directed at the harp seal harvest in eastern Canada gained strength during a period in which scientists were assembling convincing evidence of the viability of the harvested harp seal stocks.[38] None of the animal populations involved in the burgeoning conflict over fur trapping is endangered or even threatened. Although concerns about the biological status of animal stocks and populations can influence the course of conflicts over the consumptive use of wild animals, it would be a mistake to overemphasize the role of these biological factors as determinants of the outcomes of the conflicts. Beyond this, it is worth noting that those embroiled in these conflicts sometimes use information regarding the status of animal stocks or populations in a manipulative or self-serving fashion.[39] It is probable, for example, that the efforts of antisealing advocates to persuade the CITES parties to add numerous species of seals (specifically, all phocids, or earless seals) to the convention's Appendix II list[40] have been inspired more by tactical considerations than by unbiased assessments of the biological evidence regarding the status of the relevant populations.

Finally, shifts in the broader sociopolitical context regularly affect conflicts over the consumptive use of wild animals in ways that are highly significant but largely beyond the control of the protagonists and difficult to predict. The growth of government deficits and the rising interest in privatization schemes, for example, have clearly influenced the course of several of the conflicts under consideration. The desire to economize on funding for research on bowhead whales and for monitoring the bowhead hunt, for instance, has made it attractive for the U.S. federal government to cooperate with the AEWC, backed by the resources of the NSB and the energy industry in this realm. But this, of course, means that the federal government must take a meaningful stand in support of the continuation of the Alaskan Eskimo bowhead hunt. By contrast, heightened concerns about deficit spending and the growing popularity of privatization schemes clearly played a role in the dismantlement of the Pribilof Islands Program.[41] These developments undoubtedly served to deter government initiatives to stabilize or revitalize the sealing industry and, in the process, had a significant impact on the outcome of the conflict over the commercial harvest of·fur seals.

The emergence of common foes can also serve to redefine relations among those involved in conflicts over the consumptive use of wild animals. In the northern cases under consideration, the obvious example is the rising threat to animal populations and critical habitat associated with nonrenewable resource development.[42] The Alaskan Eskimo whalers and the preservationists can agree, for example, on the importance of protecting migrating bowhead whales from the side effects of offshore oil development in the Beaufort Sea. In recent years, Native groups and environmental groups have begun to make common cause in their efforts to defend the living resources of the Bering Sea against potential threats posed by outer continental shelf hydrocarbon development.[43] Similarly, fur trappers and preservationist groups can unite in opposition to the destruction of habitat for wild animals resulting from large-scale hydroelectric projects or water diversion schemes in the North. Certainly, the emergence of common foes does not eliminate conflicts of interest between consumptive users and preservationists, but it can make the resultant clashes more tractable as the protagonists realize that they have compelling reasons to work cooperatively on other issues.

Broader sociological and political trends also come into play at this point. There is something to the proposition, for example, that the rise of affluent, urbanized populations cut off almost entirely from personal contact with the land has played an impor-

tant role in generating receptive audiences for the antiharvesting
views of the preservationist lobby. By the same token, the cultural
resurgence of Native peoples and the rise of an indigenous peoples movement worldwide have clearly made it easier for northern hunters and gatherers to organize effectively in defense of
practices involving the consumptive use of wild animals. The
AEWC in the bowhead case and ISI in the fur trapping case have
emerged as major players capable of influencing the course of the
relevant conflicts. But they did not come into existence in a vac-
uum.[44] The growth of political consciousness and sophistication
among indigenous peoples has undoubtedly played a key role in
preparing the ground for the emergence of organizations like the
AEWC and ISI.[45]

These illustrations should suffice to demonstrate that conflicts
over the consumptive use of wild animals are heavily influenced
by developments in the broader sociopolitical context over which
the protagonists have little control. There is nothing surprising
about this observation; virtually all social conflicts share this
characteristic. It does, however, have important implications for
groups embroiled in specific conflicts over the consumptive use
of wild animals. Those who wish to succeed in securing their own
objectives with regard to such conflicts must resist the temptation
to become preoccupied with the proximate details of the case at
hand and remain attuned to developments in the broader sociopolitical context. Though the protagonists in specific conflicts
may not be able to control these developments, those who are
quick to perceive such developments and grasp their implications
can frequently gain decisive advantages. By the same token, the
prospect of shifts in the broader sociopolitical context sometimes
adds to the difficulties of resolving such conflicts. Parties feeling
disadvantaged in such conflicts are often motivated to hold out
in the hope that shifts in the broader context of the conflict will
strengthen their hand and weaken the hand of their opponents.

Conclusion

Conflicts pitting preservationists against consumptive users in
the Circumpolar North will undoubtedly occur with some regu-
larity during the foreseeable future. Additional cases are easy

enough to identify. These include current or prospective conflicts over the harvest of migratory geese in the Yukon/Kuskokwim Delta region of western Alaska, narwhals in the eastern Canadian Arctic, caribou belonging to the George River herd in northern Quebec, and polar bears throughout the Arctic.[46] Each of these cases is complex, involving a number of players and a variety of factors that may affect the course of the interaction significantly. The preceding analysis does not point to any master variable that is likely to determine the outcome of all of these conflicts over the consumptive use of wild animals. Rather, it identifies an array of factors that play a role in shaping the course of specific conflicts of this type.

All the same, the analysis does suggest certain lessons that any party involved in such conflicts would do well to bear in mind. Ultimately, political action of one type or another plays a crucial role in all of these conflicts. It follows that parties desiring to promote their own interests must do everything in their power to maximize their ability to operate effectively in political arenas. Among other things, this means paying attention to organizational details and maintaining a willingness at all times to form tactical alliances with others whose interests are compatible on the issue at hand, whether or not they are likely to emerge as allies with regard to other issues.[47] Beyond this, the advantage generally goes to parties who can maintain perspective in the sense that they remain sensitive to developments in the broader sociopolitical context. Though they cannot control these developments, alert parties can often exploit such developments to their own advantage in the context of specific conflicts.

CHAPTER 7

The Petrodollar Trap: Oil Revenues and the Political Economy of Alaska

Starting in the late 1970s, a surge of oil revenues flowing into Alaska's treasury propelled the state government into a position of dominance in Alaskan society virtually unparalleled in American politics. Awash in newfound wealth, the state government found it easy and initially rewarding not only to discard more secure sources of revenue (for example, the statewide personal income tax) but also to expand its role in Alaskan society by embarking on an array of costly programs with little concern about their longer-run financial implications. Understandable as this reaction was, it led the state government to assume a set of far-reaching commitments, not to mention a central position in Alaskan society, that it has found difficult to relinquish even when dramatic fluctuations in world market prices for oil have led to sharp declines in the revenues available to the state. In effect, the initial rewards associated with the expansion of the state government's role caused policymakers to ignore the problems

This chapter originated as a presentation to the Arctic Science Conference held in Anchorage, Alaska, 24–26 September 1987. A version of the chapter appeared in Rebecca Allard, ed., *Running the North: The Getting and Spending of Public Finances by Canada's Territorial Governments* (Ottawa: Canadian Arctic Resources Committee, 1989), 195–221. Over the past several years, world market prices for oil have recovered partially from the collapse of 1986. But given the boom/bust cycles characteristic of the Circumpolar North, the analysis of social traps set forth in this chapter remains relevant to the study of Arctic politics.

that would arise in the event that sharp declines in available revenues engendered pressures to contract the role of state government in Alaska.

Approached in this way, recent events in Alaska exhibit the hallmarks of what students of human affairs have come to know as social traps. Just as "an ordinary trap entices its prey with the offer of an attractive bait and then punishes it by capture," social traps "draw their victims into certain patterns of behavior with promises of immediate rewards and then confront them with consequences that the victims would rather avoid."[1] Traps arise in connection with such activities as smoking or drug addiction, in which "our generally successful learning strategy leads us astray."[2] In a social trap, initial rewards channel "behaviors along lines that seem right every step of the way but nevertheless end up at the wrong place."[3] Because behavior of this sort emerges from processes involving reinforcement learning or instrumental conditioning, victims cannot easily discard the resultant habits, even after the costs become apparent.

In this chapter, I endeavor to show in some detail that this is exactly what happened to Alaska's state government as a result of the surge in oil revenues that began in the late 1970s. But the processes involved in this case are generic; they can be expected to occur in many other jurisdictions in which the flow of public revenues is subject to rapid and substantial swings. Because the prices of raw materials are well known for their tendency to fluctuate and because public authorities throughout the Far North are unusually dependent on income derived from the exploitation of natural resources, Alaska's experience with this petrodollar trap should be a subject of considerable interest to policymakers throughout the Circumpolar North.

The State Takes Charge

Almost effortlessly, and without any searching consideration of the longer-run consequences, the state government adapted to the flow of oil revenues by expanding its role in Alaskan society. The evidence of the resultant transformation is straightforward and dramatic. With remarkable speed, the state government assumed a preponderant position in Alaska's public sector. Table 1

TABLE 1

Revenue* Sources, State and Local Governments, Alaska and the U.S. Average, Selected Fiscal Years, 1962–1980
(Percent Distribution)

Combined State and Local Government Revenues	1962		1967		1974		1977		1980	
	U.S.	Alaska	U.S.	Alaska	U.S.	Alaska	U.S.	Alaska	U.S.	Alaska
State sources	41%	47%	41%	33%	43%	44%	42%	62%	44%	74%
Local sources	46	19	42	15	37	22	36	17	34	14
Federal sources	13	34	17	52	20	34	22	21	22	12
All sources	100%	100%	100%	100%	100%	100%	100%	100%	100%	100%

SOURCES: U.S. Department of Commerce, Bureau of the Census, *Census of Governments*, 1962, 1967, and 1977; and *Governmental Finances*, 1973–74 and 1979–80.

*Includes all revenues except utility revenue, liquor store revenue, and insurance-trust revenue.

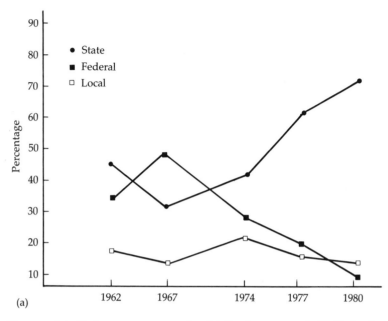

Figure 1. (a) *Alaska revenue sources for state/local government.* (b) *National revenue sources for state/local government.* Source: *Alaska Review of Social and Economic Conditions* 24 (February 1987).

and Figures 1a and 1b tell the story graphically. In 1974, state sources accounted for 44 percent of the revenues available to state and local governments in Alaska, a proportion directly comparable to the national average of 43 percent. By 1980, however, state sources were contributing 74 percent of the public sector revenues in Alaska, far in excess of the national average, which then stood at 44 percent. Federal sources of revenues for state and local governments, by contrast, shifted sharply in the opposite direction. In 1974, federal sources of revenue for Alaska's public sector exceeded the national average—34 percent to 20 percent, respectively. Six years later, the situation had reversed itself, with federal sources contributing 12 percent to the Alaskan public sector in comparison with a national average of 22 percent.

Not only was the state government overshadowing the role of the federal government in Alaska, it was also becoming a con-

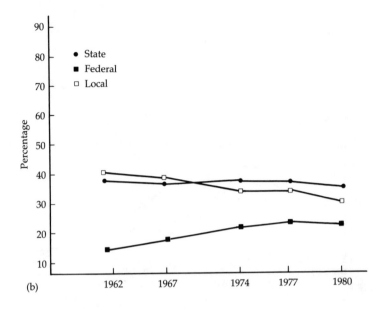

(b)

trolling force vis-à-vis local governments at the same time. As Figure 2 shows, local government revenues declined rapidly relative
to state government revenues, falling to a level of 29 percent of
state government revenues by 1982. And this figure includes state
transfers to local governments, a source accounting for 47.2 percent of local government revenues in that year (compared with a
34 percent average for other states).[4] By contrast, local government revenues across the United States amounted to 64.2 percent
of the state government revenues in 1984, a figure not matched
in Alaska since 1975.[5] Directly or indirectly, therefore, the state
government had assumed a preponderant role in Alaska's public
sector by the early 1980s.

Equally striking, the state became an immensely important
player in the overall economy of Alaska during these years. As
Figure 3 indicates, state revenues as a percentage of gross state
product (GSP) soared as the oil revenues derived from the Prudhoe Bay development came on stream. From a low of 9.3 percent

in 1975, state revenues mushroomed to account for 25 percent of GSP by 1982. By way of comparison, state revenues summed over all fifty states amounted to only 10.5 percent of gross national product (GNP) in 1984.[6] In short, the state government in Alaska dwarfed the average American state government as a player in the state's economy.

As Figure 4 suggests, this transformation allowed the state government in Alaska to devise programs requiring a far greater expenditure per capita than the programs of the average state government. Whereas the average expenditure of state *and* local

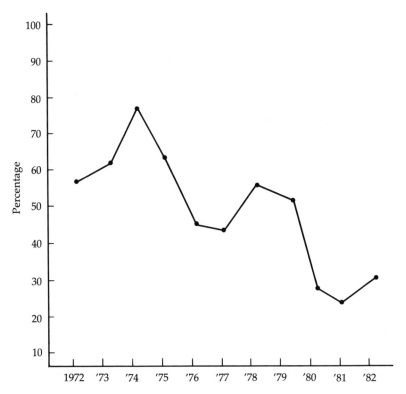

Figure 2. Local government revenues as a percentage of state government revenues (includes state transfers to local governments). Source: *Alaska Review of Social and Economic Conditions* 21 (February 1984).

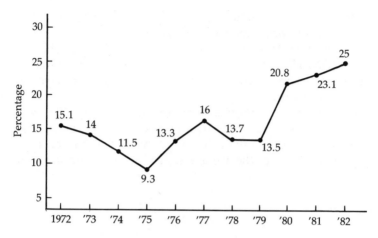

Figure 3. State revenues as a percentage of gross state product (GSP). Source: *Alaska Review of Social and Economic Conditions* 21 (February 1984).

governments per capita nationwide was $2,543 in 1984, the state government *alone* was spending $9,063 per capita in Alaska.[7] And this was well below the state's peak expenditure per capita of $13,590, which occurred in 1981. From the point of view of the typical individual in Alaska, the state had clearly become the single most important player on the economic horizon. Whether we choose to focus on Alaska's public sector or to take a broader view of the overall economy of the state, then, it is apparent that the state government had emerged as a dominant player by the early 1980s.

The Habit Forms

It is tempting to suppose that there is a certain symmetry in such matters so that contractions in the roles state governments play can occur just as effortlessly as expansions. In this view, the state government in Alaska would simply revert to a more typical role in Alaskan society following a major drop in available revenues. But, in fact, this supposition is *not* correct. Having assumed an expanded role in Alaskan society, the state government found itself under heavy pressure to continue to act as a dominant player, regardless of the flow of revenues accruing to the state treasury. Several differentiable factors have contributed to this asymmetry between expansion and contraction in the role of the state government in Alaskan society.

Controlling about a quarter of Alaska's GSP and exercising

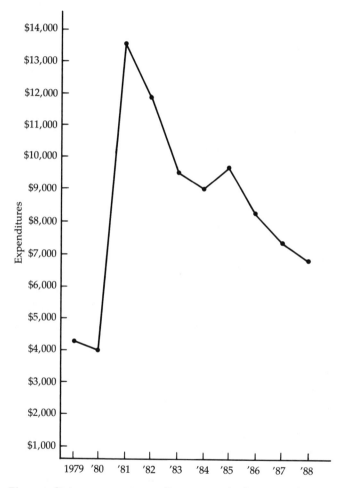

Figure 4. State government expenditures per capita (in current dollars; includes all general funds). Source: *Alaska Economic Trends* (7 August 1987).

TABLE 2
Government Employment in Alaska, 1970–1982
(in thousands)

Year	Total state and local	State	Local
1970	18.5	10.4	8.1
1971	20.7	11.7	9.0
1972	23.3	13.3	10.0
1973	24.6	13.8	10.6
1974	25.8	14.2	11.6
1975	28.8	15.5	13.3
1976	29.3	14.1	15.2
1977	31.1	13.9	17.2
1978	34.3	14.3	19.8
1979	36.6	15.0	21.6
1980	36.3	15.4	20.9
1981	38.5	16.6	21.9
1982	40.9	18.0	22.9

SOURCE: Thomas A. Morehouse, "Resource Development and Alaska Wealth Management," in Thomas A. Morehouse, ed., *Alaska Resources Development* (Boulder, Colo.: Westview, 1984), 179.

management authority over the Permanent Fund (the largest source of potential investment capital for new economic initiatives in Alaska), the state government soon reached a point where it could not *avoid* playing a major role in Alaska's economy.[8] In a sense, moreover, the sharp declines in the activities of the oil industry in Alaska, beginning in 1986, merely accentuated the role of the state government in Alaska's economy. In a slumping economy lacking attractive private alternatives to the oil industry, the state quickly discovered that it could not simply rely on the private sector to take up the slack, much less to initiate productive new ventures to breathe life into Alaska's economy. Under the circumstances, the state government came under intense pressure to pump money into new enterprises, such as the Red Dog mine, and to conduct a vigorous search for other economic activities suitable for state investment.[9]

As well, the state government found itself holding the key to Alaska's employment picture by the early 1980s. As Table 2 indicates, state and local government employment in Alaska rose from 18,500 in 1970 to almost 41,000 in 1982.[10] At this point, state and local governments employed more than 20 percent of the total labor force in Alaska.[11] Of course, the state government possesses the authority to cut back on state employment if it sees fit to do so. Also, sharp reductions in state transfers to local governments would certainly result in sizable reductions in local government employment. But with unemployment reaching double digits in Alaska in any case, a state policy aimed at reducing government employment substantially would have served only to drive up overall unemployment, push the state's economy into a deeper recession, and impose other costs (for example, unemployment compensation and welfare payments) on the state.

To make matters more complicated, a number of programs devised during the period of rising revenues had the effect of increasing sharply the dependence of local governments on transfers from the state government. Infrastructure (for example, airports, harbors, roads), built with state capital construction funds during a period of rising revenues, requires regular servicing and

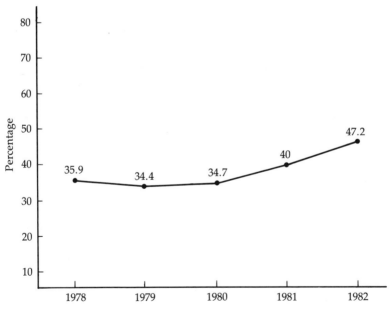

Figure 5. Transfers from state as a percentage of local government revenues.
Source: *Alaska Review of Social and Economic Conditions* 21 (February 1984).

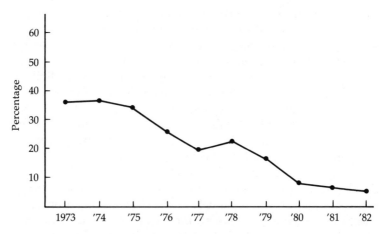

Figure 6. Federal grants-in-aid as a percentage of state revenues. Source: *Alaska Review of Social and Economic Conditions* 21 (February 1984).

maintenance over an indefinite period. The establishment of local educational facilities and the creation of Rural Education Administrative Areas (REAAs) entail rising operating costs that cannot now be avoided. Moreover, as mentioned above, local governments expanded their workforces rapidly through the 1970s and early 1980s. Figure 5 demonstrates that local governments came to depend heavily on state funds to cover the resultant expenses. By 1982, transfers from the state paid for 47.2 percent of the expenditures of local governments in Alaska, compared with a nationwide average of 34 percent. And there is little prospect of local governments finding alternative sources of revenue to cover such expenses in the foreseeable future. In effect, therefore, the state found itself facing a situation in which its own policies produced a continuing need for large transfers of funds to local governments.

Nor can the state depend on the federal government to bail it out of such financial commitments. As Figures 6 and 7 show, federal transfers have declined markedly as a source of revenue for Alaska. Between 1972 and 1982 federal grants-in-aid fell from 35.8 percent to 3.8 percent of state revenues in Alaska, and by

1982 transfers from the federal government made up only 4.1 percent of local government revenues in the state. By contrast, federal transfers accounted for 7.5 percent of local government revenues nationwide in 1982. What is more, there is no basis for expecting these trends to be reversed in the near future. With the continuation of massive budget deficits at the federal level, decision makers in Washington are more likely to cut federal transfers to state and local governments further than to increase them. This is particularly true in the case of a state like Alaska, which is widely perceived in other parts of the country as a wealthy state.

To be sure, none of this means that the state government is entirely without options in endeavoring to limit its role in Alaskan society and therefore to curtail its expenditures. But it does suffice to demonstrate why it is easier to expand programs during periods of rising revenues than to contract them when revenues decline. By the mid-1980s, then, the state government in Alaska found itself heavily committed to a set of programs requiring the continuation of a sizable flow of revenues. It had, in effect, become addicted to oil revenues.

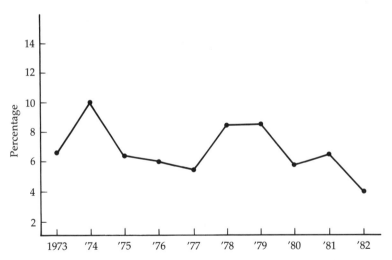

Figure 7. Transfers from federal government as a percentage of local government revenues. Source: *Alaska Review of Social and Economic Conditions* 21 (February 1984).

The Trap Is Sprung

The pitfalls inherent in this situation might have been avoided, of course, if oil revenues had continued to flow at a steady rate indefinitely. Not surprisingly, however, this was not to be. In fact, the collapse of oil revenues accruing to the state during the mid-

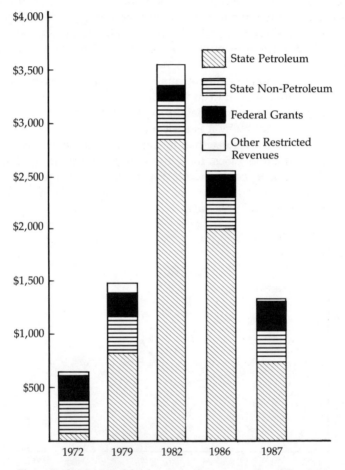

Figure 8. State general fund revenues by source, selected fiscal years 1972–1987 (in 1979 dollars). Source: ISER calculations based on Alaska Department of Revenue, *Revenue Sources,* January 1987.

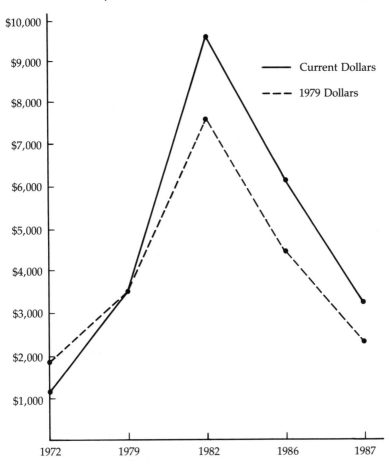

Figure 9. General fund revenues per capita,[a] for selected fiscal years. Source: *Alaska Review of Social and Economic Conditions* 24 (February 1987).

	1972	1979	1982	1986	1987[b]
Current dollars	$1,115	$3,574	$9,670	$6,260	$3,347
1979 dollars	$1,993	$3,574	$7,694	$4,692	$2,456

[a]Based on population figures of: 1972—330,000; 1979—414,000; 1982—461,000; 1986—542,000; and 1987—539,000 (estimates as of early 1987).
[b]Based on Alaska Department of Revenue projections as of January 1987.

1980s closed the trap on Alaska's state government with a vengeance. Figures 8 and 9 depict this development in a dramatic fashion. Just as the state's general fund revenues rose sharply from $1.48 billion (in 1979 dollars) in 1979 to about $3.5 billion in 1982, they fell again to less than $1.5 billion in 1987. As Figure 9 shows, the state government had considerably less to spend per capita in 1987 than it had in 1979.

Of course, thoughtful observers had been predicting a decline in the revenues available to the state government for some time.[12] Even so, the speed and magnitude of the drop occurring in 1986 and 1987 took almost everyone by surprise. This crash, brought on by the collapse of the world oil market during the first six months of 1986, demonstrated with shocking clarity the extent to which the state of Alaska had come to depend on revenue sources subject to extreme fluctuations that the state government was powerless to control.

Toward a More Stable Future

Escaping social traps is never easy. Sometimes, as in the case of the longtime smoker who contracts emphysema, there is no escape. An added complication in the case of Alaska's state government arises from the collective-choice processes characteristic of policy-making in democratic systems.[13] Periods of contraction are bound to prove painful for politically powerful interest groups; such periods often yield outcomes that are redistributive in nature, whether intended or not. Under the circumstances, efforts to contract the role of the state government in an orderly and thoughtful manner are apt to be opposed by groups capable of mustering blocking coalitions in the state legislature, thereby magnifying the disruptive impact of the petrodollar trap.

Even so, we must consider measures that the Alaska state government can adopt to avoid falling prey to the petrodollar trap in the future. In essence, what is needed is a strategy designed to reduce the preponderant role of the state government in Alaskan society while securing more stable sources of revenue to sustain the continuing activities of the state government. This suggests an approach featuring the following elements.

The state government should move vigorously to encourage

the development of a sustainable economy in Alaska, reducing its own longer-term role in the state's economy in the process. What is required is an aggressive effort to build stronger industries based in Alaska. Such industries might focus on the exploitation of renewable resources (as in the case of mariculture) or on the processing of raw materials (as in the case of refined petroleum products for consumption in Alaska).[14] In every case, however, the choice of industries to form the core of a development strategy for Alaska should be guided by the principle of comparative advantage.

In pursuing this goal, the state government could treat at least a portion of the Permanent Fund as a source of investment capital for the development of Alaska-based enterprises rather than as a portfolio to be invested in outside securities in the form of stocks and bonds. This would involve taking some risks, and it might necessitate a termination of the current policy of distributing part of the income from the fund to individual residents of Alaska in the form of annual dividend checks. But it would permit the state government to make use of the Permanent Fund to build a viable economy in Alaska rather than to sustain the growth of industrial enterprises located elsewhere in the United States or abroad. Implemented with care, such a policy should allow the Permanent Fund to function as a source of investment capital in Alaska indefinitely.

At the same time, the state government must develop more secure sources of revenue to sustain its own continuing (if somewhat diminished) role in Alaskan society. Faced with similar concerns, many states are now experimenting with innovative taxes (for example, rooms and meals taxes, statewide property taxes) as well as unconventional revenue-generating devices, such as state lotteries. In the final analysis, however, it is hard to avoid the conclusion that Alaska should reinstitute a statewide personal income tax at the first available opportunity. This would, of course, involve abandoning some efforts to shift the tax burden in Alaska away from Alaskan residents and onto outsiders (for example, corporations with headquarters in the lower forty-eight states or tourists visiting Alaska for short periods of time). But calibrated properly and combined in a sensible fashion with corporate income taxes, personal income taxes remain the most secure and equitable sources of revenue available to state governments.

Finally, the state government must shy away from quick fixes whose only effect is to put off for awhile the day of reckoning with the petrodollar trap. Oil development in the Arctic National Wildlife Refuge (ANWR), for example, seems attractive to many Alaskans today not only because it could send a new surge of oil revenues into the state's treasury but also because it might reinvigorate the state's economy as a whole. But it is apparent that this would do nothing to resolve the underlying problems associated with the petrodollar trap. In fact, such a development would serve only to rebait the trap, encouraging the state government to expand its activities in response to a renewed flow of oil revenues while giving little consideration to the disruptive consequences of contraction following the subsequent decline or collapse of oil revenues.

Undoubtedly, a strategy of this sort would be hard to implement politically in Alaska. Still, periods of crisis often create opportunities for the initiation of major political changes. Just as the Great Depression of the 1930s gave rise to an extraordinary transformation in the overarching American political system, crises facing the state government as a result of the petrodollar trap may provide an opportunity to introduce major changes in Alaska. In the long run, the dramatic fashion in which the trap was sprung as a consequence of the collapse of the world oil market in 1986 may even come to be regarded as a blessing in disguise.

Should Alaska achieve success in this realm, it will not only place its own economy on a sounder footing, but it may also become a model for policymakers in other northern areas seeking solutions to similar problems. The relevance of this point is particularly striking today with the collapse of the Soviet Union and the initiation of efforts to guide Russia's administration of the Eurasian Arctic. Given the magnitude of the nonrenewable resource endowments of northern Siberia and the financial pressures facing Russia, all of the ingredients for a recurrence of the petrodollar trap in this part of the Arctic are in place. The need for models that can help northern governments to avoid this trap has never been greater.

CHAPTER 8

Arctic Shipping:
A Tale of Two Passages

The Northeast and Northwest Passages have much in common. They are both complex coastal waterways threading their way for several thousand kilometers through ice-infested waters adjacent to the Arctic fringes of the major land masses of the Northern Hemisphere. Both passages have earned worldwide reputations as magnets for adventurous Europeans spurred by a desire to discover unknown lands and seas but ultimately supported by hardheaded commercial interests hoping to open lucrative East-West trade routes. After several centuries of unsuccessful attempts, which resulted in considerable loss of life as well as numerous tales of heroism, Nordenskjöld completed the first transit of the Northeast Passage in the *Vega* during 1878–1879. Amundsen, in the *Gjoa*, followed shortly thereafter, completing the first transit of the Northwest Passage during 1903–1906. Today much of the international interest in the two passages arises from the promise these waterways seem to offer as marine arteries capable of serving as trade routes between Europe and the Orient, routes that would be shorter and quicker than alternatives like the Panama Canal and the Suez Canal, not to mention

This chapter came into existence in response to a request from Dr. Alexander Arikainen of the Institute for Systems Studies of the Soviet Academy of Sciences in Moscow. An earlier version was published in Russian, during the fall of 1990, in *Morskoy Flot*, the journal of the Soviet Ministry of the Merchant Fleet.

the much longer passages around Cape Horn and the Cape of Good Hope.

In any assessment of the actual development of commercial shipping in the Northeast and Northwest Passages, however, sharp contrasts quickly supersede these superficial similarities. Under Soviet administration, the Northeast Passage became a major commercial artery, plied each year by hundreds of vessels carrying millions of tons of freight.[1] (Although jurisdiction over Arctic shipping is now passing to Russia, there is little reason to expect this change to cause drastic shifts in policy in this area.) For the most part, these operations involve coastal trade rather than through shipments moving from one end of the passage to the other. They focus on the transport of raw materials, such as timber and minerals, harvested or extracted from the hinterlands of the Russian Federation and the shipment of equipment and other supplies to the industrial and population centers of Siberia. At present, ships navigate these waters routinely at least five months of the year, and passage is possible (though not necessarily economically attractive), with the support of the world's largest icebreaker fleet, during virtually any month of the year. The development of the Northeast Passage into a commercial artery, a matter of explicit Soviet policy from the 1930s onward, has also occasioned sizable investments in infrastructure, in such forms as port facilities, aids to navigation, and an extensive administrative apparatus. Taken as a whole, the resultant system is known today as the Northern Sea Route. Under Soviet jurisdiction, a separate agency—the Administration of the Northern Sea Route, located within the Ministry of the Merchant Fleet—assumed responsibility for its administration.

The contrast between the development of the Northern Sea Route and the course of commercial shipping in the Northwest Passage could hardly be more striking.[2] Fewer than fifty vessels have made complete transits of the passage during the years since 1906, when Amundsen arrived off the coast of Alaska. Given the paucity of powerful icebreakers available for use in the North American Arctic, shipping in this passage is largely confined to the months of August and September. For the most part, these operations involve the movement of relatively small vessels to supply fuel oil and consumer goods to the scattered human settlements of the Canadian Arctic. A larger vessel, the M/V *Arctic*, makes several trips a year to pick up lead and zinc from the Nanisivik Mine on Baffin Island and the Polaris Mine on Little Cornwallis Island. In recent years, there have been some shipments of oil eastward from Panarctic's Bent Horn field on Cameron Island and several experimental shipments of oil westward from Gulf Oil's Amauligak field in the Canadian Beaufort Sea. An annual barge convoy, carrying industrial equipment destined for use in the oil fields of Alaska's North Slope, goes by way of Seattle and does not make use of the waters of the Northwest Passage proper. There are no deepwater ports in the North American Arctic. The icebreaker fleets of Canada and the United States together amount to a small fraction of the Russian fleet.[3] There is no administrative apparatus, analogous to the Administration of the Northern Sea Route, responsible for shipping in the Northwest Passage.

Accounting for the Differences

What accounts for these striking differences in the scale and organization of shipping in the two Arctic passages? It is impossible to single out any one factor as the cause of these differences. Rather, a number of factors interacting with each other account for the differences in the evolution of commercial shipping in the Northeast Passage and the Northwest Passage. No doubt, these divergent patterns of development are attributable, in part, to prominent features of the relevant natural systems (for example, the configuration of navigable channels and the behavior of ice in the two passages). But human factors have clearly played a role of great importance as determinants of the development of Arctic shipping in the two passages. In this chapter, I direct attention to those human factors, exploring in the process the impact of five differentiable sets of considerations: (1) jurisdiction, (2) demography, (3) political economy, (4) geopolitics, and (5) culture.

Jurisdiction

Whereas shipping in the Northeast Passage developed without serious controversy under Soviet administration, the jurisdictional status of the Northwest Passage has become a focus of conflict, pitting Canada against an array of other states led by the United States. This long-running dispute features intermittent testing behavior (as in the voyages of the *Manhattan* in 1969 and the *Polar Sea* in 1985), which frequently provokes Canadian reactions in the form of more encompassing jurisdictional claims. Today, Canada claims all of the waters of the Northwest Passage and, more generally, the waters of the Canadian Arctic Archipelago as internal waters. This claim rests on an argument featuring historic waters as delimited through a liberal application of the doctrine of straight baselines.[4]

In fact, the contrast between the two passages with regard to jurisdiction is a little more subtle than this tale of Canadian jurisdictional claims suggests. For its part, the Soviet government proceeded in a cautious manner in asserting jurisdictional claims in the maritime Arctic.[5] Despite the views expressed by some publicists, for example, the Soviet Union never officially and unambiguously advanced claims to the Kara, Laptev, and East Siberian seas as internal waters. Even the well-known confrontations of the 1960s regarding innocent passage in the Arctic straits of Siberia and, more specifically, the Vilkitski Straits incident of 1967, in which the Soviet government refused permission for the American Coast Guard icebreakers *Edisto* and *Eastwind* to use the straits to pass between the Kara and Laptev seas, did not center on conflicting positions concerning the delimitation of internal waters. Rather, the Soviets claimed these straits as territorial waters and argued that it was impermissible for foreign warships to transit them in the absence of prior authorization.[6]

On the other hand, the Soviet Union made it clear that the Northern Sea Route, a complex administrative and logistical system, was not only differentiable from the Northeast Passage but also unquestionably subject to Soviet (now Russian) jurisdiction. Because commercial vessels registered in other countries cannot hope to ply these waters without making use of the infrastructure provided by the Northern Sea Route (for example, pilotage, icebreaker escorts, ice reconnaissance), the Russians can exercise effective control over shipping in the waters of the Eurasian Arctic without any need to advance controversial jurisdictional claims to the waters of the Northeast Passage.

Canada, by contrast, has launched increasingly expansive jurisdictional claims relating to the waters of the North American Arctic without making any vigorous effort to develop infrastructure analogous to that of the Northern Sea Route. This has generated a continuing dispute that undoubtedly constitutes a barrier to enhanced use of the Northwest Passage for commercial shipping. Whereas the Russians, who have undisputed control over the Northern Sea Route, can offer the services of the route to prospective foreign shippers on specified terms, the Canadians are in the position of threatening to prevent prospective shippers from using the waters of the Northwest Passage on the basis of jurisdictional claims that are not universally accepted by members of the international community. No doubt, the Canadian dilemma is easy to explain on the basis of the fact that the Canadian government is not in a position to commit resources to Arctic shipping on anything like the scale that the Soviet Union did in developing the Northern Sea Route. But the differences between the two passages with respect to jurisdictional status and the availability of infrastructure certainly go far toward explaining the contrast between them regarding commercial shipping.

An Arctic Cooperation Agreement signed by Canada and the United States in January 1988 has helped to alleviate the friction between the two countries over the status of the waters of the Northwest Passage. Yet this accord is hardly sufficient to eliminate the jurisdictional impediment to the development of commercial shipping in the North American Arctic. With regard to the central issue of the legal status of the waters of the Northwest Passage, the two sides agreed to disagree.[7] The fact that the United States undertakes to seek prior permission or authorization for transits of American icebreakers through the passage does not signify acceptance of Canada's internal waters claim. The accord applies only to icebreakers (though some have argued that this also implies a de facto coverage of commercial vessels). And the agreement is bilateral; it has no effect as far as other countries are concerned. It seems fair to say, therefore, that the jurisdictional ambiguities affecting the waters of the Northwest Passage constitute a continuing problem for those interested in commercial shipping in these waters.

Demography

Up to 80 percent of the residents of the Far North are citizens of the Russian Federation. For the most part, these Russian northerners are grouped into sizable urban centers associated with the extraction of raw materials (for example, Norilsk, Igarka) or with the conduct of northern commerce (for example, Murmansk, Archangel).[8] Murmansk alone has a population of half a million, and there are a number of other Arctic communities in the Russian Federation whose populations run into the hundreds of thousands. In the northern reaches of North America, by contrast, the only community of over one hundred thousand is Anchorage, which lies at or beyond the southern boundary of the Arctic region. Moreover, Anchorage's commercial lifeline, which runs southward to Seattle, provides no stimulus for commercial shipping in the waters of the Northwest Passage.

The importance of the Northern Sea Route owes much to the links that have grown up between coastal shipping in the marginal Arctic seas and river traffic reaching far into the Siberian interior. In fact, the traditional economic justification for Arctic shipping in the Soviet Union stressed the role of the Northern Sea Route in connecting the riverine communities of Siberia with the outside world rather than any desire to transport cargoes between Europe and the Far East over the entire route. Thus, equipment and supplies needed for oil and gas development in northwestern Siberia move into place by way of Ob Bay and the rivers running into it.[9] Timber from Igarka and ores from Dudinka/Norilsk move out to the Northern Sea Route along the Yenisei River. To the east, the Lena River constitutes Yakutsk's lifeline to the outside world, despite the fact that the city is hundreds of kilometers upriver from the port of Tiksi on the Laptev Sea. Taken together, these links form a complex commercial network tying the sizable urban centers of Siberia to the rest of the Russian Federation.

There is nothing remotely comparable to this commercial network in the North American Arctic. The entire population of Alaska approximates that of the city of Murmansk. The combined population of the Yukon and the Northwest Territories in northern Canada is under one hundred thousand. The only river in the North American Arctic that bears any significant commercial traffic is the Mackenzie. Shipping on this river generally takes the form of the movement of goods from the south to resupply more northerly communities; there is no link to commercial shipping making use of the waters of the Northwest Passage. Whereas the Northern Sea Route constitutes a vital link in a coastal/riverine commercial network serving a number of urban centers in Siberia, therefore, the demography of the North American Arctic offers no basis for the evolution of a parallel trading system encompassing the waters of the Northwest Passage.

Political Economy
Yet another factor that affects the course of Arctic shipping centers on the relationship between politics and economics in the relevant coastal states. In part, this is a matter of differences between the capitalist systems of North America and the socialist system that long prevailed in the Soviet Union. The Soviet government, for example, followed a conscious policy of developing the Northern Sea Route from the 1930s onward.[10] In support of this policy, the Soviet Union created a government agency to administer the Northern Sea Route and invested heavily from public funds in the infrastructure needed to transform the route from a paper operation into a physical reality.

The contrast between this political decision to develop the Northern Sea Route and the situation facing those interested in commercial shipping in the Northwest Passage is striking. To be sure, even the American government, which normally espouses the virtues of private enterprise, is willing, under some conditions, to take steps to encourage large-scale investment in industrial development. Consider, by way of illustration, the ultimately unsuccessful efforts of the Carter and Reagan administrations to facilitate the construction of the proposed Alaska Natural Gas Transportation System.[11] But there is no comparison between these modest steps and the capacity of the former Soviet government simply to decide, as a matter of public policy, to invest the resources needed to develop a commercial network like the Northern Sea Route.

Even if we set aside the role of the state in providing infrastructure, the economics of commercial shipping differ substantially between the North American Arctic and the Eurasian

Arctic. In the North American case, potential shippers must reckon with the fact that world market prices for goods of the type likely to move through the Northwest Passage (for example, hydrocarbons or nonfuel minerals) are notoriously volatile. This greatly complicates financial calculations and tends to shorten the time frame employed by those making investment decisions. Under the circumstances, projects (such as commercial shipping in the Arctic) that can be expected to produce profits only over a longer time period tend to fall by the wayside.[12] By contrast, fluctuations in world market prices have loomed less large for Soviet/Russian planners concerned with the economics of Arctic shipping. For the most part, the goods in question have traded on domestic Soviet/Russian markets that are not significantly affected by world market prices. As a result, Russian planners can count on somewhat more predictable income streams than their North American counterparts can in calculating the net benefits of relying on Arctic shipping to move bulk cargoes.

Beyond this, some commentators envision a future for Arctic shipping that features through passages in contrast to coastal trade of the sort that presently characterizes the Northern Sea Route. The usual scenario underlying this vision involves potential Japanese interests in moving cargo to and from Europe by way of the Northern Sea Route or the Northwest Passage. In times of financial stress and budget deficits, this scenario has obvious economic attractions. Some such idea almost certainly motivated the Soviet offer, made in the context of the 1987 Murmansk initiative, to open the Northern Sea Route to foreign shippers willing to pay for using the services that the route provides.[13] But it seems doubtful whether anything will come of such proposals during the immediate future. In the case of the Northern Sea Route, there are political uncertainties, arising from the collapse of the Soviet Union and the emergence of new political systems, to be overcome. Through traffic in the Northwest Passage, on the other hand, would require a resolution of outstanding jurisdictional issues as well as an investment in infrastructure of a magnitude that may well deter all parties concerned. And it is perfectly possible that new technologies, such as cost-effective submarine tankers, soon will make shipping routes running directly across the Arctic Basin more attractive than either the Northern Sea Route or the Northwest Passage.[14]

Geopolitics

A motivating force behind Soviet policies emphasizing the development of the Far North (including the transportation system of which the Northern Sea Route is a major component) was the emergence of the Arctic as an important region in geopolitical terms. As the preeminent Arctic state, the Soviet Union long felt compelled to maintain a high profile in the region. Murmansk is the northernmost ice-free port in the world, and the Barents Sea provided the Soviet Union's most reliable access to the waters of the Atlantic Ocean. The Soviet Northern Fleet, based at Polyarny and Severomorsk on the Kola Peninsula, developed into one of two principal concentrations of Soviet naval power and the largest Soviet fleet in terms of strategic firepower.[15] Additional land-based forces on the Kola Peninsula have given that area, by many measures, the greatest concentration of military power in the world. As well, the marginal Arctic seas acquired importance as patrol stations for Soviet nuclear-powered, ballistic-missile submarines (SSBNs) capable of delivering nuclear weapons to targets throughout North America.[16] The Arctic coastline stretching eastward from the Kola Peninsula is dotted with radars and interceptors constructed as part of an air defense system intended to knock out American manned bombers or cruise missiles coming in over the Arctic Basin. Shortly before its collapse, the Soviet government moved to conduct all of its underground nuclear tests at the Novaya Zemlya test site.

Contrast this picture, from a geopolitical point of view, with the situation prevailing in the North American Arctic. Canada has its hands full simply maintaining effective occupancy in the sparsely populated Canadian Arctic, much less deploying substantial military capabilities in the region. Even the proposed fleet of ten to twelve nuclear-powered submarines, which the Mulroney administration had sold to the Canadian public in considerable part as a means of enhancing the country's presence in the Arctic region, has now fallen to the rigors of budget constraints. Under the circumstances, Canada lacks the military capability to

patrol its Arctic domains effectively, much less to defend them
against hostile incursions.[17] For its part, the United States does
not station either nuclear-powered submarines or high-endurance manned bombers in the Arctic, though it has often asserted
the right to deploy such forces in the region as a counter to Soviet
military activities in the Far North, and the putative Soviet threat
provided the impetus for the construction of air defenses in the
North American Arctic.[18] While American nuclear submarines
regularly roam the waters of the Arctic Basin, moreover, there is
no comparison between American Arctic deployments and the
profile the Soviet Union maintained in this region.

What we see here, then, is yet another dimension of the contrast between the Eurasian Arctic and the North American Arctic.
The Soviet Union (and now Russia) is an Arctic country in terms
of geopolitics as well as conscious policy. Sizable concentrations
of people live in the Russian Arctic. The region is thoroughly
linked to the rest of the country in economic terms. And the Arctic has loomed large in Soviet strategic thinking for geopolitical
reasons. The North American Arctic, on the other hand, is
sparsely populated and far less important than the Russian Arctic
in economic terms. For the vast majority of Canadians and Americans, whose vision is still shaped by the Mercator projection, it
is an area of little geopolitical significance as well. Whereas Arctic
shipping is just one interlocking piece in the larger picture of
Soviet/Russian activities in the Far North, marine transportation
seldom occurs to North Americans as a human endeavor appropriate to the Arctic.

Culture

To complete this picture of the human factors accounting for
differences in the commercial use of the Northeast Passage and
the Northwest Passage, it is important to add some notes on cultural predispositions. The role of culture as a determinant of national behavior is notoriously difficult to pin down with any
precision. Culture is almost always better understood as a force
predisposing groups of human beings to act in certain ways than
as a causal factor that explains specific actions.[19] Yet the Arctic or
the Far North does loom large in both Canadian culture and So-
viet/Russian culture. The contrast between these visions of the

Arctic serves to reinforce the factors reviewed in the preceding paragraphs in accounting for the differences between the North American Arctic and the Eurasian Arctic with regard to commercial shipping.

The central element of the Canadian vision of the Far North is captured in the concept of the Arctic sublime.[20] The Arctic is awesome and alluring, fascinating and mysterious. Its cultural significance requires that the region remain remote and undeveloped. This accounts for the extreme sensitivity of Canadians to the intrusions of others (for example, the United States) into the Arctic, even though most Canadians have no personal experience in the Arctic and the Canadian government has no coherent policy covering the activities of its own citizens in the region. To the Soviets, by contrast, the Arctic has been a frontier region containing natural resources of great value. Like any frontier, the Arctic is to be confronted with the best available technology and ultimately tamed so that its wealth can be used to enhance the material well-being of Soviet/Russian citizens living elsewhere. This accounts for the conquering mentality that observers have long noted in describing Soviet activities in the Far North.[21]

Given these predispositions, the contrast between the Eurasian Arctic and the North American Arctic with regard to commercial shipping is no cause for surprise. Nothing could be more mundane than the development of a transportation network encompassing (though not confined to) a system of sea routes. For those whose vision rests on some notion of the Arctic sublime, the materialism and pragmatism associated with industry and commerce will seem alien. But for those who see the Arctic as a frontier to be colonized and as a storehouse of natural resources to be exploited or extracted, the development of a network of trade routes is apt to be taken for granted as a necessary concomitant of the growth of human activities in the region. Viewed from this perspective, the differences between the Northern Sea Route, which provides infrastructure for the economic development of the Soviet/Russian North, and the Northwest Passage, which merely fires the imagination of visionaries and adventurers, seem perfectly natural and indeed almost inevitable.

Concluding Observations

What can we conclude from this brief account of the role of human factors as determinants of the course of commercial shipping in the Northeast Passage and the Northwest Passage? More specifically, what is the likelihood of a counterpart to the Northern Sea Route emerging in the North American Arctic during the foreseeable future? Such a development would require, at a minimum, a resolution of the Canadian/American jurisdictional disputes in the region coupled with a coherent Canadian northern policy that would both justify substantial public investments in the necessary infrastructure and encourage large-scale private investments in Arctic enterprises.

In the light of recent events in the North American Arctic, the chances of such a development occurring are slim. The Mulroney administration's decision to dismantle the National Energy Program articulated in the early 1980s under Trudeau signaled a decline in the inclination of the Canadian federal government to provide public incentives for northern development. The gathering movement to transfer control and even ownership of large segments of the Canadian North to groups of indigenous peoples seems likely to reduce further the influence of those interested in large-scale economic development in the region.[22] To be sure, the *Polar Sea* incident of 1985 temporarily stiffened the resolve of the federal government to go forward with the construction of the *Polar 8,* an icebreaker designed to be the world's most powerful at the time of its commissioning.[23] But this project, like the proposed fleet of nuclear-powered submarines, has fallen to the budgetary ax, a fact that marks it more as a momentary response to public passions than as the beginning of a serious effort to build up Canada's icebreaking capability. With regard to the Arctic, then, Canadian federal budget deficits, which are larger in per capita terms than their better-known American counterparts, clearly take precedence over the pursuit of concrete measures intended to lend substance to Canada's vision of itself as a northern nation.

Under the circumstances, it seems fair to conclude that the Northwest Passage is destined to remain, for the foreseeable future at least, an object of vision and romance rather than to serve as the basis for a commercial artery comparable to the Northern Sea Route. Despite the apparent similarities between the two passages, any other course of development would require profound changes, not only in Canadian and American public policies regarding the Arctic but also in the cultural predispositions that most North Americans bring to Arctic affairs.

Postscript—January 1992

With the unraveling of the Soviet Union during 1991, responsibility for the administration of the Northern Sea Route has shifted to the government of the Russian Federation, which has asserted its jurisdiction over all of the Soviet North. Undoubtedly, financial constraints will limit the ability of Russia to support the operation of the Northern Sea Route as a matter of public policy. One probable response to this development features a growing effort to encourage foreign shipping in the Northeast Passage as a means of defraying some of the costs of amortizing and operating the existing infrastructure of the Northern Sea Route. In North America, meanwhile, there are signs of renewed interest in economic development in the Canadian Arctic. But this time, planners are focusing on the construction of a system of roads in the Northwest Territories, in contrast to envisioning an enlarged role for commercial shipping in the Arctic.

PART THREE

International Studies

Prologue

Two sharply contrasting trends have stimulated a marked increase in the attention that practitioners and scholars alike devote to Arctic international relations. Though seldom thought of as a prize to be fought over, the Far North has become an important deployment zone for strategic weapons systems and, as a result, a focus of considerable interest among those concerned with the global strategic balance. At the same time, the Arctic has emerged, somewhat unexpectedly, as an active arena for those endeavoring to foster sustained cooperation through the establishment and operation of international regimes. Although these trends are at odds with one another in some respects, they are similar in the sense that they both have the effect of highlighting Arctic issues for those concerned with world affairs.

The remarkable growth of the Arctic's strategic significance during the 1980s is attributable to mounting concerns about the vulnerability of land-based intercontinental ballistic missiles coupled with the realization that the Far North offers exceptionally favorable operating conditions both for nuclear-powered submarines carrying sea-launched ballistic missiles and for manned bombers equipped with air-launched cruise missiles. Will this role of the Arctic continue during the 1990s in the wake of the end of the cold war, substantial (and possibly dramatic) reductions in stockpiles of nuclear weapons, and the profound economic and political transformations associated with the collapse of the Soviet Union?

176   INTERNATIONAL STUDIES

The answer to this question is far from simple. Still, there are reasons to believe that the Far North will continue to be an arena of considerable strategic significance during the foreseeable future. Its role in an overall strategic balance restructured to reflect a shared interest in maintaining some form of finite or minimal deterrence could actually increase. Even as political pressure for deep reciprocal cuts in strategic weapons systems (especially land-based intercontinental ballistic missiles) grows, most knowledgeable observers believe that some form of deterrence among nuclear-armed states will continue to characterize the global strategic balance. As a result, the hospitality of the Arctic to sea-based and air-breathing strategic weapons seems destined to remain a highly attractive asset to military planners.

Whereas the problems leading to the demise of the Soviet Union have generated intense pressure to reduce sharply overall expenditures on armaments, there are few signs as yet of any drastic reductions in forces stationed in the Russian North. At this writing, it seems probable that Russian military planners (or former Soviet planners reemerging as Russian officials) will continue to find the Arctic an attractive deployment zone. Their American counterparts will experience strong incentives to follow suit in maintaining a supply of strategic forces capable of operating comfortably under Arctic conditions.

None of this has had the effect of dampening the enthusiasm of those who now see the Circumpolar North as an attractive setting for the pursuit of a variety of cooperative ventures. Two features make this trend particularly distinctive. Above all, recent efforts to stimulate international cooperation in the Arctic have come to center increasingly on activities involving the Arctic Eight, a grouping of countries that joins together five Western allies (the United States, Canada, Denmark/Greenland, Iceland, and Norway), two neutral states (Sweden and Finland), and Russia (as the successor to the Soviet Union in the Far North). Though this development is surely a sign of the times, it has come as a surprise to many to see it manifested so quickly and effectively in a region where the superpowers confronted each other at close quarters for decades. In addition, both subnational governments (for example, states, provinces, territories, counties, autonomous regions) and nongovernmental organizations (for instance, indig-

enous peoples groups, scientific establishments) have emerged
as prominent players in the international relations of the Arctic,
a fact that has given rise to a number of interesting efforts to
bridge the gap between state and nonstate actors in the pursuit
of international cooperation.

The results are becoming visible today in a variety of settings.
A nongovernmental International Arctic Science Committee is up
and running. The Arctic Eight have agreed formally to launch an
Arctic Monitoring and Assessment Program as part of an emerging Arctic Environmental Protection Strategy. A sizable grouping
of subnational governments have initiated a Northern Forum to
explore and advance their common interests. The indigenous
peoples of the Circumpolar North have taken initial steps toward
creating a pan-Arctic aboriginal association. Responsible and
well-informed voices, especially but not exclusively in Canada,
are calling for the establishment of an international Arctic Council, envisioned as an ongoing organization capable of providing
a forum in which all of those possessing legitimate interests in
Arctic issues would be able to exchange ideas on a regular basis.

Predictably, the links between these developments and the
strategic considerations outlined above have become a source of
concern to some. Both the Soviets and the Americans have often
asserted, at least in formal terms, that security issues are off-lim-
its with regard to the activities of the newly emerging cooperative
arrangements in the Arctic. But this does not diminish the significance of the growth of cooperative ventures in the Far North;
it may prove to be little more than a declaratory policy in the not
too distant future. As the chapters to follow suggest, it is even
possible that the Arctic will emerge as a microcosm in which to
experiment with devices designed to link military and civil concerns in the interests of broadening the movement toward international cooperation.

The chapters of Part Three explore the emerging role of the
Arctic in world affairs from several perspectives. Chapter 9 provides an overview of recent developments in the international
relations of the region. In the process, it lays the foundation for
a sustained effort to take stock of the rising tide of efforts to foster
international cooperation in the Circumpolar North. Chapter 10
focuses on the militarization of the Arctic, examining the impli-

cations of this development both for political alignments in the region and for the prospects of Arctic arms control. The original version of the chapter was written prior to the most dramatic recent changes in the Soviet Union and the East-West relationship, but its central concern with the strategic significance of the Arctic remains a subject of considerable interest today. Chapter 11 addresses the issue of sustainable development in the Circumpolar North; it asks whether there are opportunities to launch constructive international initiatives in an area long dominated by core/periphery relations running from south to north within individual countries.

The concluding chapter poses the question of whether the Circumpolar North is emerging as a distinctive region in the thinking of those responsible for policy-making in the Arctic Eight. In the process, it demonstrates that this is by no means a technical or politically neutral matter, subject to resolution on the basis of some objective analysis. Both the conceptual lenses and the interests of those who make decisions on behalf of a variety of actors (at the nongovernmental, subnational, federal agency, and national levels) exert a profound influence on how individuals and groups react to the proposition that the Arctic is becoming a distinctive region in international society. Accordingly, this discussion should be of interest not only to those concerned with the future of the Arctic but also to those struggling to come to terms with similar issues involving regional security and cooperation in other parts of the world.

CHAPTER 9

The Arctic in World Affairs

Long dismissed as a frozen wasteland, of interest only to a handful of explorers, traders, missionaries, scientists, and indigenous peoples, the Arctic has emerged over the past several decades as an international region of major significance. As the possibilities for military, economic, and environmental benefits and losses rise, so too do the stakes of all of the Arctic nations in devising ways to work together. It would be pointless and wasteful for people in different parts of the Circumpolar North to attempt to solve the same problems without benefiting from each other's experiences.[1]

All Arctic states can gain from cooperating to devise ways of exploiting northern resources while protecting the region's ecosystems and indigenous cultures. The Russians, for example, could teach the West much about constructing multistoried buildings on permafrost, about Arctic marine transportation, and even about providing a measure of self-government to northern indig-

Based on the Donald L. McKernan Lecture delivered at the University of Washington in Seattle, 10 May 1989, this essay appeared as Oran R. Young, "Global Commons: The Arctic in World Affairs," *Technology Review* 93 (February/March 1990): 52–61. The current version draws on material developed in Oran R. Young, "La Politique internationale dans l'Articque: Une perspective américaine," *Etudes internationales* 20 (March 1989): 97–114; and Oran R. Young and Arkady I. Cherkasov, "International Cooperation in the Arctic: Opportunities and Constraints," a paper prepared for the International Conference on Arctic Cooperation held in Toronto, October 1989.

enous peoples. Canada and the United States could share their experience in building small dwellings for northern conditions; using specialized transportation, such as snowmobiles and all-terrain vehicles; and designing and implementing environmental safeguards. Scandinavian countries, which have the most effective systems of reindeer husbandry, could further Russian practices in this field. And capitalist and socialist nations alike want to reduce the high cost of extracting Arctic raw materials and transporting them to distant markets.

Fortunately, policymakers are grasping, albeit slowly, the potential for regional collaboration. The most recent formal expression of American Arctic policy, a 1983 National Security Decision Directive that declares that the United States has "unique and critical interests in the Arctic region," speaks explicitly of "promoting mutually beneficial international cooperation in the Arctic."[2] In 1987, Joe Clark, then Canada's secretary of state for external affairs, called regional cooperation a "trend of enormous importance," stating that Canada "wishes to see peaceful cooperation among Arctic Rim countries developed further."[3] Even clearer and stronger exhortations have come from the Soviet Union. In a major speech in Murmansk in 1987, Mikhail Gorbachev laid out a program for cooperation and pledged the Soviets' "profound and certain interest in preventing the North of the planet, its Polar and sub-Polar regions, and all Northern countries from ever again becoming an arena of war."[4] In the ensuing years, the Soviets repeatedly advocated an initiative to roll back the militarization of the Arctic by declaring it a "zone of peace." There is every reason to anticipate that the government of Russia will adopt a similar perspective.

For a region in which international cooperation was until recently considered either unnecessary or—because the superpowers were directly involved—infeasible, this growing sentiment signals a welcome change. It is transforming the region, even as it stimulates an awareness of the need to maintain the integrity of the Arctic.

Global Stakes

The growing concern for cooperation has arisen as the Arctic Rim states have increased their activities in the Far North.

Whereas military analysts in the 1960s and 1970s considered the Arctic a remote periphery over which missiles might fly, the relatively empty spaces are now convenient locales for operating both nuclear submarines and bombers equipped with long-range cruise missiles. Accordingly, the Pentagon has taken an interest in pursuing Arctic air and sea defenses, such as the North Warning System being built by the United States and Canada and the U.S. Navy's SSN-21 attack submarine.

The Arctic also has gained prominence as a secure source of raw materials. Alaska's North Slope is North America's largest oil-producing area, and the U.S. Northeast is coming to rely on electricity from massive hydroelectric plants in northern Quebec. Fossil fuels off Norway's north coast have helped to limit Western Europe's dependence on Soviet natural gas. The region looms even larger in Soviet, and now Russian, plans. Giant Siberian gas fields at Urengoi and Yamburg dominate efforts to expand fossil-fuel production, and the Russians have become leaders in industrial hydropower by harnessing Siberian rivers.

With the growing human presence has come attention to the region's environment. Atmospheric phenomena peculiar to the Arctic can interfere with radar and other communications systems, endangering both military and commercial aviation. Arctic ice can pose obstacles to submarines or hinder the operation of drilling rigs on continental shelves. Dramatic evidence of links between Arctic phenomena and human activities elsewhere has surfaced. Interactions among Arctic sea, ice, and air are major determinants of weather throughout the Northern Hemisphere. Heavy metals and other toxic substances originating far to the south show up regularly in Arctic fish and marine mammals and subsequently in the breast milk of Native women. Winds blow carbon dioxide, sulfates, soot, sulfur dioxide, chlorofluorocarbons, and even radioactive materials toward the Far North. Because of the prevailing water and air currents, these pollutants accumulate in the Arctic atmosphere, and the region is plagued each winter and spring by a dense blanket of haze that can reduce visibility as much as the smog of Los Angeles does.

Arctic air masses are also particularly effective traps for greenhouse gases, including carbon dioxide. There is consensus within the scientific community on projections that global warming will raise temperatures two to three times as much in the high latitudes as in the midlatitudes over the next fifty to one hundred years. That would increase Arctic snowfall and glacial activity, significantly raising sea levels worldwide. Eventually, the warming trend could also melt Arctic sea ice and the Greenland icecap, resulting in more warming as the surface reflects less sun.

As the significance of the Arctic grows, decisions tend to be made by outsiders, who are seldom well informed about, or sensitive to, the concerns of the Arctic's 10 million human inhabitants. Because what is happening to the region presents a growing threat to these peoples, especially those anxious to protect their distinctive ways of life, they are expressing their legitimate interests regarding all of the military, economic, and environmental issues. They have sought to be heard, not only by intervening in state, provincial, and federal arenas but also by organizing themselves across national borders.

At the same time, the international community of scientists working on Arctic issues is growing and becoming more politically active. In the United States, the Arctic Research and Policy Act of 1984 has given a powerful shot in the arm to scientific endeavors. In 1990, representatives of the eight Arctic nations formally established the International Arctic Science Committee (IASC) to promote cooperation in the realm of Arctic studies. This body will give scientists an effective voice in international circles as well as providing them with a forum for discussing and coordinating their research.

Precedents for Cooperation

As the Arctic Rim nations step up their joint activities, they can build on a substantial body of experience with Arctic international cooperation. This ranges from scientific and technical collaboration to agreements on the environment and even on military security.[5] On the one hand, the record includes relatively modest bilateral arrangements. For example, an agreement between Norway and the Soviet Union (now Russia) governs the exploitation of marine resources in a disputed area of the Barents Sea. The Marine Environmental Cooperation Agreement between Canada and Denmark/Greenland protects the ecosystems of Baffin Bay and the Davis Strait. On the other hand, several

Arctic agreements are more far-reaching and multilateral. Three merit particular attention: an agreement about rights to the Svalbard Archipelago, an accord to conserve polar bears, and a pact centered on the protection of northern fur seals.[6]

The Svalbard Archipelago, located 600 miles (960 km) northwest of Norway, is about the size of Belgium and the Netherlands combined. Once a bone of contention among Great Britain, Norway, Russia, and Sweden, the archipelago's status was settled in the Treaty Relating to Spitsbergen, which went into force in 1925. Now encompassing the United States, Russia, and thirty-eight other nations, this agreement recognizes Norwegian sovereignty over the archipelago. In return, Norway respects previously established rights in the area, allows the signatories access to Svalbard's natural resources on an equal footing, and keeps the archipelago demilitarized. Throughout World War II and the cold war, the Svalbard regime has remained intact, proving that state sovereignty need not foreclose international cooperation.

The polar bear, a quintessential symbol of the Arctic, has long been a target of trophy hunters from affluent societies. By the 1960s, growing concern about the status of polar bear stocks led to a remarkable set of scientific initiatives, culminating in a 1973 agreement among Canada, Denmark, Norway, the Soviet Union, and the United States to protect the species. This success shows that both superpowers and smaller nations can cooperate. It also offers a distinctive model for collaboration, since the scientific community—rather than politicians or diplomats—provided the leadership for both its creation and its implementation.

Open-sea harvesting severely depleted stocks of northern fur seals, an animal prized for its skin, toward the end of the nineteenth century. Unilateral U.S. efforts to regulate the harvest created sharp conflict with Great Britain. But in 1911, after the decline had reached crisis proportions, Great Britain (acting for Canada), Japan, Russia, and the United States negotiated an agreement to protect the North Pacific fur seal. The resultant regime banned sealing in the open sea and placed all harvesting operations on the islands of the eastern Bering Sea under American control and those in the western Bering Sea under Russian control. Widely credited with halting the depletion of fur seal stocks and even allowing their numbers to grow, this pioneering arrangement worked for decades. Recently, the population has declined again, amid controversy over the reasons. In 1984, the U.S. Senate failed to extend American participation in the treaty, in part because animal protectionists opposed an agreement that would allow any killing of wild animals. This led to the collapse of the fur seal regime.

Polar Contrasts

With the experience of Antarctica in mind, outside observers often focus on explicit, multilateral, and comprehensive arrangements in thinking about international cooperation in the Arctic.[7] But the two poles are antipodes in more than geography. Even in an era of creeping jurisdictional claims affecting "global commons," the sovereignty of states reaches farther into the Arctic than it does into the oceans, the atmosphere, or Antarctica. No one questions the authority of Canada, Denmark (Greenland is part of Denmark), Norway, the Soviet Union, or the United States over their Arctic sectors, even if ice sometimes masks the boundary between land and sea. By contrast, when the Antarctic Treaty was signed in 1959, none of the nations advancing territorial claims in Antarctica could have met even the most lenient standard of effective occupancy.

Nor has Antarctica been a major military arena. Demilitarization under the 1959 treaty simply recognized a prevailing situation. Contrast this with the strategic significance of the Arctic to the great powers. Whatever the prospects for cooperation on other matters, demilitarization appears a distant prospect in the Arctic.

Another difference is that no commercial ventures were taking place in Antarctica in 1959, except for some whaling operations in Antarctic waters that the treaty's negotiators were able to ignore. Nor are such activities expected to take on major proportions, a fact that facilitated the negotiations leading to the 1988 Convention on the Regulation of Antarctic Mineral Resource Activities and to the even more restrictive Environment Protocol, adopted in 1991 as an alternative to the 1988 convention. The contrast with Arctic oil and gas production and other world-class industrial operations could hardly be sharper.

Moreover, because the South Polar region has no permanent residents, diplomats and scientists have been able to devise cooperative arrangements for the region without considering local reactions. But the indigenous peoples of the Circumpolar North rightfully demand a voice in developing Arctic policies.

Finally, the Antarctic treaty grew out of the interests of a global scientific community. It was formalized in the aftermath of the International Geophysical Year, and the International Council of Scientific Unions has worked hard to keep the continent dedicated to science. Despite the emergence in recent years of controversies regarding some of the practices of the scientific community in Antarctica, there is no comparison between the polar regions in these terms.

Thus, simplistic analogies between the two polar regions merely confuse the prospects for international cooperation in the Arctic. The issues requiring coordination in the Arctic are in many ways more serious than those that spurred agreements in Antarctica. This does not rule out international cooperation in the Far North. But because the stakes are higher, parties are apt to have a harder time reaching consensus on the provisions of Arctic agreements.

The Rising Tide

Recent years have been marked by an unusual ferment of joint activities relating to the Arctic. Among several bilateral initiatives, Canada and the United States signed an Agreement on Arctic Cooperation in 1988. In it, the United States pledged to obtain Canadian consent for American icebreakers to navigate in areas claimed as internal waters by Canada, though the two nations have agreed to disagree on the legal status of the waters of the Arctic Archipelago. Since then, the *Polar Star* has crossed the Northwest Passage from west to east without provoking even a ripple of the angry Canadian response that followed the 1985 east-to-west transit of its sister ship, the *Polar Sea*.

The Soviet Union signed a series of bilateral agreements with Norway, Sweden, and Finland at the end of the 1980s. One agreement with Norway provides a framework for environmental cooperation. It includes agreed measures for cleaning up oil spills in the Barents Sea and for resolving conflicts over air and water pollution emanating from the Kola Peninsula. The Soviets also agreed to notify Norway about nuclear accidents that could produce radioactive contaminants. This agreement, as well as a similar one between the Soviet Union and Sweden, stemmed from concerns about a Soviet nuclear power plant on the Kola Peninsula. Soviet bilateral ventures with the United States and Canada expanded during the same period as well. An agreement setting forth a Soviet/American oil-spill contingency plan for the Bering Sea and its northern neighbor, the Chukchi Sea, was signed in May 1989.[8] And a framework agreement with Canada on Arctic cooperation, widely discussed since 1987, was finalized during Prime Minister Brian Mulroney's visit to the Soviet Union in November 1989.

Among the smaller Arctic states, Denmark and Norway appear to be settling a long-standing dispute over maritime boundaries between Greenland and the island of Jan Mayen. In August 1988, Denmark submitted the case to the International Court of Justice, and Norway accepted the jurisdiction of the court over the case.

Even more encouraging than bilateral initiatives is the growing recognition that many Arctic problems require multilateral responses. The Soviet Union's zone-of-peace initiative, coupled with innovative responses on the part of other Arctic states, has nourished interest in a comprehensive international regime in contrast to a collection of issue-specific agreements. In his 1987 speech, Gorbachev called for a network of arrangements, such as nuclear-weapon-free zones, restricted naval activities, cooperative resource development, coordinated scientific research, cooperation to protect the environment, and opening the Northern Sea Route to foreign ships. He acknowledged as well the interests of the indigenous population of the Far North.

The establishment of the International Arctic Science Committee (IASC) to foster research is particularly significant. Despite impressive achievements during the International Polar Years of 1882–1883 and 1932–1933, the Arctic has lacked an organized international scientific community of the sort that has played a prominent role in the Antarctic. Starting with a meeting in the United States in 1986, the IASC negotiations culminated in

1990 with the adoption of a set of founding articles for the committee. All parties made concessions. In particular, the Soviets abandoned their initial insistence on restricting participation to the five states bordering the Arctic Ocean.

This abundance of public actions has given rise to a flurry of nongovernmental initiatives. Many of these efforts are bilateral, like the agreement on medical research between the University of Alaska and the Siberian Branch of the Soviet Academy of Sciences. But a growing number call for cooperation from several or all Arctic states. A striking example is the Inuit Regional Conservation Strategy, which is being developed under the auspices of the Inuit Circumpolar Conference (ICC), a nongovernmental organization representing Native peoples in Greenland, Canada, Russia, and the United States. This innovative effort to apply the principles of the World Conservation Strategy in a regional setting has won strong support from the United Nations Environment Programme and has become a significant force in promoting international cooperation on Arctic environmental issues.

In fact, the Arctic's indigenous peoples—Inuit, Indians, Saami, Evenki, and Chukchi, among others—have taken the lead in promoting international cooperation and awareness of the Arctic as a distinctive international region. The main transnational Arctic organizations, such as the ICC, Indigenous Survival International, and the Nordic Saami Council, are all products of initiatives taken by indigenous peoples. Recently, these groups have initiated a process aimed at exploring the feasibility and utility of establishing a pan-Arctic aboriginal association to protect and promote the interests of indigenous peoples throughout the Circumpolar North.

The Road Ahead

Although the opportunities for cooperation have grown steadily, there remains, as the former Soviet prime minister Nikolai Ryzhkov put it, a "lack of trust that has built up in a region so sensitive from the viewpoint of security interests."[9] Most important, the strategic or military perspective on the Arctic conflicts with cultural, scientific, and environmental viewpoints. Military planners see the Arctic as a theater of operations for weapons and, potentially, for combat. That idea is antithetical to collaborative research and efforts to protect shared ecosystems; it is regarded with horror by the permanent residents of the Arctic, for whom the region is a homeland, not a battleground for alien powers.

Cooperative efforts suffer as well because no state has a clear-cut decision-making process for Arctic matters, much less a coherent policy. Most Arctic states have made valiant attempts at interagency coordination, but none has produced unambiguous success. Canada had an Advisory Committee on Northern Development for some years, but it is now defunct. The U.S. Interagency Arctic Policy Working Group, operating under the auspices of the National Security Council, has struggled to coordinate twelve to fifteen independent agencies but without a lot to show for its efforts. The Soviet Union's high-level State Commission for Arctic Affairs, created in 1988, has fallen by the wayside as a result of the political upheaval in that country.

A number of generic problems, such as the choice of actors to participate in any cooperative initiative and the impact of positional bargaining tactics, further complicate efforts to realize joint gains through cooperation. For example, the Soviets wanted the IASC to be inaugurated on their territory, where it would have advanced the zone-of-peace initiative. But the United States blocked that move. As a result, the committee was actually founded in Canada.

Still, such problems can be solved or swept aside when the will to act is strong. Although the Soviets and now the Russians have signaled a clear desire to make progress in this realm, there is room for skepticism about American intentions in this regard. The unmistakable enthusiasm of American scientists is not matched by unambiguous support from senior politicians or from the federal bureaucracy. A related obstacle arises from a lack of leadership. Neither the United States nor Russia dominates Arctic politics; efforts by one of the great powers often provoke skepticism, if not outright opposition, from the other. The United States and Russia could exert effective pressure together, but Washington has given a low priority to Arctic matters.

This leaves the smaller Arctic states best suited to take the initiative. In many ways, such a role appeals to these states. Canada, in particular, may find it attractive. Not only would it fit many

Canadians' image of their place in international society, but it would also alleviate some of their fears of being sandwiched between the great powers in the Circumpolar North.[10] Admittedly, some of the efforts of the lesser Arctic states have not been particularly well conceived or effective, and whether these nations can pull together to offer leadership is open to question. Although the Finns have vigorously promoted multilateral environmental arrangements, others had trouble taking the initiative in the complex IASC talks. For example, the talks revealed a division between Canadians who hoped to promote their nation's political agenda regarding Arctic sovereignty and those who wanted to separate scientific goals from the rest of the agenda.

Although these obstacles cannot be ignored, they do not alter the fact that the Arctic is coming into its own as a focus of attention among policymakers in all of the Arctic Rim states. The rising tide of human activities in this environmentally sensitive region demands an increased effort to coordinate actions, not only to reap mutual benefits but also to avoid mutual losses. The result is a growing challenge requiring both innovative political thinking and effective leadership. Under the circumstances, the Arctic seems destined during the 1990s to become a proving ground for new approaches to international cooperation.

CHAPTER 10

The Militarization of the Arctic: Political
Consequences and Prospects for Arms Control

The Arctic has long possessed an irreducible significance in
strategic terms. This is a consequence of geopolitics. The
United States and Russia (the successor state encompassing all of
the northern realms of the former Soviet Union) are immediate
neighbors in the Arctic. Western Alaska and eastern Siberia are
only 57 miles (91 km) apart at the Bering Strait, and the Bering
Sea itself is essentially enclosed by Russian and American territories. Both the United States and Russia front directly on the
Arctic Basin; Russia alone exercises direct control over about half
of the Arctic littoral. The shortest air route between the homelands of the two countries is across the Pole, a fact of inescapable
significance in an age of intercontinental bombers and ballistic
missiles.

Yet a series of developments in military technology unfolding
largely during the 1980s dramatically increased the role of the
Arctic as a theater for the operations of strategic weapons sys-

This chapter began life as a paper presented at a conference, "Sovereignty, Security, and the Arctic," held at York University in Toronto,
8–9 May 1986. The first several sections of the chapter appeared as
Oran R. Young, "The Militarization of the Arctic," in Edgar J. Dosman,
ed., *Sovereignty and Security in the Arctic* (London and New York: Routledge, 1989): 9–23. The chapter also provided raw material for chapters
2 and 9 of Gail Osherenko and Oran R. Young, *The Age of the Arctic: Hot
Conflicts and Cold Realities* (Cambridge: Cambridge University Press,
1989).

tems, transforming the region into an area of intense interest to those concerned with the global strategic balance. This chapter examines these technological developments and explores their implications, both for the foreign policies of the Arctic Rim states and for the prospects of devising generally acceptable arms control arrangements to deal with the specific problems of the Arctic region.

Written prior to the end of the cold war and the disintegration of the Soviet Union, the chapter does not include any sustained analysis of the impact of these changes on the strategic significance of the Arctic. Although it is difficult to project the consequences of these transformations for Arctic international relations in any detail, the alleviation of concern about the security of Europe and the reemergence of Russia as an independent Arctic state will surely have far-reaching effects. Accordingly, the analysis presented here should be treated as a starting point or baseline for efforts to address the strategic significance of the Arctic during the 1990s.

The Militarization of the Arctic

As land-based intercontinental ballistic missiles (ICBMs) became increasingly vulnerable to counterforce strikes during the 1980s, submarine-launched ballistic missiles (SLBMs) came to occupy an increasingly important place in the strategic calculations of both the Soviet Union and the United States. Simultaneously, the capabilities of ballistic-missile nuclear submarines (SSBNs) and SLBMs developed in ways that have made them particularly well suited for deployment in the Arctic. For one thing, SSBNs operating in Arctic waters can command virtually all enemy targets from fixed patrol stations located remarkably close to their respective homelands. They no longer need to penetrate dangerous choke points, such as the Greenland/Iceland/United Kingdom (GIUK) gap, or to endure the costs and hazards of using remote and widely scattered patrol stations in the North Atlantic or North Pacific. Soviet-built SS-N-8 and SS-N-18 missiles mounted on Delta-class submarines can deliver nuclear warheads to military targets both in North America and in Europe from Arctic patrol stations. Similarly, American Trident submarines carrying C-4 missiles are capable of attacking military targets throughout the former Soviet Union from Arctic waters.

The latest generations of SSBNs, the Soviet-designed Typhoon-class submarine and the American Ohio-class submarine, are even more effective. Though all late-model SSBNs can perform well in the Arctic Basin, the large, ice-reinforced Typhoon is designed specifically to operate in Arctic waters. There are numerous points in the polar pack ice where these submarines can break through to the surface to fire their missiles. The pack ice is also frequently interrupted by stretches of open water, or polynias. The new SSBNs are, or soon will be, equipped with the latest delivery vehicles, such as the Soviet-designed SS-N-20 (six to nine warheads) or the even newer SS-NX-23 and the American Trident II (also known as the D-5), with eight to ten warheads. These missiles have ranges of more than 8,000 kilometers (4,800 miles) and are nearly as accurate as land-based missiles.

At the same time, SSBNs can operate in Arctic waters with remarkable safety because of the difficulties of locating submarines, much less tracking them closely, under Arctic conditions. The ambient noise of the pack ice drastically reduces the effectiveness of acoustical monitoring devices (for example, sonar systems). Similarly, the opaqueness of the Arctic Basin's ice cover makes visual monitoring methods of little use. The Arctic therefore offers a unique combination of ease of operations and comparative safety for seaborne strategic delivery systems.

The Soviet Union moved vigorously to exploit these military attractions of Arctic waters during the 1980s. Well over half of all of the SSBNs of the former Soviet Union are stationed with the Northern Fleet at Polyarny and Severomorsk on the Kola Peninsula. These submarines are now active in the Arctic Basin, constituting a virtually invulnerable strategic force that has no need to penetrate Western defenses stationed along the GIUK gap or even to move from the protected waters of the Eurasian Arctic. Additionally, they are capable of repositioning themselves between Severomorsk in the European Arctic and Petropavlovsk in the North Pacific (one of the home ports of the Pacific fleet developed under Soviet auspices) by passing back and forth largely under the cover of Arctic ice The United States does not have an Arctic base comparable to Severomorsk. Yet American SSBNs based in Bangor, Washington, are fully capable of operating in Arctic waters for extended periods. The United States has moved rapidly to build up its fleet of Ohio-class submarines and to fit these submarines with Trident II or D-5 missiles. And the ease of operations and comparative safety attainable in the Arctic Basin are also attractive to American military planners, despite the fact that the United States does not have to contend with problems such as penetrating the GIUK gap. Though the details are not public knowledge, there are good reasons to expect that the United States has followed the Soviet lead in this realm. Overall, then, the Arctic Basin today may well be the world's most important theater of operations for seaborne strategic delivery systems.

A similar story emerges from an analysis of air-launched cruise missiles (ALCMs), which are already capable of delivering nuclear warheads to distant targets with great accuracy. Unlike ballistic missiles, cruise missiles are subject to guidance and control at all points along their flight paths. They fly at slow speeds and low altitudes, endeavoring to evade conventional air defense systems by means of their maneuverability and their ability to come in under or confuse ordinary radar scanners. Long-range cruise missiles now in service can travel up to 3,000 kilometers (1,800 miles) from their launch site. Cruise missiles mounted on nuclear submarines are currently operational and fully capable of functioning in Arctic waters. Although some observers are particularly struck by this fact,[1] the most significant strategic development in this realm arises from the deployment of long-range ALCMs suitable for use in standoff attacks initiated from Arctic airspace. The United States has equipped five squadrons of B-52G bombers with a total of 1,150 long-range cruise missiles and plans to add 600 more ALCMs to its inventory. Work is also proceeding on an advanced cruise missile, of which as many as 1,500 air-launched models may be deployed.

In contrast to the case of seaborne delivery systems, the Soviet Union has lagged somewhat behind the United States in this field. Yet the Soviets moved during the late 1980s to deploy long-range ALCMs on existing Backfire and Bear H bombers. It was expected that by the early 1990s each country would have a substantial force of long-range ALCMs mounted on the latest generations of high-endurance bombers. Prominent among these are one hundred B1-B bombers, which have a combat radius of 7,500 kilometers (4,500 miles) and which have now entered service in the United States, and the Blackjack-A bombers, which have a combat radius of 7,300 kilometers (4,380 miles) and which the Soviets began to deploy prior to the collapse of the Soviet Union.

The deployment of long-range ALCMs on the latest genera-tions of manned bombers has greatly enhanced the role of the Arctic as a theater for military operations. The great circle route over the Pole remains the shortest air route between North America and Eurasia. Long-range ALCMs launched from high-endurance bombers operating in the airspace over the Arctic Basin will be capable of reaching most important military targets in North America and Western Europe as well as in the former Soviet Union. This will permit each side to initiate standoff nuclear strikes against enemy targets from comparatively safe launch sites. It will also allow them to give serious consideration to policies designed to avoid or minimize political complica-tions arising from forward basing strategies for ground-launched cruise missiles (GLCMs) in areas like Western Europe.

The Arctic offers an attractive environment for military oper-ations involving cruise missiles mounted on manned bombers. It is a large, sparsely populated region in which military activi-ties can be carried out largely unnoticed. Also, ionospheric irregularities in the Arctic interfere with the use of long-range, over-the-horizon-backscatter (OTH-B) radar systems for defense against the operations of high-endurance bombers (especially those equipped with protective devices like the B1-B). As a result, it is safe to say that the Arctic has come to rank as the major theater for the operations of manned bombers equipped with ALCMs as well as for the operations of SSBNs.

Not surprisingly, these developments in the Arctic operations of offensive systems stimulated a surge of interest in both sea and air defense systems in the region. With respect to sea defense, the critical problem arises from the facts that conventional naval vessels are not capable of patrolling ice-covered Arctic waters and that most of the current methods of monitoring the activities of submarines from satellites, aircraft, or sea-bottom-mounted acoustical devices are of little use in tracking the movements of

SSBNs operating under the pack ice of the Arctic Ocean or in the marginal ice zones of the Arctic Basin rim. As Critchley has observed, "[a]t present, the only method of submarine monitoring that can be used in ice-covered and ice-infested waters is the nuclear-powered attack submarine."[2] Despite serious questions regarding the cost-effectiveness of deploying attack submarines in the Arctic, over half of the Soviet fleet of these submarines (many equipped with SS-N-15 or SS-N-16 nuclear antisubmarine missiles) is stationed with the Northern Fleet, and there are good reasons to believe that American Los Angeles–class nuclear submarines (SSNs) fitted with Harpoon antisubmarine missiles are active in the Arctic region. Given the growing role of the Arctic as a theater for the operations of SSBNs carrying advanced SLBMs and SLCMs, each of the superpowers has experienced powerful incentives in recent years to devote increasing attention to the problems of sea defense under Arctic conditions.

The deployment of ALCMs precipitated a similar surge of interest in air defense systems for the Arctic region. In North America, the 1950s Distant Early Warning (DEW) Line, which had been allowed to become obsolete, is being renovated and modernized. The resultant North Warning System, scheduled for completion in 1992, will include at least fifty-two sites strung along the 70th parallel. These sites will contain thirteen medium-range microwave radars and thirty-nine unattended circular phased-array short-range radars. Long-range OTH-B radars located on the east and west coasts of the United States will supplement the North Warning System by providing coverage of the eastern and western approaches to the North American Arctic.[3] Arrangements governing the construction and operation of the North Warning System figured prominently in the military agreement signed by the United States and Canada on 18 March 1985. In a separate but complementary arrangement, the United States and Iceland agreed to construct two radar stations in Iceland to monitor Soviet air and sea traffic in the Arctic. The United States and Canada also devised a new North American Air Defense Master Plan that envisions the dedication of at least six additional Airborne Warning and Control System (AWACS) aircraft to northern defense and the development of Arctic air-intercept capabilities (authorized to use airstrips located in Arctic Canada under emergency conditions), as well as the construction of ground-based warning systems to counter the emerging threat from long-range ALCMs in the Arctic region. Given the traditional Soviet emphasis on strategic defense systems, it will come as no surprise that in the years preceding its disintegration the Soviet Union undertook comparable programs for the enhancement of intercept capabilities and early warning devices throughout its segment of the Arctic. As a result, "the [Eurasian] Arctic is easily the most heavily militarized part of the [Arctic] littoral."[4]

Several related observations will help to round out this picture of the emergence of the Arctic region during the 1980s as a theater for military operations of utmost strategic significance. The Arctic is characterized by numerous atmospheric phenomena capable of posing problems for certain types of communications and defense systems. As Johnson, Bradley, and Winokur have put it, "Ionospheric irregularities caused by an aurora can modify electromagnetic waves, thereby affecting communications with satellite systems and affecting the utilization of over-the-horizon detection radars for defense against strategic transpolar bomber attack. Additionally, currents induced during large geomagnetic storms in long conductors such as telephone cables, power lines, or pipelines can cause failure or serious damage."[5]

These features of the Arctic environment may seem advantageous to planners concerned with ensuring the survivability of retaliatory capabilities, such as ALCMs mounted on manned bombers or SLBMs deployed on nuclear submarines stationed in the Arctic Basin. But they also pose potential problems for those charged with guiding cruise missiles (in contrast to ballistic missiles) over the Arctic Basin under adverse conditions or with maintaining communications with commanders of submarines carrying SLBMs. To the extent that the Arctic remains a critical theater for military operations, therefore, we can expect a growth of interest in the unique problems of military communication, command, and control (C^3) posed by the atmospheric conditions of the Arctic.

Finally, the construction of industrial facilities of vital economic significance to both Russia and the United States has added yet another dimension to the militarization of the Arctic. The Arctic has long been a remote region, subject to policies of benign neglect. Even those who have come to see the Arctic as an important strategic arena generally assume that states might fight *in* the Arctic but not *about* the Arctic. Yet by the end of the 1980s, military planners in both the United States and the Soviet Union found themselves thinking increasingly about the security of major industrial installations in the region as well as about the emerging role of the Arctic as a theater for military operations. The Prudhoe Bay/Kuparuk oil fields on the North Slope of Alaska, for example, account for approximately 25 percent of the oil produced in the United States. Both the oil fields and the Trans-Alaska Pipeline System (TAPS) used to move the oil to southern markets are highly vulnerable to disruption. Similar observations apply to the burgeoning industrial installations in Siberia. The Urengoi and Yamburg natural gas fields, for example, play a role of vital importance in the Russian energy equation, and the Soviet-built Siberian gas pipeline, running 2,750 miles (4,400 km) from northwestern Siberia to the Czech border, would be an obvious target in any effort to disrupt the Russian economy. The dependence of both the American economy and the Russian economy on secure supplies of energy and other raw materials from the Arctic is virtually certain to increase. Concerns for the security of major industrial installations in the Arctic, therefore, could easily add fuel to the militarization of the region during the foreseeable future.

Political Consequences

How has the militarization of the Arctic affected the interests and policy calculations of the various Arctic Rim states? The implications of this trend seemed comparatively straightforward for Soviet decision makers; there is every reason for their Russian successors to adopt similar perspectives. Russia is the preeminent Arctic state. Well over 40 percent of the land area of the Circumpolar North lies within the boundaries of Russia; the country exercises direct control over about half of the coastline of the Arctic Basin. Geopolitically, therefore, Russia is well placed to exploit the strategic attractions of the Arctic. Additionally, over three-quarters of the human population of the entire Circumpolar North is located in the Russian North. The North American Arctic contains nothing remotely comparable to population centers like Murmansk and Archangel, each of which has a population of over three hundred thousand. What is more, there is a long history of Soviet industrial, scientific, and military activities in the Far North. These include the development of the world's largest naval base, at Severomorsk on the Kola Peninsula; the construction of a cluster of strategic airbases in the Far East; and the use of Novaya Zemlya as a site for underground nuclear weapons tests.

Under the circumstances, the Soviets and their Russian successors have every reason to act to maintain the paramount position of Russia in a region that has become an increasingly important theater for military operations. This means that the Russians will endeavor to maintain their effective control over the portion of the Arctic Basin adjacent to their coastline, treating the Barents, Kara, Laptev, and East Siberian seas as enclosed seas or historic waters and exercising control over access to the Northeast Passage on the part of foreign vessels. The effect of this stance will be to create a secure Arctic sanctuary for the operation of Russian SSBNs as well as for the installation of forward air defense systems designed to counter American ALCMs. At the same time, the Russians, like their Soviet predecessors, may well experience powerful incentives to maintain freedom of movement in the water column, on the surface, and in the airspace of the remainder of the Arctic Basin. Though it is politically convenient to let the Americans carry the ball with regard to issues like access to the Northwest Passage, Russian interests coincide with American interests on such matters; and Russia will likely oppose initiatives on the part of other Arctic Rim states (for example, Canada in the Arctic archipelago) that would have the effect of restricting freedom of movement in the Arctic Basin. The geopolitical position of Russia in the Arctic makes it possible for the Russians to operate in this region without regard to the interests or sensibilities of other Arctic states. Yet Russia does have a growing interest in making common cause with the lesser Arctic Rim states (for example, Norway, Iceland, and Denmark/Greenland) in an effort to dilute their ties with the United States. This appears to have been one of the considerations underlying Soviet maneuvers during the late 1980s, like the offer to discontinue work on a major radar system at Krasnoyarsk in central Asia in exchange for an American agreement not to modernize the ballistic missile early warning system (BMEWS) site located at Thule, Greenland.

The militarization of the Arctic also has several more-specific implications for Soviet and now Russian security policies. Objectively, it has reduced the significance of the GIUK gap and the Norwegian flank, since Soviet-built SSBNs can operate safely and efficiently in the Arctic Basin with no need to move out into the North Atlantic. Given the Soviet propensity to plan for protracted wars involving efforts to interdict supply lines even in the nuclear era, however, it may be some time before Russian planners cease to worry about penetrating Western defenses stationed along the GIUK gap. Beyond this, the geopolitical position of Russia in the Arctic has some consequences that will inevitably complicate efforts to devise arms control arrangements for this region. Whereas the United States can deploy SSBNs into the Arctic from a base in Bangor, Washington, and from ALCMs mounted on bombers based in the lower forty-eight, Russia possesses large and strategically critical bases (for example, the naval base at Severomorsk) in the Arctic itself. Though the United States may find it tempting to exploit this asymmetry for negotiating purposes, it rests on fundamental geopolitical facts that cannot be ignored in any serious effort to regulate the militarization of the Arctic.

By contrast, the consequences of the militarization of the Arctic for the United States are more complex. The United States has never regarded itself as an Arctic power. The country did not even possess a physical presence in the Far North before the purchase of Alaska from Russia in 1867. Though Alaska is about a fifth the size of the entire lower forty-eight, it contains less than a quarter of 1 percent of the American population. World War II briefly directed American attention toward the North because of the Aleutian campaign of 1942–1943 and dramatic engineering feats like the construction of the Alcan Highway and the Canol Pipeline. But with the introduction of ICBMs, many Americans reverted to an attitude of benign neglect regarding the Arctic.

Nonetheless, the contemporary emergence of the Arctic as a theater for military operations makes such attitudes increasingly inappropriate. Without doubt, the key political implication of this trend for the United States centers on the growing importance of relations with northern allies, such as Norway, Iceland, Denmark/Greenland, and Canada. Not surprisingly, the United States has stepped up its efforts to collaborate with these lesser Arctic Rim states on security issues. American leaders have worked hard to nurture Norway's somewhat ambivalent commitment to the Western alliance, as well as to establish good working relations with the Home Rule government in Greenland (the political system established in 1979 in recognition of Greenland's growing autonomy from Denmark). Currently, the United States is endeavoring to maintain the support of Greenland's leaders for its plan to modernize the BMEWS site at Thule. After a period of increasing friction during the 1970s, American relations with Iceland have taken on a more cooperative cast. The American airbase at Keflavik seems secure for the moment, and the two countries signed an agreement in 1985 calling for the construction of two radar sites in Iceland, intended to contribute to Western defenses in the Arctic though they are not formally a component of the North Warning System. The triumph of the Progressive Conservative Party in Canada during the 1980s has provided a generally positive environment for Canadian/American collaboration in the Arctic. The North Warning System is a fully cooperative venture. Canada agreed to pay about 40 percent, or $600 million to $700 million of the construction cost (this does not include the supplemental OTH-B radars), handle construction of the sites located in Canada, and assume substantial responsibility for the management of the system. Similarly, the two countries have collaborated on a new North American Air Defense Master Plan within the context of the reorganized and expanded North American Aerospace Defense Command (NORAD).

Even so, the militarization of the Arctic carries with it considerable potential for friction between the United States and its northern allies. Though there is cause for genuine concern in this realm in dealings with Iceland and Greenland, the problems are particularly severe when combined with Canadian sensitivities relating to the Arctic. In part, this is a consequence of an apparent inability on the part of American leaders to recognize the depth and intensity of Canadian feelings about the Far North. Thus, the American government exerted substantial pressure on Canada to acquiesce in the testing of ALCMs (without nuclear armaments) over northern Canada. But the eventual concurrence of the Trudeau government triggered a widespread outpouring of protest on the part of the Canadian public. American icebreakers and nuclear submarines are now active in the waters of the Canadian Arctic archipelago (including the waters of the Northwest Passage). The fact that the American government, as part of its general unwillingness to acknowledge Canadian sovereignty in the waters of the Arctic archipelago, refused until 1988 to seek explicit permission for transits on the part of these vessels raised hackles in many Canadian quarters regarding the sensitive issue of jurisdiction in the Canadian Arctic. The transit of the American icebreaker *Polar Sea* through the Northwest Passage during the summer of 1985, for example, prompted the Mulroney government (ordinarily disposed to adopt a friendly posture toward the United States) to issue a formal declaration asserting Canadian jurisdiction over all of the waters of the Arctic archipelago as internal waters.

Partly, Canadian/American friction in the Arctic arises from the fact, surprising to most Americans, that many Canadians regard the United States as a principal threat to the maintenance of Canadian sovereignty in the Far North.[6] Thus, Canadians have expressed real concern about the resurgence of interest in air defense in the Arctic because "the new air-defense system might commit Canada to accept American weapons" stationed on Canadian territory.[7] More generally, influential Canadians often react with genuine unease to any pattern of developments leading to an increase in American military activities in the Far North. Though each initiative may take the form of a cooperative Canadian/American venture, Canada does not possess the military capabilities or the resources to participate as an equal partner in such arrangements. Nor is Canada sufficiently confident of its ability to exercise effective occupancy in the Arctic archipelago to respond to a growing American military presence in the area without concern. Such developments are bound to remind many Canadians of the immediate postwar period, when American bases and military personnel dominated the Canadian Arctic.

This brings us directly to the interests and policy calculations of the lesser Arctic Rim states. In a general way, any militarization of the Arctic must seem worrisome to policymakers in these states. They are bound to fear being caught in the middle as the dominant Arctic powers deploy growing arsenals of both offensive and defensive weapons in the region. Such a trend is only too likely to lead to developments that infringe on the rights of the lesser states in the region (for example, in the form of demands for unrestricted transit of military vehicles) and that subject these states to pressure to cooperate with the military activities of the United States and Russia (for example, in the form of requests for forward basing facilities). The history of lesser states positioned geographically in areas that are attractive to great powers as theaters for military operations is not a happy one; this fact can hardly escape the attention of leaders in Norway, Iceland, Greenland, and Canada as the strategic significance of the Arctic grows.

Predictably, these states have experienced growing incentives to take steps to prevent or to counter the dangers associated with the militarization of the Arctic. They may well become strong advocates of proposals for arms limitations in the region. Already there is interest in ideas such as extending the notion of a Nordic nuclear-free zone to the Arctic proper, and it seems highly likely that the lesser Arctic Rim states will take the lead in exploring ways to prevent a continuing rise in the level of military operations in the Arctic. Similarly, these states will experience incentives to form a bloc or de facto alliance to further their common interests in the Arctic. Among other things, such a bloc might provide mutual support for the jurisdictional claims of the lesser Arctic states (for example, the Norwegian claims in the area around Svalbard or the Canadian claims in the Arctic archipelago) or offer to provide buffer zones to minimize any risks associated with inadvertent confrontations of Soviet/Russian and American naval vessels or military aircraft operating in the Arctic. This last point suggests that a bloc of lesser Arctic Rim states might find it increasingly expedient to adopt a neutralist or nonaligned posture with respect to the interactions of the dominant powers in the Arctic. Given the existing ties between the United States on the one hand and Norway, Denmark, Iceland, and Canada, on the other, this may seem politically far-fetched. Yet there are domestic groups in each of these states (for example, the powerful peace movements in the Scandinavian countries and in Greenland) that would respond favorably to developments along these lines, and the continuing militarization of the Arctic could well enhance the attractions of some sort of nonaligned posture for the lesser Arctic Rim states. It does not take much insight, for instance, to imagine a situation in which the leftist Inuit Ataqatigiit (IA) party could gain electoral success in Greenland on a platform calling for the elimination of the American military bases located on the island.[8] Russia would undoubtedly welcome such developments and might well be willing to make political concessions to encourage realignments along these lines.

In many ways, Canada occupies a special place among the lesser Arctic Rim states. Geopolitically, Canada is second only to Russia as an Arctic state. The country fronts on a huge stretch of the Arctic Basin, and about 40 percent of Canada's land area lies in the Far North. There is also no denying "the prominent place that the Arctic has in Canadian political consciousness and in a broad range of domestic policies."[9] Nonetheless, under one hundred thousand people, or only a fraction of 1 percent of all Canadians, live in the Canadian North; the density of human population in this area is lower than anywhere else in the Arctic except Greenland. And Canada lacks the capabilities to initiate large-scale activities in the region or, in some cases, even to monitor the activities of other countries, such as the United States, in its own sector of the Arctic.

The result is a certain ambivalence in Canada's response to the militarization of the Arctic. The country is closely tied to American military planning for the region, as the arrangements for the North Warning System and the North American Air Defense Master Plan, not to mention NORAD more generally, clearly indicate. But there is also a distinct sense in many Canadian circles that the United States constitutes the principal threat to the country's Arctic interests, and Canada reacts with considerable passion to specific incidents, such as the voyages of the *Manhattan* in 1969 and the *Polar Sea* in 1985 or the series of cruise missile tests still underway. Under the circumstances, Canada is in need of a coherent Arctic role to complement its northern political con-

204 INTERNATIONAL STUDIES

sciousness and to allow the country to transcend its awkward and often embarrassing relationship with the United States in the region. One obvious possibility would be for Canada to assume the role of leader of a bloc of lesser Arctic Rim states. If such a bloc were to emerge, Canada would certainly be its natural leader. There are indications that such a role is of interest to some Canadian leaders. Steps have already been taken to expand ties with the Home Rule government in Greenland, and influential Canadians have proposed upgrading relations with Iceland and taking a stand in support of Norway in its Arctic jurisdictional conflicts with Russia. Such a redefinition of Canada's role would also be compatible with the suggestions of influential Canadian writers who have called for the articulation of a distinctive northern foreign policy for Canada.[10]

Arctic Arms Control

The militarization of the Arctic does not bode well for sweeping proposals aimed at insulating the Arctic region as a whole from the global strategic balance, along the lines of the provisions for the demilitarization of Antarctica set forth in the Antarctic Treaty of 1959. Ironically, the fact that the intensification of military interest in the Arctic is a recent development whose strategic consequences are not yet clear only reinforces this conclusion. The great powers will certainly experience incentives to explore the full potential of the Arctic with regard to SSBNs, SLBMs, SLCMs, manned bombers, ALCMs, antisubmarine warfare, air defense systems, and command and control arrangements before entering into restrictive arms control agreements covering the region. But this is no excuse to throw up our hands in despair, allowing the militarization of the Arctic simply to proceed under its own steam. It is important to examine the strategic consequences of this recent trend with some care. Above all, we need to make inquiries about various forms of arms control (in contrast to complete demilitarization) that might serve to secure the military balance in the Arctic and to minimize the disturbing consequences of the militarization of the region.[11]

Is the militarization of the Arctic fundamentally stabilizing or destabilizing in strategic terms? The available evidence pertaining to this question cuts both ways. Manned bombers and especially SSBNs operating in the Arctic are remarkably safe from hostile attacks of any kind. They can therefore play an important role in stabilizing any deterrent system based on the idea of mutual assured destruction. This is particularly important in the light of growing concerns regarding the vulnerability of land-based strategic missiles (ICBMs) to carefully orchestrated counterforce strikes. It follows that the relative security of the Arctic as an operating environment for strategic weapons may well remain an important consideration in stabilizing the global strategic balance during the foreseeable future. In fact, serious efforts to achieve deep, reciprocal reductions in existing inventories of vulnerable land-based missiles may be premised, in part, on the stabilizing role of the Arctic as a theater of operations for SSBNs and manned bombers equipped with ALCMs.

Yet there is another, less reassuring side to this picture of the implications of the militarization of the Arctic for the strategic balance. This trend has the inevitable effect of extending the strategic arms race into a new and comparatively unfamiliar arena. Thus, production schedules for the Typhoon and the Trident II, premised in part on Arctic deployment plans, played a role in the decision to set aside the limitations on strategic weapons systems articulated in the SALT II agreement. There is considerable potential for an offense/defense arms race in the Arctic as both sides endeavor to develop more sophisticated nuclear attack submarines (SSNs) and other antisubmarine warfare (ASW) devices as well as improved air-intercept capabilities to counter the threat of ALCMs. Many knowledgeable observers regard offense/defense races as constituting the most dangerous, as well as the most costly, type of arms race. We must also bear in mind the facts that atmospheric conditions in the Arctic pose unusual problems for command and control and that the great powers lie in remarkably close proximity to each other in the Arctic region. The margin for error in the Arctic is accordingly small. It would not take much to precipitate an inadvertent clash in the region that could escalate in an unpredictable fashion. Under the circumstances, there is no basis for complacency about the strategic consequences of the militarization of the Arctic. We must give serious consideration to proposals designed to regulate this development, even if there is little chance of reaching agreement on the demilitarization of the region as a whole.

Strategic Stabilization

Perhaps the place to begin in thinking about specific arms control proposals for the Arctic is with a discussion of possible stabilization or confidence-building measures. The emphasis here is on the development of effective codes of conduct designed to minimize first-strike incentives and reduce the dangers of accidental or inadvertent clashes, rather than on actual arms reductions. A major attraction of the Arctic as a theater for military operations is the comparative safety it affords manned bombers and SSBNs. This suggests the possibility of an agreement, either explicit or implicit, between Russia and the United States to avoid wasteful expenditures on Arctic countermeasures. Such an arrangement would allow for the deployment of detection devices such as the North Warning System or improved measures to track nuclear submarines under Arctic conditions. But it would proscribe the development and deployment of air-intercept systems capable of combating manned bombers or ALCMs operating in the Arctic theater and of improved ASW systems, such as attack submarines specially designed for Arctic operations (for example, the American SSN-21, or Seawolf). There is considerable evidence that such systems are unattractive in terms of cost-effectiveness.[12] They are unlikely to be able to hold their own against improved offensive weapons designed for use in the Arctic. And an arrangement along these lines would help to alleviate growing fears about the stability of nuclear deterrence arising from the increased vulnerability of land-based missiles. It follows that an agreement to leave the Arctic as a secure sanctuary for strategic weapons systems might substantially improve the prospects for a subsequent agreement on more or less drastic reductions in ICBMs deployed on the home territories of the nuclear powers.

The dangers of accidental or inadvertent clashes in the Arctic stem, essentially, from limited reaction times attributable to the geographical proximity of the major powers in the region, problems of command and control associated with Arctic atmospheric conditions, and misunderstandings or miscalculations arising

from military exercises or even deliberate testing behavior. In all
these cases, there is room to minimize, though probably not to
eliminate, the dangers through the initiation of confidence-building measures or the development of informal conventions or
codes of conduct coupled with improved communications systems capable of clearing up ambiguous situations quickly.[13] A
useful first step in this connection would be to make provisions
for a substantial increase in scientific exchanges regarding Arctic
issues. This would not only serve to give the nuclear powers a
common pool of knowledge regarding Arctic phenomena relevant to the operation of military systems (for example, the aurora
borealis, polynias), but it would also give rise to a network of
personal contacts that would help each side to interpret the other's behavior. Beyond this, it is well worth considering proposals
for a jointly operated tracking and monitoring system for the Arctic. The agreement among the United States, the Soviet Union,
and Japan to establish a joint radar tracking system for aircraft in
the North Pacific region (an outgrowth of the destruction of KAL
007) is distinctly encouraging in this connection. A joint tracking
and monitoring system designed to minimize the dangers of accidental or inadvertent military clashes in the Arctic would be
considerably more ambitious. But it would serve the interests of
the region's dominant powers to have such a system. What is
more, the two sides could collaborate on such a mechanism with
little fanfare, given the geographical remoteness of the region and
the fact that the system would be little noticed by anyone other
than the scientists and engineers responsible for its operation.

Arms Limitations
There is a natural temptation to compare the Arctic with other
remote areas and, consequently, to suppose that it is both desirable and feasible simply to demilitarize the whole region. Article
1 of the Antarctic Treaty of 1959, after all, states that "Antarctica
shall be used for peaceful purposes only." In much the same way,
Article 4 of the Outer Space Treaty of 1966 specifies that the
"moon and other celestial bodies shall be used by all States parties to the treaty exclusively for peaceful purposes." The 1920
Treaty Relating to Spitsbergen even offers a limited precedent for

demilitarization in the Arctic region itself. Article 9 of that treaty specifies that the Svalbard Archipelago shall "never be used for warlike purposes."[14]

Enough has already been said in the preceding discussion, however, to make it clear that demilitarization is an unlikely prospect for the entire Arctic region during the foreseeable future. On a more limited scale, however, proposals for one or more Arctic nuclear-free zones strike a responsive chord in many circles.[15] Regional nuclear-free zones have proven politically attractive in other parts of the world. The Treaty of Tlatelolco of 1967, for example, establishes a regime designed to denuclearize Latin America. In 1985, the South Pacific Forum nations adopted a treaty establishing a South Pacific nuclear-free zone. Closer to the Arctic, proposals for a Nordic nuclear-free zone have surfaced repeatedly since the Soviets first introduced the idea in 1958. Though some of these proposals have certainly taken the form of political ploys, it is undeniable that they have a genuine appeal for many Scandinavians wishing to opt out of the strategic contest between the United States and the Soviet Union/Russia.[16] In the Arctic proper, the Inuit Circumpolar Conference (ICC) has persistently advocated the creation of an Arctic nuclear-free zone. Even though the ICC is not a powerful actor capable of compelling the Arctic Rim states to accede to its policy preferences, it does have a certain moral standing as the voice of the Arctic's permanent residents. It is also fair to say that the idea of a nuclear-free zone in the Arctic has a strong appeal in many Greenlandic circles and that proposals along these lines may well become an important topic of political debate in Greenland during the near future. Under the circumstances, the idea of an Arctic nuclear-free zone seems worthy of further consideration.

To address this idea in a meaningful fashion, it is important to recognize at the outset that the phrase "nuclear-free zone" encompasses an extensive family of possible arms limitations arrangements. Functionally, an Arctic nuclear-free zone might include any of a number of restrictions on nuclear weapons or materials, such as prohibitions on the manufacture or acquisition of nuclear weapons, on permanent basing or stationing of nuclear weapons (or delivery vehicles for nuclear weapons) in the area, on periodic deployment or movement of nuclear weapons through the area, on testing of nuclear weapons or delivery systems, on peaceful uses of nuclear devices, and on the disposal of nuclear wastes. Likewise, proposals for nuclear-free zones may involve plans for security belts or negative guarantees to provide reassurance to those agreeing to forswear the use of nuclear weapons in certain areas. In spatial terms, a nuclear-free zone for the Arctic could encompass the entire region or only certain well-defined portions of the region. It might also involve different provisions for the seabed, the water column, the surface of marine areas, land surfaces, and Arctic airspace. With respect to membership, such an arrangement might include all of the Arctic Rim states or only some subset of these states. There might or might not be a role for nonstate actors, such as the ICC, in a nuclear-free zone arrangement for the Arctic.

This is not the place to examine all of these options exhaustively. But it is possible to comment on a few key considerations relating to any such proposals. There is little likelihood that either Russia or the United States will agree to any plan limiting its ability to deploy strategic weapons systems in the Arctic. The limits imposed by Soviet and now Russian military configurations and deployment patterns are particularly severe in this connection. Over half of the Soviet/Russian fleet of SSBNs is permanently stationed in the Arctic. The Soviets developed a concentration of strategic airbases in the Arctic. In the absence of a comprehensive nuclear test ban, Russia will have an incentive to continue underground tests on Novaya Zemlya, an area that emerged as the major Soviet nuclear test site in recent years. The United States has less need, in geopolitical terms, to station nuclear weapons at Arctic bases. But the United States will certainly want to retain the freedom to deploy nuclear weapons in the region on a regular basis and to test delivery vehicles (for example, ALCMs) in the Arctic. Any proposals for an Arctic nuclear-free zone that ignore these basic facts will stand little chance of being taken seriously. Though some players may nonetheless find such proposals attractive as expressions of moral preferences or as devices intended to embarrass the nuclear powers (especially Russia) politically, they will not prove generally acceptable to the key Arctic Rim states in practice.

Those who have the most to gain from the creation of some

sort of nuclear-free zone in the Arctic are the lesser Arctic Rim states. Although several of these states are allies of the United States, most of them already prohibit the deployment of American nuclear weapons on their territory.[17] It would not, therefore, require any radical departure from existing policies for states like Canada, Norway, Denmark, and Iceland to advocate extending existing limits on the deployment of nuclear weapons to cover the marine areas or airspace of the Arctic region. Moreover, the development of proposals along these lines might serve as an attractive vehicle for the emergence of an effective bloc of lesser Arctic Rim states endeavoring to protect themselves from great-power pressures arising from the militarization of the Arctic. This is particularly true in the case of Canada, an Arctic Rim state that has no "combat aircraft based in the north, no ground combat units, no warships, and no missile installations" but that nonetheless seeks to assert sovereign authority over a huge segment of the Arctic.[18]

The ultimate question, then, is whether the lesser Arctic Rim states can devise a plan for a nuclear-free zone in the Arctic that the nuclear powers will not simply reject out of hand. Any such plan would have to involve a restricted arrangement, in contrast to a comprehensive Arctic nuclear-free zone, at least at the outset. The lesser Arctic Rim states might, for example, formally prohibit the deployment of nuclear weapons (or delivery vehicles capable of carrying nuclear weapons) on their territory or within the exclusive economic zones (EEZs) adjacent to their Arctic coasts. They might advocate the designation of certain marine sanctuaries (for example, areas used extensively by indigenous peoples for subsistence purposes) in which all of the Arctic Rim states would agree not to station or deploy nuclear weapons. Following the precedent of the Antarctic Treaty, they might separate out the issue of nuclear waste disposal and propose an agreement (similar to that codified in Article V of the Antarctic Treaty) prohibiting any disposal of radioactive wastes in the Arctic.

It is certainly legitimate to raise questions concerning the value of such limited measures, given the militarization of the Arctic in more general terms. Nonetheless, even modest arms limitations can prove worthwhile when they signal a willingness on the part of the participants to maintain some restraints on inherently dan-

gerous military developments. And as suggested above, the very
process of developing even a limited nuclear-free zone in the Arctic might prove politically beneficial for the lesser Arctic Rim
states as they seek methods of protecting their interests in the
face of the growth of great-power military operations in the
region.

Peacetime Impacts

Short of an actual military clash, some of the most disturbing
problems arising from the militarization of the Arctic involve the
peacetime impacts of the use of the region as a theater for military
operations. Airbases, radar sites, and other military installations
often prove disruptive to sensitive northern ecosystems, the subsistence practices of local residents, or the social fabric of nearby
communities. The testing of weapons (for example, the recent
American program of testing cruise missiles in the Canadian Arctic) constitutes an unwelcome intrusion from the perspective of
local residents and heightens the desire of Native peoples to protect themselves through the assertion of sovereign rights. Even
more concretely, military exercises carried out in the Arctic are
not only capable of producing costly disruptions, they are also
indicative of an extraordinary disregard for the concerns of local
residents.[19] The use of the airspace over Labrador to conduct exercises involving low-flying jet aircraft from Western Europe provides a striking recent illustration. Labrador was chosen as a site
for such exercises because influential groups in Western Europe
opposed the continuation of such exercises in European airspace
and because military planners regarded Labrador as a remote
area of little political consequence. Yet no one thought to make a
study of the impact of jet aircraft flying at altitudes as low as 30
meters (100 feet) on animal populations (for example, caribou
herds) in the region or to inquire about the reasonable concerns
of the indigenous people resident in the area.[20]

Without prohibiting military operations in the Arctic, much
could be done to avoid or limit these peacetime impacts arising
from the militarization of the Arctic region. Reliance on unattended or minimally attended radars in connection with the
North Warning System is a constructive step in this regard. But
there is no valid justification for the failure in both the United

States and Canada to conduct serious environmental and socio-economic impact studies in connection with projects like the North Warning System. Military planners should consciously avoid construction or maintenance programs offering local residents employment opportunities that pay well for a time but that require lengthy absences from home communities and that provide no prospect of permanent employment. It would not be difficult to create sanctuaries—in areas heavily used by indigenous residents for subsistence purposes—in which military operations would be banned during part of the year or even permanently. Regardless of the attractions of the Arctic as a theater for military operations, in short, there is simply no reason to disregard the peacetime impacts of military operations in the region. The Arctic is no longer a remote area of little concern to anyone but a small band of Native people and a handful of scientists. It is a region of great importance in both human and ecological terms that deserves as much protection as any other region of the world.

Conclusion

Recent developments in military technology have transformed the Arctic into one of the world's major theaters for military operations. It is naive, therefore, to compare the Arctic with other remote areas, such as Antarctica or the moon, and to propose to insulate the region from the pressures of world politics through some system of demilitarization. Nonetheless, it is important to think carefully about both the strategic and the political implications of the militarization of the Arctic rather than simply throwing up our hands in despair. Interestingly enough, this trend provides Russia and the United States with significant common interests in the Arctic region. Both powers can be counted on to take a stand, for example, against any jurisdictional developments that would limit their freedom of movement in the Arctic Basin or in the airspace over the Arctic Basin. Conversely, the militarization of the region will serve to increase substantially the incentives of the lesser Arctic Rim states to join forces to protect themselves from infringements of their rights or disturbing political pressures arising from the actions of the nuclear powers.

Nor should we simply dismiss out of hand proposals for more

modest arms control arrangements in the Arctic in contrast to grand but unworkable demilitarization schemes. Any plan for a comprehensive nuclear-free zone in the region will prove just as unrealistic as proposals calling for demilitarization. But codes of conduct designed to eliminate first-strike incentives or minimize the dangers of accidental clashes might prove beneficial to everyone with a significant stake in the Arctic. Restrictions on the deployment of nuclear weapons or delivery vehicles in specified areas are worthy of consideration. Above all, there is no excuse for a failure on the part of any of the Arctic Rim states to take concerted steps to limit the peacetime impacts of the militarization of the Arctic.

CHAPTER 11

Sustainable Development in the Arctic:
The International Dimensions

The modern history of the Arctic is, for the most part, a history of interactions between advanced industrial metropoles located to the south and resource-rich hinterlands located to the north.[1] It is not surprising, therefore, that discussions of domestic or intranational economic and political relationships dominate most accounts of contemporary Arctic affairs. Thus, we have a steady stream of commentaries describing and often criticizing the relationships that have evolved between Ottawa and the northern territories, Copenhagen and Greenland, Moscow and the Soviet/Russian North, and Seattle/Houston/Washington/New York and Alaska. Those who have analyzed these relationships have understandably experienced few incentives to turn their attention to the international dimensions of Arctic affairs. Compared with the prevailing metropole/hinterland relationships, interactions between Alaska and the Soviet/Russian North, Greenland and the Canadian North, or Fennoscandia and the Soviet/Russian North have paled into insignificance.

As we begin to focus on requirements and strategies for achieving sustainable development in the Circumpolar North during the next two or three decades, however, it seems essential to ask whether the metropole/hinterland relationships that char-

This chapter originated as a discussion paper prepared for the second session of the Working Group on Arctic International Relations held in Ilulissat and Nuuk, Greenland, 19–24 April 1989.

acterize the region are part of the problem rather than part of the solution. This, in turn, suggests the importance of asking whether there are benefits to be derived from international interactions in the pursuit of sustainable development under the conditions prevailing in the Arctic today. This chapter examines this question in a preliminary manner. Because it focuses on future prospects in contrast to current realities, its approach is necessarily speculative and policy-oriented. But this should not detract from the usefulness of the analysis to follow as a basis for a wide-ranging and vigorous discussion.

Requirements of Sustainable Development

The concept of sustainable development became common currency worldwide as a result of the attention devoted to the idea in the World Conservation Strategy. Published in 1980 by the International Union for the Conservation of Nature and Natural Resources (IUCN), the strategy carries the subtitle "Living Resource Conservation for Sustainable Development."[2] More recently, the World Commission on Environment and Development (also known as the Brundtland Commission) has accorded the concept of sustainable development an even more prominent place in its analysis of international environmental issues. *Our Common Future,* the report of the Brundtland Commission, defines sustainable development as "development that meets the needs of the present without compromising the ability of future generations to meet their own needs";[3] it establishes development of this kind as a key standard in terms of which to formulate and evaluate public policies.

In the Arctic, it seems reasonable to interpret this general and somewhat imprecise formula as requiring, among other things, the establishment of economic systems capable of maintaining themselves over time without disrupting major Arctic ecosystems or destroying the distinctive cultures of the Arctic's permanent residents. Construing sustainable development in this way, we can set about identifying goals that any strategy designed to promote sustainable development in the Arctic must strive to achieve. Having done so, we can proceed to ask whether there is a role for international initiatives in making headway toward the fulfillment of these goals.

Decoupling Arctic Economies

As long as the Arctic remains tightly linked to the advanced industrial economies of the southern metropoles, it will continue to be treated as a storehouse of raw materials waiting to be exploited or, to use Thomas Berger's apt phrase, as a northern frontier rather than as a northern homeland.[4] This way of thinking about the Far North is not altogether without merit, but it poses a number of problems for the attainment of sustainable development in the region. Industrialists located in the metropoles will take an interest in the Arctic when they see opportunities to initiate large-scale projects aimed at extracting nonrenewable natural resources (for example, hydrocarbons, nonfuel minerals). But such projects pose more or less severe problems for the pursuit of sustainable development because they depend on finite deposits of nonrenewable resources subject to relatively rapid exhaustion, they tie local economies to volatile world market prices, they are apt to be disruptive in environmental terms, and they cannot be integrated easily into the mixed economies otherwise prevailing in Arctic communities.

Additionally, this pattern of development serves to maximize the extent to which Arctic economies are subject to "decisions beyond [their] knowledge and control."[5] In effect, powerful individuals and groups located in the metropoles make the key decisions about economic activities in the Arctic and reap the lion's share of the economic returns accruing from these activities. In return, they supply Arctic communities with a considerable array of social services. But these services are sustained by transfer payments whose administration remains in the hands of outsiders. It follows that efforts to achieve sustainable development in Arctic communities must aim to limit the exposure of these communities to outside forces by working to decouple, or at least to insulate, the economies of the Arctic from the economies of the dominant metropoles.

Diversifying Arctic Economies

Like many developing countries, Arctic communities are often heavily dependent for their cash income on a single industry or product. This accounts for the dramatic economic swings or boom/bust cycles that commentators on Arctic affairs have often described. Sometimes this dependence involves nonrenewable resources, like gold during gold rush days or black gold (that is, oil) during more recent times. But the same problem can afflict communities whose cash economy centers on the sale of a single product derived from renewable resources. When the bottom dropped out of the fur market during the 1930s, many Arctic communities found themselves facing an economic crisis of dire proportions. The economic dislocations in numerous Arctic communities caused by the collapse of the market for seal skins during the 1980s have been amply documented.[6] Likewise, the economic consequences of the contamination of reindeer in Sweden as a result of the 1986 Chernobyl accident have been drastic for many Saami herders. In each case, the underlying problem is the same: a lack of economic diversity capable of cushioning the shock of disruptions affecting individual industries and dampening economic fluctuations to avoid boom/bust cycles. It follows that any strategy aimed at achieving sustainable development in the Arctic must strive to promote economic diversification in the region.

Sustaining Informal Arctic Economies

While the importance of the cash economy in Arctic communities has grown substantially over time, the traditional or informal economy has remained an essential component of economic life for the permanent residents of the Arctic. Given the remoteness, sparse population, and limited infrastructure of the region, it seems likely that a healthy informal economy constitutes a necessary condition for sustainable development in the Arctic over the foreseeable future.[7] The informal economy of the region centers on domestic production, largely in the form of subsistence hunting and gathering, coupled with distribution mechanisms based on social conventions that do not involve monetized transactions. Sustainable development in the Arctic consequently requires a concerted effort to secure and nurture the informal economies already in operation in the region.

This means, in part, devising programs designed to protect the region's renewable resource base through land banks, comanagement arrangements, regimes to control air and water pollution, and so forth. Partly, it means taking into account key cultural norms and social conventions in formulating economic programs for the region. The introduction of new economic activities that have the effect of undercutting the sociocultural bases of the existing informal economies are just as detrimental to the achievement of sustainable development in the Arctic as the initiation of economic enterprises that prove disruptive to the region's ecosystems.

Given the centrality of metropole/hinterland relationships in the Arctic, it seems undeniable that many efforts to meet these requirements of sustainable development in the Far North must be organized primarily in domestic terms. At the same time, it is well worth asking whether there are international initiatives that can and should be taken to facilitate the achievement of sustainable development in the Arctic. The remainder of this chapter offers an initial response to this question. The options discussed, grouped under the headings of environmental protection, economic initiatives, and political actions, are presented in no particular order of priority. Moreover, this account of international initiatives is not intended to diminish in any way the importance of domestic initiatives in the pursuit of sustainable development in the Arctic. Taken together, however, these options do suggest that it would be a serious mistake to overlook the international dimensions in devising strategies for achieving sustainable development under the conditions prevailing in the Arctic today.

Environmental Protection

It takes little insight to realize that the protection of habitat and of ecosystems more generally constitutes one of the keys to sustainable development in the Arctic. The link between sustainable development and environmental protection is, of course, direct and obvious in the case of the hunting and gathering activities that form the backbone of the informal economy. But maintaining the well-being of natural systems is no less important to the prospects for achieving economic diversification in the Arctic and, through diversification, a decoupling of Arctic economies from the economies of southern metropoles. In the Arctic, the relationship between environmental protection and international cooperation is particularly clear. New initiatives and sustained efforts in at least three areas merit careful consideration in this context.

Pollution Control

The major forms of pollution occurring in the Arctic are traceable to human activities centered far to the south; the pollutants reach the high latitudes through long-range transport mechanisms involving airborne or waterborne particulates. Ordinarily, these mechanisms involve transboundary flows of harmful substances, such as radioactive fallout, heavy metals, PCBs, carbon dioxide, chlorofluorocarbons, or the complex of airborne particulates that together give rise to Arctic haze. The adverse consequences of these pollutants for sustainable development in the Arctic are easy enough to document. We have only to consider the contamination of Saami reindeer in Sweden as a result of the Chernobyl accident or the extraordinary levels of toxic substances found in polar bears and in the breast milk of Inuit women to appreciate the significance of these threats. Under the circumstances, it is heartening to note the growing interest in devising multilateral arrangements for environmental protection (for example, the Arctic Environmental Protection Strategy) in the Arctic region.[8] In the absence of progress along these lines, it would be difficult to sustain optimism about the prospects for devising an effective strategy for securing sustainable development in the Arctic.

Wildlife Management

For the most part, the Arctic's economically important animal populations are common property resources vulnerable to the classic problems associated with the tragedy of the commons. Equally important, many of these populations move through the jurisdictions of several nations in the course of their annual migratory cycles. Bowhead whales in the western Arctic, for example, summer in Canadian waters in the eastern Beaufort Sea, winter in Soviet waters in the western Bering Sea, and pass back and forth through American waters during the course of their spring and fall migrations.[9] Harp seals in the eastern Arctic annually spend time in waters under the jurisdiction of Canada and Denmark/Greenland as well as in waters lying beyond the jurisdiction of any nation-state. Many species of birds that breed in the Far North during the Arctic summer migrate far to the south—as far as Antarctica in some cases—during the winter months.

To the extent that the economies of Arctic communities are dependent on the availability of these animals for subsistence harvesting, commercial use, or both, therefore, sustainable development in the Arctic necessarily requires international action. The development of a cooperative regime for polar bears during the 1960s and 1970s—a five-nation international agreement on polar bears was signed in 1973—constitutes a heartening development in this context.[10] Conversely, the collapse of the venerable international regime for northern fur seals during the 1980s can only be regarded as a discouraging development, despite the fact that the regime was not well adapted to contemporary conditions.[11] The Arctic agenda today includes a number of issues requiring the (re)formation of bilateral or multilateral arrangements to manage shared stocks of living resources.

Habitat Protection

By now, we are well aware that the establishment of management regimes to guide human harvesting of wild animals is not sufficient to ensure the viability of stocks that are economically important to Arctic communities. What is needed, in addition, are effective measures to protect the habitats these animals depend upon during every phase of their migratory cycles. There are significant problems involving the protection of habitat in the Arctic itself. It is becoming clear, for example, that the destruction of habitat resulting from the development of the Prudhoe Bay oil field has been more severe than initially anticipated, and there is compelling evidence that habitat destruction associated with the development of oil and gas fields in northwestern Siberia has been even more extensive.[12]

At the same time, it is important to recognize that some of the most serious threats to habitat of importance to Arctic wildlife lie far to the south in waters and wetlands where the animals winter. Perhaps the most dramatic examples involve migratory birds. The destruction of wetlands in the coastal areas of the Caribbean Basin or the disruption of winter feeding areas in California and in southern Asia, for example, can cause more damage to bird populations than any misuse associated with harvesting activities far to the north. It follows that habitat protection, too, is a matter that cannot be handled effectively in the absence of international cooperation.

Economic Initiatives

Although environmental protection constitutes a necessary condition for the achievement of sustainable development in the Arctic, it is far from sufficient. What is needed to complement environmental protection in this context is a program featuring more direct economic initiatives. No doubt, some of the most important of these initiatives can and will be articulated and administered largely within domestic political arenas. But there are opportunities in this realm for international activities as well. To acquire a feel for these opportunities, consider the following examples.

An Arctic Technical Assistance Program

There are fundamental structural similarities among the various parts of the Arctic with regard to obstacles to the achievement of sustainable development. Whatever the nature of the local situation, communities throughout the Arctic need to decouple their economies from those of the relevant metropoles, pursue economic diversification based on small-scale enterprises making use of appropriate technologies, and shore up the informal economy as an integral part of economic life. It follows that the lessons learned from both successes and failures in individual Arctic communities should be of considerable interest to those located elsewhere in the Arctic. What, for instance, can we learn from comparing and contrasting the experiences of the regional and village corporations established in Alaska under the terms of the Alaska Native Claims Settlement Act of 1971 with the experiences of the Native economic development corporations established in the Canadian North during the 1970s and 1980s (for example, Makivik, Nunasi, Inuvialuit Development Corporation, Denendeh Development Corporation)?[13] Are there instructive conclusions to be drawn from a comparison of the arrangements for reindeer husbandry that have evolved in Fennoscandia and the parallel arrangements that the Soviets introduced in the Soviet/Russian North?[14]

What is needed, in this context, is an advisory service capable of evaluating the results of existing strategies for the achievement of sustainable development in the Arctic and providing informed technical advice to those endeavoring to devise new strategies in this realm. Such a service would be most useful if it were international in character rather than being compelled to operate under the auspices of a single national government. Perhaps there is even a role for the United Nations here; an Arctic economic advisory service lodged within the United Nations Development Programme or operated jointly with the United Nations Environment Programme might prove quite attractive to fourth world constituencies.

An Arctic Development Bank

Regional development banks, such as the Inter-American Development Bank, the African Development Bank, and the Asian Development Bank, have become a prominent feature of programs designed to provide the capital needed to achieve economic development in the Third World. The idea of instituting a similar arrangement for the Arctic may seem strange at first, given the fact that the region is composed of the northern hinterlands of advanced industrial metropoles in contrast to the independent nation-states of the Third World. Even so, an Arctic Development Bank is an idea worthy of serious consideration.

As those who use the phrase "Fourth World" in speaking about the Arctic (as well as other regions of the world containing sizable populations of indigenous peoples) have pointed out, Arctic communities exhibit a number of features that are characteristic of less-developed economies (for example, a tendency to become monocultures oriented toward the supply of raw materials to industries located elsewhere).[15] And they cannot count on policymakers located in the southern metropoles to adopt and implement appropriate development strategies for Arctic economic environments, much less to provide the capital necessary to implement such strategies. These observations also suggest, however, that those interested in establishing a regional development bank for the Arctic should be alert to the problems that have plagued similar institutions operating in the Third World. Development banks have often based their actions on inappropriate models or theories of development in providing assistance to Third World countries, for instance, and it is hard to avoid the conclusion that they have contributed to the debt crisis that has become a severe and unyielding constraint on economic policymaking in much of the Third World.

Transnational Joint Ventures
   When Arctic communities own or exercise management authority over valuable natural resources but lack the expertise or the capital required to exploit these resources in a profitable manner, opportunities for mutually beneficial joint ventures may arise. But as those who have tried can attest (for example, the North Slope Borough and the NANA Corporation in Alaska or the Home Rule in Greenland), such joint ventures can become a mixed blessing, especially from the point of view of sustainable development. They offer neither an assurance of permanence nor a guarantee of an accumulation of wealth usable for other purposes once the initial enterprise is gone. They are apt to intensify sensitivity to world market prices, known for their volatility. Because of asymmetries in bargaining strength, the local owners of the resources frequently have a hard time negotiating on equal terms with the outside suppliers of the necessary technical expertise and capital.
   When they do prove mutually advantageous, however, such joint ventures will often take on a transnational or international character. An interesting case in point is the Red Dog lead/zinc mine in northwestern Alaska, which has been developed as a joint venture between NANA, an Alaskan regional corporation, and Cominco, a multinational corporation headquartered in Canada. A similar arrangement, which is currently in a state of suspended animation because of relatively low world market prices for oil, is the joint venture agreement between the Greenland Home Rule and ARCO regarding hydrocarbon development in Jameson Land along the east coast of Greenland.

North/North Commerce

An obvious way to decouple Arctic economies from southern metropoles as well as to promote economic diversification in the region would be to encourage the growth of mutually beneficial commerce among the northern regions of the several Arctic states. Conventional wisdom suggests that this is a long shot for purely economic reasons, quite apart from any political obstacles that may have to be overcome.[16] What could such communities, whose economic life revolves around subsistence harvesting and the export of raw materials to southern metropoles, profitably trade with each other? Even if they could find goods or services to trade with each other, how could these communities cope with the costs arising from the long distances between northern communities and transportation systems structured on north/south lines?

Yet, north/north commerce is not altogether without precedent. Archaeologists have found ever increasing evidence of the operation of extensive trade networks among early Arctic peoples. The Norse developed substantial trade relations among northern centers in their time. As recently as the later part of the nineteenth century, there was a lively commercial network encompassing the circum–Bering Sea area.[17] Of course, none of this offers any assurance of success in efforts to bolster north/north commerce under contemporary conditions. But the exploration of opportunities to promote north/north commerce might well become a priority for an Arctic Technical Assistance Program or an Arctic Development Bank.

Political Action

As in the sphere of economics, the dominance of north/south interactions in the Arctic has produced an emphasis on domestic politics in the search for institutional arrangements to cope with problems of sustainable development in the Far North. Thus, the North Slope Borough in Alaska, the Home Rule in Greenland, the Saami Parliament in Finland, and the newly emerging territory of Nunavut in northern Canada are all institutional arrangements designed to give the permanent residents of the Arctic a greater say in decisions made within domestic arenas affecting the welfare of Arctic communities.[18] In each of these cases, in fact, international affairs are explicitly excluded from the authority granted to the new political entities emerging in the Arctic. Yet, as the preceding discussion indicates, a number of the threats to sustainable development in the Far North are international in scope and can be countered effectively only through the creation of transnational political institutions. It should come as no surprise, therefore, that the Arctic has become an active arena for transnational political initiatives relating to issues that are relevant to sustainable development. To grasp the significance of this phenomenon, consider the following examples.

Responses to Antiharvesting Campaigns

Antiharvesting campaigns waged by animal protectionist groups strike directly at the prospects for sustainable development in the Arctic.[19] This threat is of obvious significance in connection with the subsistence practices that form the backbone of the informal economy in Arctic communities. But in some ways, the results are even more troublesome when antiharvesting activities take the form of measures that are disruptive to the fragile cash sector of Arctic economies (for example, bans on the importation of seal skins or labeling requirements on the furs of animals captured in leghold traps). The activities of the animal protectionists are fundamentally transnational in character. Thus, the International Whaling Commission has become a battleground for efforts to eliminate or sharply curtail the subsistence harvest of bowhead whales in northern Alaska. The European Parliament has emerged as an arena for campaigns aimed at halting the use of the leghold trap in the Canadian North. The biennial conferences of the parties to the Convention on International Trade in Endangered Species have become forums for efforts to restrict walrus hunting throughout the Arctic.

It follows that actions designed to protect the economies of Arctic communities against these threats must encompass transnational responses. This accounts for the energetic interventions of Arctic organizations such as the Inuit Circumpolar Conference in the deliberations of the International Whaling Commission and in the conferences of the International Union for the Conservation of Nature and Natural Resources. It explains also the creation

226 INTERNATIONAL STUDIES

of transnational organizations, such as Indigenous Survival International, devoted to protecting responsible harvests of wild animals in the Arctic. Even so, the odds against those whose livelihood depends upon the harvesting of wild animals are hardly reassuring. Accordingly, any strategy designed to promote sustainable development in the Arctic must include effective measures to protect Arctic economies from the disruptive impact of a growing array of antiharvesting campaigns.

Institutional Innovations

The renewable resources that are essential to the achievement of sustainable development in the Arctic show no respect for the political or jurisdictional boundaries imposed and administered by nation-states. Thus, reindeer move regularly across international boundaries in Fennoscandia; bowhead whales move in and out of the jurisdictions of Canada, the United States, and the Soviet Union; and fish stocks straddle international boundaries in many parts of the Arctic. To avoid the problems associated with the tragedy of the commons in connection with these resources, therefore, it is necessary to pursue international cooperation in efforts to manage the human use of the resources.

In responding to this challenge, there is much to be said for a policy of turning to co-management regimes. Co-management, an institutional device that has recently generated considerable interest at the domestic level in the Arctic, hinges on efforts to institutionalize the sharing of power between public authorities and user groups in guiding the human use of renewable resources.[20] In the Arctic, this ordinarily means creating boards or commissions encompassing representatives of state (or provincial/territorial) and federal governments on the one hand and representatives of the permanent (usually indigenous) residents of the relevant area on the other. Just as a co-management regime has been established for the Beverly-Kaminuriak caribou herd that ranges over parts of the Northwest Territories and several adjacent provinces, similar arrangements can be developed to manage the consumptive use of animals that migrate across international borders. Some steps have been taken toward the development of a co-management regime for the Porcupine caribou herd that migrates annually across the Alaska/Yukon border.

Similar initiatives are worth considering for other populations of shared living resources, like walruses, seals, whales, and migratory birds.

Regional Conservation Strategies

There is a growing realization that conservation strategies dealing with transnational regions or ecosystems are required to promote sustainable development in many parts of the world. The World Conservation Strategy is certainly helpful as a framework document articulating concepts and principles that are intended to be universally applicable.[21] By the same token, there can be no doubt that some conservation problems are appropriately handled in domestic arenas. Still, many issues relating to sustainable development are best dealt with at the regional level because the relevant ecosystems are regional in character, because the transaction costs of coming to terms with regional issues in global forums are apt to be prohibitively high, and because considerations of ownership suggest keeping management systems as close to the level of the relevant user communities as possible.

Nowhere is this more apparent than in the Arctic, a fact that has stimulated several significant efforts to develop regional conservation strategies in or for the region. The Inuit Circumpolar Conference, for instance, has accorded top priority to the development of an Inuit Regional Conservation Strategy. Similarly, the Canadian Department of Fisheries and Oceans has launched a plan for an Arctic Marine Conservation Strategy designed to encourage "the development of a circumpolar conservation effort in all [A]rctic marine waters."[22] To the extent that sustainable development in the Arctic requires the wise use of renewable resources, it seems evident that a continued growth of these regional conservation efforts will constitute a necessary condition for the achievement of sustainable development in the region.

Conclusion

Because Arctic affairs have long been dominated by interactions between advanced industrial metropoles located to the south and resource-rich hinterlands located to the north, there is

an understandable tendency to ignore international considerations in thinking about sustainable development in the Circumpolar North. Without denying the continuing importance of
domestic initiatives, this chapter presents the case for devoting
more attention in the future to the international dimensions of
sustainable development in the Arctic. Partly, this is a matter of
the need for international responses to the environmental threats
now facing the region. In part, it stems from the potential role of
international initiatives as part of a strategy to diversify the economies of Arctic communities and, in the process, to decouple
these economies from the advanced industrial economies of the
metropoles. Additionally, it is a consequence of the need to devise
transnational mechanisms to manage the human use of the region's shared living resources. Under the circumstances, it seems
fair to conclude that any successful strategy for the achievement
of sustainable development in the Arctic will have to deal explicitly with international interactions affecting the region as well as
with the north/south interactions taking place within domestic
economic and political arenas that have consumed most of our
energies thus far.

CHAPTER 12

The Arctic: Distinctive
Region or Policy Periphery?

No one now denies the growing international significance of events taking place in the Arctic. Technological advances in nuclear-powered submarines, submarine-launched ballistic missiles (SLBMs), and air-breathing cruise missiles, coupled with a concurrent erosion of confidence in the deterrent value of land-based intercontinental ballistic missiles (ICBMs), have transformed the Arctic into a leading theater of operations for strategic weapons systems. Though production and transportation costs are high under Arctic conditions, the region looms large in any assessment of the global energy picture. The bulk of both the crude oil and the natural gas produced in Russia—most of the world-class energy resources of the former Soviet Union are now under Russian jurisdiction—flows from giant fields (for example, the Samotlor oil field and the Urengoi and Yamburg gas fields) located in northwestern Siberia. As of the end of 1991, about 25 percent of the crude oil produced in the United States came from the North Slope of Alaska.

Nor is the rising international significance of the Arctic limited to matters of security and resource development. Northern Na-

This chapter originated as a discussion paper prepared for the first session of the Working Group on Arctic International Relations held at Hveragerdi, Iceland, 20–22 July 1988. The Working Group is an unofficial forum that allows practitioners and scholars from the eight Arctic countries to identify emerging issues and to exchange thoughts, off the record, regarding the pros and cons of alternative responses to these issues.

tives have assumed positions of leadership among indigenous peoples worldwide, a fact that makes them a force to be reckoned with in connection with the rapid evolution of the fourth world movement. Both because the Arctic is regarded as a major generator of the Northern Hemisphere's weather and because the temperature increases associated with global warming are likely to be particularly pronounced in the high latitudes, the Arctic is likely to play a key role in the global environmental changes expected to occur over the next several decades.

Yet the implications of these Arctic developments for the content of public policies in the Arctic Rim states, as well as for the processes through which Arctic policies are made in these states, are far from clear. Is the Arctic emerging as a distinctive international region—comparable to other accepted regions, like the Middle East, East Asia, or Antarctica—for purposes of policy analysis and public decision making? Concretely, are the Arctic Rim states likely, during the foreseeable future, to add substantial Arctic expertise to their policy planning staffs; create bureaus of Arctic or northern affairs in their foreign ministries, establish effective interagency coordinating mechanisms to handle complex Arctic issues, or devise new Arctic policies to replace the policies of benign neglect they have habitually relied on in dealing with Arctic matters in modern times? Or is the Arctic destined to be relegated to the status of a remote periphery of no more than passing concern to the Arctic Rim states—not to mention others—in policy terms? To be blunt about it, are public policymakers likely to continue to dispose of Arctic issues by assimilating them into broader conceptual categories or letting them run their course without any deliberate public intervention?

In this chapter, I argue that there are no unambiguous, much less analytically correct, answers to these questions. Observers can and do employ the same facts to justify treating the Arctic as a distinctive region or as a policy periphery, depending upon the character of the interpretive frameworks or conceptual lenses they use to bring order to these facts. Choices among alternative interpretive frameworks, in turn, are commonly dictated more by interests or ideological presuppositions than by unbiased assessments of conditions on the ground.[1] It follows that the questions posed in the preceding paragraph are likely to be controversial ones, subject more to the influence of political forces than to the persuasive power of analytic reasoning. We cannot, at this juncture, confidently predict the ultimate outcome of the resultant debate about different ways of thinking about the Arctic for purposes of policy analysis and public choice. Even so, we can deepen our understanding of the international significance of Arctic events by identifying the nature of the interests at stake in the debate, showing how these interests operate to structure the perspectives of the participants, and discussing the forces that shape interactions among those active in the debate.

Arctic Antinomies

It is surely significant that the essential facts regarding recent developments in the Arctic are not, for the most part, in dispute. But this is hardly sufficient to ensure that policymakers will reach consensus on treating the Arctic as a distinctive region for purposes of policymaking. Well-informed observers differ sharply in terms of the policy implications they ascribe to recent Arctic developments. Depending upon the interpretive framework they bring to the subject, individual observers conclude that the Arctic is well on its way toward taking its place among the world's major regions or, conversely, that the Arctic does not require treatment as a distinctive region at all. A few concrete examples will convey a clear sense of the Arctic antinomies that arise when the same events are viewed through divergent conceptual lenses.[2]

Some commentators see the Arctic as a predominantly marine area that fits comfortably into the comprehensive system of public order for such areas as articulated in the 1982 Convention on the Law of the Sea. As in other parts of the world, there are certain problems associated with demarcating Arctic baselines, determining the status of straits, and delimiting maritime boundaries between opposite and adjacent states in the Arctic. Because of the long-standing tendency to treat the Arctic with benign neglect, some of these problems are only now coming to public attention. Even so, there are no inherent obstacles to applying in the Arctic the general provisions of the law of the sea pertaining to internal waters, territorial waters, and exclusive economic zones, along with the complementary regimes for transit passage and areas lying beyond the bounds of national jurisdictions.

Yet there is an alternative account that emphasizes the distinctiveness of the Arctic and suggests the need for a specialized regime for this region. The ice-covered waters of the Arctic pose severe problems, not only for navigation but also for efforts to cope with marine pollution (for example, oil spills or chronic discharges). The fragility of Arctic ecosystems and the slow pace of biodegradation under Arctic conditions ensure that pollutants that would cause only moderate damage under other conditions may prove profoundly destructive in the Arctic. Taken together, these considerations serve to justify the inclusion of Article 234, a special provision dealing with the protection of ice-covered waters, in the 1982 Convention on the Law of the Sea. More fundamentally, the basic distinction between land and water, a dichotomy on which much contemporary thinking about international order rests, tends to break down under Arctic conditions. Sea ice regularly serves as a stable platform for human enterprises that are conventionally thought of as land-based activities. Conversely, land underlain by permafrost is inhospitable to many common land-based activities. Consequently, the conventional practice of proceeding from a clear-cut distinction between land and water in addressing problems of international order does not serve us well in the Arctic.

A similar story emerges from a consideration of the strategic significance of the Arctic. Some observers have approached the Arctic as little more than a northern extension of the East/West confrontation centered on the European continent, a condition that suggests a declining strategic role for the region with the termination of the cold war. The significance of the buildup of Soviet forces on the Kola Peninsula, on this account, arose from the role these forces could play in disrupting the sea lines of communication (SLOCs) between Europe and North America. Viewed from this perspective, parts of Scandinavia, together with the waters surrounding the Greenland/Iceland/United Kingdom Gap have been properly regarded as NATO's northern flank. Similarly, the American maritime strategy, with its emphasis on conventional attacks against Soviet forces in the Barents Sea and on the Kola Peninsula, was rationalized as a response to the threat of a Soviet attack against NATO's central front.

But here too there is an alternative interpretation that accords independent strategic significance to events occurring in the Arctic. On this account, the Arctic has become a distinct and critically important theater of operations for strategic weapons systems, such as nuclear-powered ballistic missile submarines (SSBNs) carrying long-range SLBMs and high-endurance manned bombers equipped with air-launched cruise missiles (ALCMs), as well as for defensive systems, such as sophisticated attack submarines and air defense facilities (for example, the American/Canadian North Warning System). The Arctic is not, of course, unrelated to other theaters of military operations. On the contrary, the region now looms large in any realistic appraisal of the global strategic balance. It is possible, for example, that the unusually secure deployment zones afforded by Arctic conditions will seem particularly attractive to military planners seeking to implement strategies of finite or minimal deterrence in the aftermath of the cold war. Although uncertainties regarding the future abound, this account licenses the conclusion that any assessment of the strategic significance of the Arctic that treats it as nothing more than the northern flank of Europe will be wide of the mark.

Turning to industrial and commercial affairs, similar antinomies emerge. On one account, there are no Arctic economic systems as such. The Arctic is segmented into a number of economic peripheries, or hinterlands, each tied to a southern industrial core. Capital and technology flow north from these cores to facilitate the extraction of raw materials needed to fuel the industrial engines of southern societies. At the same time, the lion's share of the economic returns and rents derived from these activities flows south, and decision making regarding the development of Arctic resources remains in southern hands. What is more, there is relatively little interaction among the northern hinterlands of the Arctic Rim states.

Yet the Arctic can be approached, conversely, as a distinctive outpost in an increasingly global economy, where subsistence-based economic systems remain very much in evidence and where interesting alternatives to the prevailing socioeconomic arrangements of industrial societies are everyday realities. It is true that everywhere in the Arctic Rim states these economic systems are now under siege, threatened with collapse as a result of the inroads of the modes of production and forms of socioeconomic organization characteristic of advanced industrial societies. Given the profound problems that currently plague these societies, however, this state of siege only reinforces the need to understand the distinctive socioeconomic systems of the Arctic and to take steps to protect the subsistence-based economies of this region.

If anything, this pattern of Arctic antinomies becomes even more pronounced when we turn our attention to environmental matters. On one account, the natural environment is strikingly homogeneous throughout the Arctic region. The ecosystems we associate with tundra and taiga biomes are so similar that knowledgeable individuals dropped blindfolded into the Arctic might well experience some difficulty ascertaining their location. Not only are the plant and animal communities of the Arctic typically circumpolar in their distribution, but the dynamics of Arctic ecosystems are also similar throughout the region. Phenomena like diminished biological productivity, coupled with occasional thermal oases, protracted cycles of regeneration, and lowered rates of biodegradation, are common to all Arctic ecosystems.

But others, emphasizing physical processes like ocean/ice/atmosphere interactions, have shown that the Arctic (like the Antarctic) is intimately linked to global dynamics; they generally conclude that it is not helpful to treat the Arctic as a distinctive region. Air pollution generated in the midlatitudes shows up in the Far North in the form of Arctic haze. The global warming trend, largely attributable to human activities far to the south, is expected to produce a rise in temperatures in the Far North two to three times the comparable temperature increases in the midlatitudes. This, in turn, could have dramatic consequences for the midlatitudes themselves, resulting partly from the simple mechanism of the melting of the Greenland icecap and partly from the determinative role of the Arctic in the climate system of the Northern Hemisphere. It will come as no surprise, then, that those who adopt this perspective stress the importance of the Arctic in systemic processes of the sort emphasized by the International Geosphere/Biosphere Programme (IGBP) even while they reject proposals to treat the Arctic as a distinctive or separate region of the world.

Nor does this picture of Arctic antinomies change as we shift our focus to the peoples and cultures of the region. On one account, the Arctic is a well-defined cultural mediterranean. The indigenous cultures of the region are based on strikingly similar adaptations to the natural systems prevailing in the Arctic. The region is one of the few remaining strongholds of hunter/gatherer cultures. What is more, the indigenous peoples of the Arctic are becoming increasingly conscious of their common concerns and interests. We are witnessing today the emergence of effective transnational organizations among Arctic peoples in such forms as the Inuit Circumpolar Conference, Indigenous Survival International, and the Nordic Saami Council.

On the other hand, the indigenous peoples of the Arctic also form an integral part of the emerging Fourth World movement, a social force that has unleashed a rising tide of political consciousness among aboriginal peoples—estimated to number about 200 million worldwide—locked into states they can never hope to control. Whether we look to the work of the World Council of Indigenous Peoples, the International Working Group on Indigenous Affairs, or the Working Group on Indigenous Peoples of the United Nations Economic and Social Council, northern Natives have been quick to assume leadership roles in the Fourth World movement. The growing consciousness of the Arctic as a cultural mediterranean, therefore, is currently unfolding side by side with feelings of solidarity linking the indigenous peoples of the Arctic with their brethren in Australia, Central America, and elsewhere.

A Choice of Perspectives

What, then, prompts public officials or private analysts to adopt one or another of these interpretive accounts as a guide to thinking about the significance of the Arctic for purposes of policy analysis and public policy-making. In this section, I argue that interests (or perceptions of interests) hold the key to such choices. The perspectives identified in the preceding section are *not* neutral with respect to their implications for the interests of various stakeholders in the Arctic. On the contrary, the acceptance of an interpretive framework can go far toward sustaining or undermining the causes espoused by specific groups. It should come as no surprise, therefore, that preferred perspectives on the Arctic vary across nations, groups, and individuals in a predictable fashion.

At least three distinct classes of interests figure prominently in choices among interpretive frameworks: (1) national interests, (2) bureaucratic interests, and (3) group interests. A brief discussion of each will help to concretize the argument regarding the place of the Arctic in terms of policy analysis and public decision making.

National Interests

Consider first the national interests of the principal Arctic states: Canada, the United States, and Russia (the Soviet Union's successor when it comes to Arctic affairs). Canada seeks to exercise authority over a huge, sparsely populated segment of the Arctic, but it lacks the capabilities required to compete effectively in the region in military or economic terms, a fact of increasing significance in the face of the militarization and industrialization of the Arctic. Canada's paramount interests in the Arctic, therefore, are to entrench Canadian sovereignty in the Far North through effective occupancy and to alleviate anxieties arising from the dangers of being sandwiched between the dominant powers in this increasingly important region of the world. By contrast, the United States, which exercises direct control over a relatively small segment of the Arctic, exhibits the interests of a superpower in maintaining freedom of access to all parts of the region and in opposing Arctic developments that could prove detrimental to American interests in other parts of the world.

The Arctic interests of Russia (as of the Soviet Union before it) are more complex and, on occasion, contradictory. Russia is undoubtedly the preeminent Arctic power. Almost half of the Arctic coastline is under Russian control; over 75 percent of the inhabitants of the Arctic are Russian citizens; no other Arctic Rim state depends on the Arctic economically or militarily to the extent that Russia does. It is perfectly natural, therefore, for the Russians to regard the Arctic as an international region that is distinctive in many ways. Yet Russia has also inherited the mantle of the Soviet Union as a major world power with far-reaching interests extending to all corners of the globe. As a result, it cannot avoid concerning itself with the implications of Arctic developments for Russian interests worldwide.

How would we expect those endeavoring to promote these different interests to approach the Arctic in policy terms? For Canada, there is much to be said for treating the Arctic as a distinctive region. Such a perspective can provide a rationale for efforts to entrench Canada's jurisdictional claims in the Far North. Arguments regarding the distinctiveness of the Arctic played a prominent role, for example, in justifying Canada's Arctic Waters Pollution Prevention Act of 1970 as well as Canada's successful campaign for the inclusion of Article 234 (the ice-covered waters provision) in the Law of the Sea Convention. Similarly, approaching the Arctic as a distinctive region can help to undergird economic policies (for example, the frontier development provisions of the Trudeau administration's National Energy Program) designed to bolster Canadian control or effective occupancy in the Far North. Treating the Arctic as a distinctive region may even produce beneficial results for Canada in the field of security. As long as the Arctic is conceptualized as a northern extension of Europe, progress toward arms control arrangements tailored to Arctic conditions is unlikely, and the region will continue to seem attractive as a deployment zone for major weapons systems, a pattern that cannot work to Canada's advantage. Accepting the Arctic as a distinctive theater of military operations, by contrast, opens up the prospect of promoting Arctic-specific arms control agreements (for example, arrangements imposing limits on anti-submarine warfare or air defense) that would alleviate Canada's fears of being caught in the crossfire of an Arctic arms race involving the United States and a nuclear-armed Russia as the successor to the Soviet Union.

The United States, by contrast, can hardly avoid reacting with skepticism to arguments emphasizing the distinctiveness of the Arctic in policy terms. Because the United States is a superpower with worldwide interests, it is impelled to oppose initiatives that would not only restrict its freedom of access within a specific region but that could also inspire those in other regions seeking strategems to protect themselves against superpower incursions. Emphasizing the distinctiveness of the Arctic seems suspect on both counts. It is understandable, for instance, that the United States has long rejected Canadian efforts to exploit the distinctive characteristics of the Arctic as a basis for Canadian jurisdictional claims in the waters of the Arctic archipelago and opposed occasional moves on the part of the Soviet Union to extend Soviet jurisdiction in the Kara, Laptev, and East Siberian seas (Russian policy in this area has yet to be formulated). In both cases, American freedom of access to Arctic waters and the superjacent airspace is at stake.

Should Canada succeed in its efforts to enclose the waters of the Arctic archipelago—including the Northwest Passage—by emphasizing the distinctive features of the Arctic region, moreover, a number of states could well be encouraged to make use of similar arguments applying to other regions. Indonesia and Singapore, for instance, might be tempted to reevaluate their attitudes toward the Straits of Malucca; Libya might renew its claims to the Gulf of Sidra. What is more, the fact that the United States has direct control over only a small segment of the Arctic means that it will frequently have reason to engage in economic or military activities (for example, the testing of cruise missiles) involving Arctic lands controlled by others. Under the circumstances, the United States is bound to reject arguments appealing to the distinctiveness of the Arctic as a rationale for developing policies, such as those that surfaced in Canada's National Energy Program, that would have the effect of impeding American efforts to exploit Arctic resources or to operate military installations in Canada, Greenland, or Iceland.

Although Russia's Arctic policies are still in embryonic form, it seems probable that the new Russia will inherit the Soviet Union's somewhat ambivalent attitude toward treating the Arctic as a distinctive region. As the region's preeminent power, Russia will exhibit an almost instinctive propensity to emphasize both the importance and the distinctive character of the Arctic. Whether this takes the form of efforts to justify expansive jurisdictional claims in the marginal Arctic seas or enthusiastic endorsements of the idea of the Arctic as an international zone of peace, Russian actions in the Arctic will reflect a profound involvement in the region, an involvement that goes back to the early days of the Soviet Union and beyond. Indications of Soviet, and now Russian, sympathy for Canada's efforts to portray the region in distinctive terms to buttress Canadian jurisdictional claims in the Arctic may reasonably be read in a similar light.

Yet Russia has also inherited the Soviet Union's role as a great power with interests extending far beyond the confines of the Arctic region. The Russians therefore will find that they have good reasons to avoid lending credibility to restrictive measures initiated by states in other parts of the world that cite as precedents assertions of control over Arctic matters on the grounds that the Arctic is a distinctive region. This may account for the distinction the Soviets, and now the Russians, draw between the Northeast Passage, regarded as an international waterway, and the Northern Sea Route, treated as a Russian-owned and -operated transportation system, as well as for the care they take to avoid articulating dubious jurisdictional claims in the Eurasian Arctic. It seems highly probable, therefore, that the Russians will follow the Soviets in becoming increasingly sensitive about arguments emphasizing the distinctiveness of the Arctic as their own international interests come to encompass matters extending well beyond the confines of the Arctic.

Bureaucratic Interests

It is widely understood today that individual government agencies, as well as factions operating within political systems, have well-defined interests of their own.[3] These interests may coincide with or reinforce national interests, but they need not do so. The Arctic is no exception in these terms. In each of the Arctic Rim states there are individual agencies or factions that stand to benefit from emphasizing the distinctiveness and the importance of the Arctic in policy terms. But in each case there are also agencies or factions that have little or no interest in singling out the Arctic.

In Canada, the Department of Indian Affairs and Northern Development (DIAND) has much to gain from treating the Arctic as a distinctive region and viewing Canada as a northern nation that should devote considerable time and energy to the formulation of a coherent (and more activist) Arctic policy. Ultimately, developments along these lines could propel DIAND from its present secondary status into the front rank of Canadian government departments. But the same cannot be said of other government agencies in Canada. The Department of Fisheries and Oceans, for instance, deals with marine issues generally and has little interest in singling out the Arctic, where marine activities such as fishing are less significant in commercial terms than comparable activities in the Atlantic or the Pacific. The Ministry of External Affairs is heavily populated with Europeanists who have little knowledge of or interest in the Arctic. Certain elements in the Department of National Defense may see political opportunities in emphasizing the Canadian North. Witness the role assigned to the Arctic in efforts to sell the proposed acquisition of nuclear-powered submarines to the Canadian public in the late 1980s. But there is no indication that this will lead to any deep-seated commitment to the Arctic as a distinctive region in policy terms. Though Canada's national interest may benefit from treating the Arctic as a distinctive region in policy terms, then, it is by no means apparent that this is an interest widely shared among the individual agencies that make up the Canadian government.

Similar comments are in order regarding the Arctic interests of government agencies in the United States. The United States Navy, profoundly concerned with maintaining freedom of movement for surface vessels throughout the world, certainly has reasons of its own to subscribe to the thesis that the Arctic is a marine area much like other marine areas in policy terms rather than a distinctive region requiring a specialized maritime regime. Yet there are government agencies in the United States that stand to benefit from treating the Arctic as a distinctive region. The Division of Polar Programs (DPP) located within the National Science Foundation, for instance, is founded on the premise that the polar regions are sufficiently distinctive to require specialized programs of scientific research set apart from the discipline-based programs that form the backbone of the foundation's normal operations. For its part, the government of the state of Alaska sees itself as facing big problems with little political influence at the federal level. Its best hope is to convince others that the Arctic is a distinctive region requiring special treatment in policy terms. Without doubt, this was a motivating force behind the efforts of

Alaska's congressional delegation, culminating in the enactment of the Arctic Research and Policy Act of 1984.

Nor is the situation much different in the Eurasian Arctic, despite differences between the political systems operative in this part of the region and those at work in the North American Arctic. Because the newly emerging Russian system has no track record, a few observations drawn from the final phase of Soviet administration in the Arctic will serve to illustrate this point. The Soviet State Committee for Hydrometeorology (Hydromet), which administered the Arctic and Antarctic Scientific Research Institute (AANII), along with a number of other northern ventures, and the Ministry of Merchant Fleet, which encompassed the Northern Sea Route Administration (Glavsevmorput), had obvious interests in stressing the importance and the distinctiveness of the Arctic. Over time, the State Committee on Science and Technology (SCST) came to share these interests. Not only did SCST establish a separate Arctic section, it also acquired added Arctic interests as the organization responsible for the staff work associated with the Soviet Arctic "zone of peace" initiative first articulated publicly in Gorbachev's Murmansk speech in October 1987.

Yet other Soviet government agencies had little reason to stress the distinctiveness of the Arctic. The Soviet Academy of Sciences, for instance, employed numerous individuals who worked in the North, but it never established a strong Arctic institute to serve as a locus of organized support for treating the Arctic as a distinctive region. Despite the buildup of military forces stationed on the Kola Peninsula, the Ministry of Defense seldom displayed any special interest in the Arctic. Nor was the Soviet Foreign Ministry organized along lines likely to give it an institutional interest in devoting increased attention to the Arctic in policy terms. With regard to bureaucratic interests, then, the situation prevailing at the end of the Soviet era tended to reinforce ambivalences regarding the treatment of the Arctic as a distinctive region arising from mainstream perspectives on the Soviet national interest.

Group Interests

All societies contain unofficial interest groups that work to influence public policies in the light of their own worldviews and policy preferences. Some of these groups are functionally specific, encompassing physicians, educators, farmers, steelworkers, sport hunters, wilderness advocates, and so forth. Other interest groups form to promote distinctive social philosophies, such as those we associate with capitalism, socialism, or environmentalism. The concerns of these groups are particularly suggestive in connection with this discussion of the treatment of the Arctic in policy terms. A few concrete examples will serve to clarify this proposition.

In both the United States and Canada, Atlanticists have long exercised a powerful influence over the formulation of foreign policy. Treating Europe as the central arena of international relations, members of this group have staunchly supported NATO and generally approached the Arctic as little more than Europe's northern flank. By and large, the Atlanticists react to the suggestion that the Arctic deserves treatment as a distinctive region in policy terms as a mistake that can only detract from a clear-cut acknowledgment of the centrality of Europe in the global balance of power. To take another example, assimilationists favor the absorption of racial and ethnic minorities into the mainstream of the dominant social and political systems. They are apt to reject the idea of treating the Arctic as a distinctive region on the grounds that any such orientation will only add fuel to the growing demands for separate treatment or self-determination among the indigenous peoples of the Far North. Much the same is true of economic liberals, who see the world as a network of voluntary exchange systems open to all on essentially equal terms and who reject structuralist arguments pointing to built-in biases ensuring that certain groups are able to capture the bulk of the gains from trade associated with economic exchange. Because treating the Arctic as a distinctive region could easily serve to reinforce the arguments of those who speak of internal colonialism and advocate protecting the subsistence-based economies of the north from the inroads of industrial society, economic liberals can be counted on to react with skepticism to proposals that highlight the distinctiveness of the Circumpolar North.

As these comments imply, however, there are countervailing groups in each of the Arctic Rim states whose interests may well be promoted by a strategy of treating of the Arctic as a distinctive

region. Promoters of the rising international significance of the
Pacific Rim and others desiring to dilute the influence of the Atlanticists may find it useful, at least in tactical terms, to support
the treatment of the Arctic as a distinctive region. Those fighting
to preserve the integrity of indigenous cultures against the forces
of assimilationism may find that emphasizing the distinctiveness
of the Arctic region provides an appealing rationale for claims on
the part of ethnic groups to self-determination, home rule, or separate treatment in other realms. Likewise, the vision of the Arctic
as an outpost of subsistence-based economies offering a viable
alternative to the socioeconomic arrangements characteristic of
advanced industrial societies can be expected to appeal to the
appropriate technology movement as well as to other critics of
industrial society. They will be attracted to treating the Arctic as
a distinctive region in order to justify policies, such as income
security programs, designed to protect the viability of the region's economies.

The Road Ahead

Can those whose interests would be served by treating the
Arctic as a distinctive region in policy terms succeed in persuad-
ing others to adopt their point of view? Any effort to answer this
question must begin with a clear appreciation of the obstacles to
the acceptance of the Arctic as a distinctive region for purposes
of policy analysis and public decision making. Traditional policies
of benign neglect, which have long characterized southern thinking about the Arctic, remain firmly entrenched in many circles.
Inertia, a powerful force in all large organizations, also favors the
continuation of existing practices that relegate the Arctic to the
status of a remote periphery in policy terms. It follows that we
must inquire whether there are forces at work today of sufficient
magnitude to alter existing practices in this area. The following
paragraphs make a case that some forces of this sort do exist. But
it is far from clear whether they will prevail in the sense of bringing about major shifts in the organization of public policy-making
regarding Arctic issues during the near future.

Perhaps the most decisive way for a region to become distinctive in policy terms is for it to emerge as the site of one or more

severe regional conflicts that engage the interests of the great powers. It seems unlikely, for example, that the Middle East would loom so large as a policy region if it were not the cockpit of the festering Arab-Israeli conflict. The Vietnam war certainly put Southeast Asia on the map as a region in policy terms. Long-running conflicts in Nicaragua and El Salvador seem to have done the same for Central America during the past decade. Similar observations may be in order regarding the Iran-Iraq and Afghan conflicts in Southwest Asia and the conflicts in Angola, Mozambique, and South Africa in sub-Saharan Africa.

Yet it is not easy to visualize regional conflicts of this sort arising in the Arctic during the foreseeable future. To be sure, there are frictions between Russia and Norway over their maritime boundary in the Barents Sea as well as the regime governing areas of the outer continental shelf adjacent to Svalbard. Tensions could mount between the United States on the one hand and Greenland or Iceland on the other over the presence of American military installations in those countries. And there are a number of real or potential sources of conflict between the United States and Canada in the Arctic. But none of these issues has the potential to become a severe regional conflict of the sort referred to in the preceding paragraph. This may well be attributable to the fact that the great powers are so deeply involved in the Arctic that there is little scope for regional conflicts breaking out between lesser powers in the region. In one sense, this is a measure of the importance of the Arctic as a factor in the global balance of power. Paradoxically, however, this circumstance could serve as an impediment to the acceptance of the Arctic as a distinctive region in policy terms.

Short of becoming a locus of regional conflict, a geographically defined area may achieve the status of a distinctive region for purposes of policy analysis and public decision making when it enters a period of political turmoil or flux as a result of the impact of realigning forces. East Asia, for example, has become a focus of attention on the part of policymakers in recent years as a consequence of the Sino-American rapprochement, rather than because it has become a site of sharp regional conflicts. Any moves toward a Sino-Russian or Russian/Japanese rapprochement during the near future would only reinforce this situation. In much the same way, the emergence of a multiplicity of new states in Africa during the 1950s and 1960s made that region a focus of increased attention. And the requirements of implementing the Antarctic Treaty System, negotiated in 1959 in the aftermath of the International Geophysical Year of 1957–1958, clearly played a major role in bringing Antarctica to the attention of policymakers as a distinctive region. In all of these cases, simple adherence to the status quo, much less reliance on policies of benign neglect, was out of the question. Policymakers were compelled to focus on the region in question in the search for adequate responses to realigning forces.

Something of this sort may well be occurring in the Arctic today. Through much of the postwar era, international relations among the ice states seemed simple and unambiguous. On one side stood the Soviet Union, controlling about half of the Arctic coastline but interested in the region primarily as a base from which to launch naval forces into the North Atlantic in conjunction with a potential war in central Europe. On the other side stood the rest of the ice states (that is, Canada, Denmark/Greenland, Iceland, Norway, and the United States), closely allied as members of NATO and primarily interested in deterring potential Soviet initiatives on the European continent. From this perspective, it was easy to treat the Arctic as a peripheral area presenting no distinctive issues in its own right.

By contrast, the situation now emerging as a result of the militarization and industrialization of the Arctic, the end of the cold war, and the breakup of the Soviet Union is far less straightforward and unambiguous. The end of the cold war has undermined the rationale for the long-standing pattern of alignments in the Circumpolar North. The Russians, as the successors to the Soviets in the Arctic, will almost certainly perceive opportunities for opening up friendly relations with several of the other ice states and be prepared to act on this perception. Some influential Canadians, fearful of the consequences of the militarization of the Arctic and increasingly disenchanted with American strategic thinking, have begun to espouse the idea that Canada should take the lead in efforts to form a bloc of lesser Arctic Rim states. Norway could easily find itself at odds with the United States, as well as with Russia, in connection with its interpretation of the

Svalbard regime. The Home Rule in Greenland, which has already declared all of Greenland (with the exception of the American base at Thule) a nuclear-free zone, could become more militant in its desire to opt out of strategic maneuvering in the Arctic. Should these or other realigning forces continue to unfold, policymakers in all of the Arctic Rim states are likely to experience growing pressures to focus on the Arctic as a distinctive region and to acquire the capability needed to deal with Arctic issues in an informed and sensitive manner.

Beyond this, there is the prospect that one or more of the Arctic states will launch policy initiatives that focus attention on the Arctic in such a way that governments in all of the Arctic Rim states experience growing pressure to treat the Arctic as a distinctive region in policy terms. Canada could become a catalyst in this connection. Pressures are mounting in a number of quarters for Canada to articulate a coherent northern or Arctic policy. One or more of the national political parties may fix on the role of the Arctic as an attractive vehicle in electoral terms. Under the circumstances, the Arctic could emerge as a focus of attention in Canadian electoral politics. Equally probable is the prospect that the leaders of the new Russia will fix on the idea of creating an Arctic zone of peace, launched initially by Gorbachev and pursued vigorously by the Soviet leadership during the intervening years. The concept of an Arctic zone of peace, configured in such a way as to underline the preeminent role of Russia in the Arctic region while avoiding both the costs and the dangers of an offense/defense arms race with the United States in the Far North, could easily emerge as a centerpiece of Russian foreign policy. Should this occur, the United States and the other ice states would all find themselves more or less compelled to focus on the Arctic in order to formulate coherent responses to the Russian initiative.

Where do these observations leave us with regard to the status of the Arctic in policy terms? In particular, do they justify an expectation that the Arctic will achieve acceptance as a distinctive region for purposes of policy analysis and public decision making during the foreseeable future? In my judgment, the jury remains out on this question. It is not difficult to sketch out good reasons for treating the Arctic as a distinctive region. But it is equally easy to identify groups whose interests (at least as their members currently perceive them) would not be served by such a development. It would be a mistake, as well, to underestimate the role of organizational inertia with regard to matters of this sort. Even so, the rise of the Arctic has now progressed far enough to trigger a lively debate regarding the extent to which the Circumpolar North should be treated as a distinctive region in policy terms. The resultant debate itself is apt to strengthen the hand of those who champion the Arctic as a distinctive region by contributing to a kind of Arctic consciousness raising among both opinion leaders and the members of attentive publics throughout the Arctic region.

Introduction

1. Barry Lopez, *Arctic Dreams* (New York: Charles Scribner's Sons, 1986); Richard K. Nelson, *Shadow of the Hunter* (Chicago: University of Chicago Press, 1980); Pierre Berton, *The Arctic Grail: The Quest for the North West Passage and the North Pole, 1818–1909* (New York: Viking, 1988); Farley Mowat, *People of the Deer* (New York: Pyramid Books, 1968).

2. For a clear and influential statement see Mikhail Gorbachev, "The North: A Zone of Peace" (Speech delivered at Murmansk, 1 October 1987) (Ottawa: Press Office of the USSR Embassy, 1988).

3. Donat Pharand, *Canada's Arctic Waters in International Law* (Cambridge: Cambridge University Press, 1988), and William E. Butler, "The Legal Regime of Soviet Arctic Maritime Areas," in Lawson W. Brigham, ed., *The Soviet Maritime Arctic* (London: Belhaven Press, 1991), 215–34.

4. Thomas R. Berger, *Northern Frontier, Northern Homeland*, rev. ed. (Vancouver, B.C.: Douglas and McIntyre, 1988).

5. For a survey of jurisdictional issues in the Arctic, see Kurt M. Shusterich, "International Jurisdictional Issues in the Arctic Ocean," in William E. Westermeyer and Kurt M. Shusterich, eds., *United States Arctic Interests: The 1980s and 1990s* (New York: Springer-Verlag, 1984), 240–67.

6. For a rich account focusing on the western Arctic, see William R. Hunt, *Arctic Passage: The Turbulent History of the Land and People of the Bering Sea, 1697–1975* (New York: Charles Scribner's Sons, 1975).

7. Franklyn Griffiths and Oran R. Young, *Managing the Arctic's Resources*, Impressions of the Co-Chairs from the Fourth Session of the Working Group on Arctic International Relations held at Kaktovik and Prudhoe Bay, Alaska in September 1990 (Hanover, N.H.: Institute of Arctic Studies, 1991).

8. For an articulate Soviet analysis of these matters, see Alexandre S. Timoshenko, "Shared Natural Resources: Conception, Evolution and Perspectives" (Paper prepared for the International Conference on the

Shared Living Resources of the Bering Sea, Fairbanks, Alaska, June 1990).

9. For a detailed account of the Mediterranean case, see Peter M. Haas, *Saving the Mediterranean: The Politics of International Environmental Cooperation* (New York: Columbia University Press, 1990).

10. For a well-informed and highly readable account of the exploits of these men, see Berton, *The Arctic Grail*.

11. I owe the phrase the "Arctic of the Imagination" to my Dartmouth colleague, Chauncey Loomis. Among the best known of Jack London's many northern tales are *The Call of the Wild* and *White Fang*.

12. Franklyn Griffiths and Oran R. Young, *Sustainable Development and the Arctic*, Impressions of the Co-Chairs from the Second Session of the Working Group on Arctic International Relations held at Ilulissat and Nuuk, Greenland in April 1989 (Hanover, N.H.: Institute of Arctic Studies, 1989).

13. Bonnie J. McCay and James M. A. Acheson, eds., *The Question of the Commons: The Culture and Ecology of Communal Resources* (Tucson: University of Arizona Press, 1987), and Fikret Berkes, ed., *Common Property Resources: Ecology and Community-Based Sustainable Development* (London: Belhaven Press, 1989).

14. Elinor Ostrom, *Governing the Commons: The Evolution of Institutions for Collective Action* (Cambridge: Cambridge University Press, 1990).

15. Gail Osherenko, "Can Comanagement Save Arctic Wildlife?" *Environment* 30 (July/August 1988): 6–13, 29–34.

16. On Native self-government and tribal sovereignty with particular reference to Alaska, consult David S. Case, *Alaska Natives and American Laws* (Fairbanks: University of Alaska Press, 1984), chaps. 8–10. For Canada, see Michael Asch, *Home and Native Land: Aboriginal Rights and the Canadian Constitution* (Toronto: Methuen, 1984).

17. Oran R. Young and Gail Osherenko, eds., *Polar Politics: Creating International Environmental Regimes* (Ithaca, N.Y.: Cornell University Press, forthcoming).

18. On joint development zones, with particular reference to the Iceland/Jan Mayen case, see Elliot L. Richardson, "Jan Mayen in Perspective," *American Journal of International Law* 82 (July 1988): 443–58. For a description of recent cooperative developments in the Bering Sea region, see David A. Shakespeare, "Recent US/USSR Agreements Relating to the Bering Region," *Arctic Research of the United States*, vol. 5 (Fall 1991), 37–47.

19. For an account emphasizing the concepts of metropoles and hinterlands see H. A. Innis, *The Fur Trade in Canada: An Introduction to Canadian Economic History* (New Haven, Conn.: Yale University Press, 1962).

20. For a general and influential account of internal colonialism, see Michael Hechter, *Internal Colonialism: The Celtic Fringe in British National Development, 1536–1966* (Berkeley: University of California Press, 1975).

21. The concept of segmentation is developed in Arctic Council Panel

(Franklyn Griffiths and Rosemarie Kuptana, co-chairs), *To Establish an International Arctic Council* (Ottawa: Canadian Arctic Resources Committee, 1991), 38–41.

22. Jens Dahl, "Greenland: Political Structure of Self-Government," *Arctic Anthropology* 23 (1986): 315–24.

23. Gurston Dacks, ed., *Devolution and Constitutional Development in the Canadian North* (Ottawa: Carleton University Press, 1990). On the recent agreement to create Nunavut, see John F. Burns, "Accord to Give the Eskimos Control of a Fifth of Canada," *New York Times,* 17 Dec. 1991, A1, A7.

24. Thomas A. Morehouse, Gerald A. McBeath, and Linda Leask, *Alaska's Urban and Rural Governments* (Lanham, Md.: University Press of America, 1984).

25. For a general account of tribal governments in the United States, see Sharon O'Brien, *American Indian Tribal Governments* (Norman: University of Oklahoma Press, 1989).

26. For the concept of "nordicity," see Louis-Edmond Hamelin, *Canadian Nordicity: It's Your North, Too* (Montreal: Harvest House, 1978), and Amanda Graham, "Indexing the Canadian North: Broadening the Definition," *The Northern Review* 6 (Winter 1990): 21–37.

27. State of Alaska Office of International Trade, "Cooperation in a Changing World" (Summary Proceedings, Third Northern Regions Conference, Anchorage, 1990). The quote is from the "Statement of Intent" to establish the North Forum, which appears on p. 8.

28. On the newly formed Association of the Small Peoples of the Soviet North, see *Indigenous Peoples of the Soviet North,* Document 67 (Copenhagen: IWGIA, 1990).

29. For a general account, see Gail Osherenko and Oran R. Young, *The Age of the Arctic: Hot Conflicts and Cold Realities* (Cambridge: Cambridge University Press, 1989), chap. 3.

30. For a variety of accounts reflecting this way of thinking, see Edgar Dosman, ed., *Sovereignty and Security in the Arctic* (London and New York: Routledge, 1989).

31. Gorbachev, "The North." The six points included a nuclear-free zone in Northern Europe, restrictions on naval activity, cooperation in developing Arctic resources, scientific cooperation, cooperation on matters of environmental protection, and opening the Northern Sea Route to foreign ships.

32. The International Arctic Science Committee was established formally at a meeting in Resolute, Northwest Territories, in August 1990; its council met for the first time in Oslo in January 1991. The Arctic Monitoring and Assessment Program will be the key operational component of the Arctic Environmental Protection Strategy, adopted by the Arctic Eight at a meeting in Rovaniemi, Finland, in June 1991.

33. Franklyn Griffiths and Oran R. Young, *Protecting the Arctic's Environment,* Impressions of the Co-Chairs from the Third Session of the Working Group on Arctic International Relations held at Moscow and

252 Notes to Pages 26–39

Murmansk, Russia in January 1990 (Hanover, N.H.: Institute of Arctic Studies, 1990).

34. For a discussion see Arctic Council Panel, *To Establish an International Arctic Council*.

35. Kari Mottola, ed., *The Arctic Challenge: Nordic and Canadian Approaches to Security and Cooperation in an Emerging International Region* (Boulder, Colo.: Westview Press, 1988).

36. Arnfinn Jorgensen-Dahl and Willy Ostreng, eds., *The Antarctic Treaty System in World Politics* (London: Macmillan, 1991).

37. For a general discussion of framework agreements, see Peter S. Thacher, "Alternative Legal and Institutional Approaches to Global Change," *Colorado Journal of International Environmental Law and Policy* 1 (Summer 1990): 101–26.

38. Jorgen Wettestad and Steinar Andresen, *The Effectiveness of International Resource Cooperation: Some Preliminary Findings*, Report 007–91 (Oslo: Fridtjof Nansen Institute, 1991).

39. For an extended discussion of this distinction and its implications, see Oran R. Young, *International Cooperation: Building Regimes for Natural Resources and the Environment* (Ithaca, N.Y.: Cornell University Press, 1989), chap. 2.

40. Arctic Council Panel, *To Establish an International Arctic Council*.

Chapter 1. Internal Colonialism or Self-Sufficiency?

1. The field experience underlying this analysis derives primarily from work conducted in Alaska. The analysis relies heavily on the works of others for information about the remaining sections of the region. Most of these are cited at various points in the text. Additionally, the analysis has benefited from discussions with numerous people familiar with the circumstances of communities in various parts of the Far North.

2. For a particularly eloquent example, see Frederick Seagayuk Bigjim and James Ito-Adler, *Letters to Howard: An Interpretation of the Alaska Native Land Claims* (Anchorage: Alaska Methodist University Press, 1974).

3. On the basic concept of internal colonialism, see Michael Hechter, *Internal Colonialism: The Celtic Fringe in British National Development, 1536–1966* (Berkeley: University of California Press, 1975). For rich descriptive accounts of its operation in the north, consult Hugh Brody, *The People's Land* (Harmondsworth, U.K.: Penguin, 1975), and Mel Watkins, ed., *Dene Nation: The Colony Within* (Toronto: University of Toronto Press, 1977).

4. Barbara Boyle Torrey, *Slaves of the Harvest: The Story of the Pribilof Aleuts* (St. Paul, Alaska: Tanadgusix, 1978).

5. For detailed accounts of specific cases, see Nelson H. Graburn, *Eskimos without Igloos* (Boston: Little, Brown, 1969), and Peter J. Usher, *The Bankslanders: Economy and Ecology of a Frontier Trapping Community* (Ottawa: Department of Indian Affairs and Northern Development, 1979), vol. 1.

6. The phrase "traditional subsistence life-style" is intended to refer to a way of life or cultural complex, not just to certain methods of hunting and gathering. Many of the social and cultural characteristics of the indigenous communities of the Circumpolar North during precontact times were linked directly to the requirements of subsistence hunting and gathering. For an account focusing on the Athapascans of interior Alaska, see Richard K. Nelson, *Hunters of the Northern Forest* (Chicago: University of Chicago Press, 1973).

7. For an extended account of a specific instance, see Graburn, *Eskimos without Igloos*.

8. For a well-known and particularly poignant account of a specific case, see Farley Mowat, *People of the Deer* (New York: Pyramid Books, 1968).

9. Usher, *The Bankslanders*, esp. vol. 2.

10. Michael Asch, "The Dene Economy," in Mel Watkins, ed., *Dene Nation: The Colony Within* (Toronto: University of Toronto Press, 1977), 47–61.

11. William Alonso and Edgar Rust, "The Evolving Pattern of Village Alaska" (Report prepared for the Joint Federal-State Land Use Planning Commission, Anchorage, 1976).

12. There are indications that the Soviets often promoted certain types of manufacturing in the larger communities of Siberia. Although it is hard to get accurate information on such developments, see the informal account in Farley Mowat, *The Siberians* (Boston: Little, Brown, 1970).

13. For an excellent survey of current estimates, see U.S. Central Intelligence Agency, *Polar Regions Atlas* (Washington, D.C.: U.S. Government Printing Office, 1978), 6–33.

14. For a case study dealing with Northern fur seals, see Oran R. Young, *Natural Resources and the State: The Political Economy of Resource Management* (Berkeley: University of California Press, 1981), chap. 3.

15. It remains to be seen whether the move toward home rule will alter this situation in Greenland. For the text of the Greenland Homerule Act of 1979, see *Arctic Coastal Zone Management Newsletter* 20 (May 1979): 5–7. For an English-language summary of the report of the Commission on Homerule, see *Arctic Coastal Zone Management Newsletter* 18 (February 1979): 15–17.

16. For a more detailed account of the St. Paul case, see Young, *Natural Resources*, chap. 3.

17. For the conceptual and theoretical underpinnings of this option, see E. F. Schumacher, *Small Is Beautiful* (New York: Harper & Row, 1972).

18. Young, *Natural Resources*, chap. 3.

19. For a discussion of the interests of environmentalists and others in the context of Arctic issues, see John S. Dryzek, *Conflict and Choice in Resource Management: The Case of Alaska* (Boulder, Colo.: Westview Press, 1983).

20. For a detailed case study, see Usher, *The Bankslanders*.

21. S. L. Albrecht, "Socio-Cultural Factors and Energy Resource Development in Rural Areas in the West," *Journal of Environmental Management* 7 (1978): 73–90.
22. Dorothy M. Jones, *Aleuts in Transition: A Comparison of Two Villages*
(Seattle: University of Washington Press, 1976).
23. Terence Armstrong, "The Administration of Northern Peoples:
The USSR," and Margaret Lantis, "The Administration of Northern Peoples: Canada and Alaska," both in R. St. J. MacDonald, ed., *The Arctic
Frontier* (Toronto: University of Toronto Press, 1966), 57–78 and 89–119.
24. For a well-known account of similar problems in metropolitan
areas, see Frances Fox Piven and Richard A. Cloward, *Regulating the Poor*
(New York: Pantheon Books, 1971).
25. For an intriguing discussion of the consequences for children, see
Robert Coles, *Eskimos, Chicanos, Indians*, vol. 4 of *Children in Crisis* (Boston: Little, Brown, 1977), 3–228.
26. June Helm, "Indian Dependency and Indian Self-Determination:
Problems and Paradoxes in Canada's Northwest Territories," in
Ernest L. Shusky, ed., *Political Organization of Native North Americans*
(Washington, D.C.: University Press of America, 1980), 235.
27. See also E. Adamson Hoebel, *The Law of Primitive Man* (Cambridge, Mass.: Harvard University Press, 1954).
28. For additional details, consult Don C. Foote, Victor Fischer, and
George W. Rogers, *St. Paul Community Study* (College, Alaska: Institute
of Social, Economic and Government Research, 1968).
29. As it turns out, the commercial harvest of 1984 was the last. During 1984–1985, the United States terminated the international fur seal
regime by failing to ratify the 1984 protocol extending the life of the regime. At the same time, the federal government dismantled the Pribilof
Islands Program under the provisions of the Fur Seal Act Amendments
of 1983. What remains is a limited subsistence harvest of fur seals to
provide for the needs of residents of the communities of St. Paul and St.
George.
30. The argument here is that such control is necessary to secure the
operations of the Coast Guard's Loran C station and the weather station
on St. Paul Island.
31. Peter Fruechen, *Book of the Eskimos* (Cleveland, Ohio: World,
1961), and Graburn, *Eskimos without Igloos*.
32. For a more extended discussion of the effects of the Alaska Native
Claims Settlement, see Young, *Natural Resources*, chap. 2.
33. Watkins, ed., *Dene Nation*, and Tom G. Svensson, *Ethnicity and
Mobilization in Sami Politics* (Stockholm: University of Stockholm, 1976).
34. Hugh Brody, *The People's Land* (Harmondsworth, U.K.: Penguin,
1975).
35. Bigjim and Ito-Adler, *Letters to Howard*.
36. See also Coles, *Eskimos, Chicanos, Indians*, for a discussion of the
effects of this situation on the children of several Eskimo villages in
Alaska.

37. For a particularly clear account of the role of racism in the Circumpolar North, see Brody, *People's Land*.

38. It would be a mistake to infer from this that any of these settlements is on the verge of collapse as an organized social entity. Human communities have a remarkable capacity to persist in the face of assaults on the quality of life of their members.

39. Peter Puxley, "The Colonial Experience," in Mel Watkins, ed., *Dene Nation: The Colony Within* (Toronto: University of Toronto Press, 1977), 103–19.

40. Brody, *People's Land*.

41. For a detailed account of the events leading up to the Alaska settlement and the terms of the settlement itself, consult Robert D. Arnold and others, *Alaska Native Land Claims* (Anchorage: Alaska Native Foundation, 1978).

42. Young, *Natural Resources*, chap. 2.

43. "Village Management Assistance," *Alaska Native Management Report* 6 (15 Dec. 1977): 4.

44. Bigjim and Ito-Adler, *Letters to Howard*.

45. "A Proposal to the Government and People of Canada," in Mel Watkins, ed., *Dene Nation: The Colony Within* (Toronto: University of Toronto Press, 1977), 182–87.

46. Schumacher, *Small Is Beautiful*.

47. Thomas R. Berger, *Northern Frontier, Northern Homeland: The Report of the Mackenzie Valley Pipeline Inquiry* (Toronto: James Lorimer, 1977).

48. For eloquent testimony concerning this danger, see the account of Eskimo children in Coles, *Eskimos, Chicanos, Indians*.

49. Bigjim and Ito-Adler, *Letters to Howard*, 82.

Chapter 2. The Mixed Economies of Village Alaska

1. Steve J. Langdon, ed., *Contemporary Alaskan Native Economies* (Lanham, Md.: University Press of America, 1986), and Peter J. Usher, "Sustenance or Recreation? The Future of Native Wildlife Harvesting in Northern Canada," in M. M. R. Freeman, ed., *Proceedings: First International Symposium on Renewable Resources and the Economy of the North* (Ottawa: Association of Canadian Universities for Northern Studies, 1981), 56–71.

2. See also the estimates of the scale of domestic production in David P. Ross and Peter J. Usher, *From the Roots Up: Economic Development As If Community Mattered* (Croton-on-Hudson, N.Y.: Bootstrap Press, 1986), chap. 5.

3. For a collection of essays exploring the emerging linkages between subsistence and other sectors of these economies, see L. Muller-Wille, P. J. Pelto, Li. Muller-Wille, and R. Darnell, eds., *Consequences of Economic Change in Circumpolar Regions* (Edmonton, Alta: Boreal Institute for Northern Studies, 1978).

4. For further discussion of the relationships between the subsistence and cash sectors of the mixed economies of village Alaska, see John S.

256 Notes to Pages 58–63

Petterson, "Subsistence Continuity and Economic Abundance in the North," in Theodore Lane, ed., *Developing America's Northern Frontier* (Lanham, Md.: University Press of America, 1987), 91–106.

5. For an early but still highly relevant account, consult William Alonso and Edgar Rust, "The Evolving Pattern of Village Alaska" (Report prepared for the Joint Federal-State Land Use Planning Commission, Anchorage, Alaska, 1976).

6. See also Ross and Usher, *From the Roots Up*, 141–53.

7. Ibid., Appendix B, for an account stressing the same proposition throughout the Circumpolar North.

8. Nonetheless, it is important to consider strategies designed to protect the subsistence sector of the mixed economies prevailing in village Alaska. For helpful discussions consult Thomas R. Berger, *Village Journey: The Report of the Alaska Native Review Commission* (New York: Hill and Wang, 1985), and Peter J. Usher, "Indigenous Management Systems and the Conservation of Wildlife in the Canadian North," *Alternatives* 14 (February 1987), 3–9.

9. On the history of these communities, see D. K. Jones, *A Century of Servitude: Pribilof Aleuts under U.S. Rule* (Lanham, Md.: University Press of America, 1980).

10. See also Thomas D. Lonner, "Subsistence as an Economic System in Alaska: Theoretical Observations and Management Implications," in Langdon, ed., *Contemporary Alaskan Native Economies*, 15–27, and the additional literature cited therein.

11. For a particularly suggestive case study, see Pertti J. Pelto, "Snowmobiles: Technological Revolution in the Arctic," in H. Russell Bernard and Pertti J. Pelto, eds., *Technology and Social Change* (New York: Macmillan, 1972), 165–200.

12. For an excellent analysis of the problems remote communities face as a consequence of high levels of exposure to outside forces, see Ross and Usher, *From the Roots Up*, Appendix B.

13. For some relevant data, consult Scott Goldsmith and J. Phillip Rowe, "Federal Revenues and Spending in Alaska," *Alaska Review of Social and Economic Conditions* 19 (1982): 1–24, and Scott Goldsmith, Teresa Hull, and Brian Reeder, "Alaska's Economy since Statehood," *Alaska Review of Social and Economic Conditions* 21 (1984): 1–36.

14. Neal Fried, Greg Huff, and Judy Hallanger, "The Oil Patch Slide—How Alaska's Economy Compares to Other Oil States," *Alaska Economic Trends* 6 (December 1986): 1–10.

15. For a study that explores the socioeconomic origins of wildlife management practices in the United States, see Thomas A. Lund, *American Wildlife Law* (Berkeley: University of California Press, 1980). For an account of the problems associated with efforts to apply these practices in Alaska, see Gail Osherenko, *Sharing Power with Native Users: Co-Management Regimes for Arctic Wildlife*, CARC Policy Paper No. 5 (Ottawa: CARC, 1988).

16. For a helpful discussion of the bureaucratic confusion that reigns

in this area, see Harry M. Luton Jr., "The Logic of Subsistence Based Economies in Alaska" (Paper presented at the meetings of the Society for Applied Anthropology, Oaxaca, Mexico, April 1987).

17. For a striking case study focusing on the impact of the antisealing movement in the eastern Canadian Arctic, see George W. Wenzel, "Threats to Traditional Native Foods: Canadian Inuit Subsistence in an Anti-Harvest Environment" (Paper presented at the meetings of the Society for Applied Anthropology, Oaxaca, Mexico, April 1987).

18. Shelagh Jane Woods, "The Wolf at the Door," *Northern Perspectives* 14(2) (1986): 1–8. For the relevant background, consult Alan Herscovici, *Second Nature: The Animal-Rights Controversy* (Montreal: CBC Enterprises, 1985).

19. For a more detailed account, see George Wenzel, *Animal Rights, Human Rights* (London: Pinter, 1991).

20. See Petterson, "Subsistence Continuity," and Peter J. Usher, "An Hypothesis on the Effects of Wage Employment on Subsistence Harvesting in the Canadian Western Arctic" (Paper presented at the American Anthropological Association annual meeting, Washington, D.C., December 1985).

21. For a concrete example of the type of analysis involved in calculations of this sort, see John F. Helliwell, "The Distribution of Economic Benefits from a Pipeline," in Mel Watkins, ed., *Dene Nation: The Colony Within* (Toronto: University of Toronto Press, 1977), 75–83.

22. Collectively, the Natives are the largest private landowners in Alaska. Between them, however, the state and federal governments continue to hold title to about 86 percent of the land in Alaska. The two governments also exercise exclusive management authority over the marine resources of the area.

23. For a more general discussion of the problem of capturing economic rents associated with natural resourcs projects, see J. W. Devanney III, *The OCS Petroleum Pie*, Report No. MITSG 75–10 (Cambridge, Mass.: MIT SeaGrant Program, 1975).

24. For a particularly clear case study, see Arvin D. Jellis, "The Loss of Economic Rents," in Mel Watkins, ed., *Dene Nation: The Colony Within* (Toronto: University of Toronto Press, 1977), 62–74.

25. Originally, all of the income from the sale of seal skins went to the federal government. Under the terms of Section 6(e) of the Alaska Statehood Act of 1958 (PL 85–805), however, the federal government agreed to turn over to the state 70 percent of revenues in excess of the costs of operating the Pribilof Islands Program. See also Oran R. Young, "The Political Economy of the Northern Fur Seal," *Polar Record* 20 (1981): 407–16.

26. A possible exception involves land exchanges of the type contemplated in the 1980s in connection with a swap of subsurface rights in the Arctic National Wildlife Refuge for land to be added to various units of the refuge system in Alaska. Typically, however, such exchanges involve Native regional corporations rather than village corporations. See also

Steve Pilkington, "Interior Details Land Exchange with Natives," *Tundra Times*, 27 July 1987, pp. 1, 5.

27. Under current practice, as required by the provisions of the Mineral Leasing Act of 1920, for example, the federal government shares royalties accruing from onshore oil and gas production occurring on federal lands with the relevant state governments. Though the normal split is fifty-fifty, the federal government has agreed to a ninety-ten split in favor of the state in the case of Alaska on the grounds that Alaska does not benefit from a variety of federal programs available to states in the lower forty-eight.

28. Any effort to intervene in local decisions regarding such matters would entail paternalism of a type that is no longer acceptable in the Far North.

29. On the Dutch Harbor/Unalaska case, see D. M. Jones, *Aleuts in Transition* (Seattle: University of Washington Press, 1976).

30. See C. W. Hobart, "Industrial Employment of Rural Indigenes: The Case of Canada," *Human Organization* 41 (1982): 54–63, and Thomas D. Lonner, "Transient Work Forces as Casualties in Northern Frontier Development," in Theodore Lane, ed., *Developing America's Northern Frontier* (Lanham, Md.: University Press of America, 1987), 181–97.

31. For an account that emphasizes the importance of renewable resources for Alaska more generally, see Robert B. Weeden, *Alaska: Promises to Keep* (Boston: Houghton Mifflin, 1978).

32. On the role of commercial fishing in village Alaska, see Stephen Langdon, "Commercial Fisheries: Implications for Western Alaska Development," in Theodore Lane, ed., *Developing America's Northern Frontier* (Lanham, Md.: University Press of America, 1987), 3–26.

33. Oran R. Young, "The Political Economy of Fish: The Fishery Conservation and Management Act of 1976," *Ocean Development and International Law* 10 (1982): 199–273.

34. Of course, the fur trade is the classic example. For a seminal account, see H. A. Innis, *The Fur Trade in Canada: An Introduction to Canadian Economic History* (New Haven, Conn.: Yale University Press, 1962).

35. Steve J. Langdon, "Transfer Patterns in Alaskan Limited Entry Fisheries" (Final report for the Limited Entry Study Group of the Alaska Legislature, Juneau, 1980); Nasser Kamali, *Alaskan Natives and Limited Fisheries of Alaska*, Commercial Fisheries Entry Commission (CFEC) Report No. 84-8 (Juneau: 1984); and E. Dinneford and B. Hunt, *Changes in the Distribution of Permit Ownership in Alaska's Limited Fisheries—1975–1985*, CFEC Report No. 86-6 (Juneau: 1986).

36. Specifically, the Marine Mammal Protection Act of 1972 prohibits the sale of ivory, baleen, and other marine mammal products unless they have been crafted by Alaskan Natives in a traditional manner.

37. For an extensive discussion of these variations on informal economic activity, see Ross and Usher, *From the Roots Up*, esp. chap. 4.

38. John S. Petterson, "Fishing Cooperatives and Political Power," *Anthropological Quarterly* 53 (1980): 64–74.

39. On the origins of the cooperative movement in Canada, see Edith Iglauer, *Inuit Journey* (Seattle: University of Washington Press, 1979).

40. For an extended account, consult Ross and Usher, *From the Roots Up.*

41. Both conservative economists, such as Milton Friedman, and Republican presidents, such as Richard Nixon, have advocated programs of this sort. For a more general account of negative tax schemes, consult Christopher Green, *Negative Taxes and the Poverty Problem* (Washington, D.C.: Brookings Institution, 1967).

42. On the operation of this program, consult I. LaRusic, *Income Security for Subsistence Hunters: A Review of the First Five Years of Operation of the Income Security Programme for Cree Hunters and Trappers* (Ottawa: Department of Indian Affairs and Northern Development, 1982). Note also that a similar program was set up for the Naskapi under the terms of the Northeastern Quebec Agreement of 1978.

43. For a generally upbeat account of experience with the Cree income security program, see Richard F. Salisbury, *A Homeland for the Cree* (Kingston: McGill–Queen's University Press, 1986).

Chapter 3. The Politics of Pathology

1. For some relevant data, see John A. Kruse, "Changes in the Wellbeing of Alaska Natives since ANCSA," *Alaska Review of Social and Economic Conditions* 21 (1984): 1–12. A particularly poignant account of the human consequences of these pathologies is contained in a special series published by the *Anchorage Daily News* under the overall title "A People in Peril," 10–20 Jan. 1988.

2. As a recent federal document puts it, "In Alaska, unintentional injuries are the leading cause of death, accounting for 27% and 18% of the deaths of Natives (Eskimos, Aleuts, Indians) and non-Natives, respectively. They are also the leading cause of years of potential life lost (YPLL) in the two populations, 52% and 43% respectively." See Interagency Arctic Research Policy Committee, *United States Arctic Research Plan* (Washington, D.C.: National Science Foundation, 1987), 222.

3. Stephen Conn, "Alaskan Bush Justice: Centralism Confronts Social Science Research and Village Alaska" (Paper delivered at IUAES Commission on Contemporary Folk Law Meeting/Symposium, Bellagio, Italy, September 1981), 28.

4. Thomas D. Lonner and J. Kenneth Duff, "Village Alcohol Control and the Local Option Law" (Report to the Alaska State Legislature, Juneau, June 1983).

5. On the tendency of efforts to control the use of drugs to provoke criminal behavior, see John G. Cross and Melvin J. Guyer, *Social Traps* (Ann Arbor: University of Michigan Press, 1980).

6. For a sympathetic account of the problems facing village Alaska today, see Thomas R. Berger, *Village Journey: The Report of the Alaska Native Review Commission* (New York: Hill and Wang, 1985).

7. For an account of the ravages wrought by tuberculosis and other respiratory diseases only a generation ago, see Federal Field Committee for Development Planning in Alaska, *Alaska Natives and the Land* (Anchorage: Federal Field Committee, 1968).

8. For the account of an experienced health care professional who makes the same point regarding the remote communities of northern Canada, see Peter Sarsfield, "Health Issues in Northern Canada" (Paper delivered at the Boreal Institute of Northern Studies, University of Alberta, Edmonton, November 1986).

9. The concept of anomie was initially developed by Emile Durkheim, a nineteenth-century sociologist, who featured the concept in his pioneering analysis of suicide.

10. See also the sensitive account presented in Robert Coles, *Eskimos, Chicanos, and Indians,* vol. 4 of *Children of Crisis* (Boston: Little, Brown, 1977).

11. John S. Dryzek and Oran R. Young, "Internal Colonialism in the Circumpolar North: The Case of Alaska," *Development and Change* 16 (1985): 123–45. Much of the analysis developed in this essay appears in chap. 1 of this volume.

12. For an account of the resultant problems in northwest Alaska, see Kotzebue Fish and Game Advisory Committee, "Regulations Review" (Kotzebue, 1986, Photocopied).

13. On the role of myths in cultural integration, see Carl G. Jung, ed., *Man and His Symbols* (New York: Doubleday, 1964).

14. Sarsfield, "Health Issues," 8.

15. The following account is based on personal communications and direct observations collected during a visit to the NANA region during the summer of 1986.

16. For an early but still unsurpassed expression of this point of view, see F. Seagayuk Bigjim and J. Ito-Adler, *Letters to Howard: An Interpretation of the Alaska Native Land Claims* (Anchorage: Alaska Methodist University Press, 1974).

17. See also Norman A. Chance, "Modernization and Educational Reform in Native Alaska," in John J. Pogie and Robert N. Lynch, eds., *Rethinking Modernization* (Westport, Conn.: 1974), 332–52; and, more broadly, Hugh Brody, *The People's Land: Eskimos and Whites in the Eastern Arctic* (Harmondsworth, U.K.: Penguin, 1975).

18. For an account of recent developments in Cree education, consult Richard F. Salisbury, *A Homeland for the Cree: Regional Development in James Bay 1971–1981* (Kingston: McGill–Queen's University Press, 1986), 117-31.

19. The following account is based on extensive conversations with a number of people involved in the Kativik education program over the past several years.

20. I. LaRusic, *Income Security for Subsistence Hunters: A Review of the First Five Years of Operation of the Income Security Programme for Cree Hunters*

and Trappers (Ottawa: Department of Indian Affairs and Northern Development, 1982).

21. For a generally optimistic assessment, see Salisbury, *Homeland*, esp. pp. 76–84.

22. Gail Osherenko, *Sharing Power with Native Users*, CARC Policy Paper No. 5 (Ottawa: Canadian Arctic Resources Committee, 1988). For a discussion of similar concerns in the Canadian North, see Peter J. Usher, "Indigenous Management Systems and the Conservation of Wildlife in the Canadian North," *Alternatives* 14 (February 1987): 3–9.

23. See Milton M. R. Freeman, "The Alaska Eskimo Whaling Commission: Successful Co-Management Under Extreme Conditions," in Evelyn Pinkerton, ed., *Co-operative Management of Local Fisheries* (Vancouver: University of British Columbia Press, 1989), 137–53.

24. For an extended account of this arrangement, see Osherenko, *Sharing Power*.

25. See also David L. Vinje, "Cultural Values and Economic Development on Reservations," in Vine Deloria, Jr., ed., *American Indian Policy in the Twentieth Century* (Norman: University of Oklahoma Press, 1985), 155–75.

26. For extensive descriptions, consult Impact Assessment, Inc., *Analysis of Aleut Institutional Response and Change: 1980–1985*, Draft Final Technical Report Submitted to Minerals Management Service (Washington, D.C.: U.S. Department of the Interior, 1987); and Charles W. Smythe and Rosita Worl, *Monitoring Methodology and Analysis of North Slope Institutional Response and Change: 1979–1983*, Final Technical Report submitted to Minerals Management Service (Washington, D.C.: U.S. Department of the Interior, 1985).

27. For background materials on Native government and tribal sovereignty in Alaska, see David S. Case, *Alaska Natives and American Laws* (Fairbanks: University of Alaska Press, 1984), chaps. 9, 10.

28. Because local governments in Alaska depend on the state for up to 50 percent of their revenues, dramatic reductions in state funding will necessarily produce drastic impacts at the local level.

29. Although this division typically surfaces in disagreements over technical issues, such as those surrounding the so-called 1991 amendments to the Alaska Native Claims Settlement Act, the roots of the division lie much deeper in questions relating to the authority of tribal entities in village Alaska.

Chapter 4. Hunter/Gatherers in Industrial Societies

1. Finn Lynge, *Arctic Wars, Animal Rights, Endangered Peoples* (Hanover, N.H.: University Press of New England, 1992), chap. 5.

2. For background, see the essays in William E. Westermeyer and Kurt M. Shusterich eds., *United States Arctic Interests: The 1980s and 1990s* (New York: Springer-Verlag, 1984), and Gail Osherenko and Oran R. Young, *The Age of the Arctic: Hot Conflicts and Cold Realities* (Cambridge: Cambridge University Press, 1989), chap. 8.

3. Recently, this interagency coordinating mechanism has been re-named the Interagency Arctic Policy Working Group (IAPWG) and given a somewhat higher profile within the federal government.

4. For a discussion of these policy shifts with particular reference to Alaska, see Thomas R. Berger, *Village Journey: The Report of the Alaska Native Review Commission* (New York: Hill and Wang, 1985).

5. For a brilliant account of differences between white and Native approaches to dispute resolution in Canada, see Hugh Brody, *Maps and Dreams* (New York: Pantheon Books, 1981).

6. For a detailed empirical account of this phenomenon, see George Wenzel, *Animal Rights, Human Rights: Ecology, Economy, and Ideology in the Canadian Arctic* (London: Pinter, 1991).

7. Marianne Stenbaek, "Forty Years of Cultural Change among the Inuit in Alaska, Canada and Greenland: Some Reflections," *Arctic* 40 (December 1987): 300–309.

8. Gurston Dacks, ed., *Devolution and Constitutional Development in the Canadian North* (Ottawa: Carleton University Press, 1990).

9. See also Robert F. Keith and Alan Saunders, eds., *A Question of Rights: Northern Wildlife Management and the Anti-Harvest Movement* (Ottawa: Canadian Arctic Resources Committee, 1989).

10. For a more general account of the 1987 amendments, see Thomas A. Morehouse, *The Alaska Native Claims Settlement Act, 1991, and Tribal Government*, ISER Occasional Paper No. 19 (Anchorage: University of Alaska, 1988).

11. Gail Osherenko, "Can Comanagement Save Arctic Wildlife?" *Environment* 30 (July/August 1988): 6–13, 29–34.

12. Lynge, *Animal Wars*.

Chapter 5. Arctic Resource Conflicts

1. There is an obvious link between the study of resource conflicts and the assessment of environmental or socioeconomic impacts. The distinguishing feature of conflict analysis, however, is an emphasis on real or apparent conflicts of interest between organized human groups.

2. The best study of the effects of pipeline construction on Fairbanks is Mim Dixon, *What Happened to Fairbanks?* (Boulder, Colo.: Westview Press, 1978).

3. See Thomas R. Berger, *Northern Frontier, Northern Homeland* (Toronto: James Lorimer, 1977), esp. chaps. 8–10. Berger advocated a temporary moratorium on megaprojects in the North to give the small, remote communities of the region a chance to develop a more stable socioeconomic footing.

4. See Peter J. Usher, "Assessing the Impact of Industry in the Beaufort Sea Region" (Report prepared for the Beaufort Sea Alliance, December 1982). Though Usher's empirical data pertain to Canada, his argument is equally applicable to the American Arctic.

5. For a highly accessible account of the problems posed by the occurrence of probabilistic events, see Anatol Rapoport, *Strategy and Conscience* (New York: Harper & Row, 1964), esp. chaps. 3, 10.

6. It is also important to bear in mind that most Arctic communities have experienced dramatic changes in the postwar era for reasons having little to do with the commercial development of natural resources. This fact makes it even harder to isolate the probable impacts of activities related to more or less large-scale resource development.

7. For a sophisticated effort to extend benefit/cost analysis to deal with a variety of natural resource issues, see John V. Krutilla and Anthony C. Fisher, *The Economics of Natural Environments* (Baltimore: Johns Hopkins University Press, 1975). For an equally sophisticated critique of such efforts, see Mark Sagoff, "Economic Theory and Environmental Law," *Michigan Law Review* 79 (1981): 1393–1419.

8. On problems involved in measuring and comparing utilities, consult Paul Samuelson, *Foundations of Economic Analysis* (Cambridge, Mass.: Harvard University Press, 1947), chap. 8, and Kenneth J. Arrow, *Social Choice and Individual Values*, 2d ed. (New York: John Wiley, 1963).

9. The North Slope Borough, village and tribal governments, and environmental organizations have initiated a steady stream of litigation challenging various aspects of hydrocarbon exploration in the Beaufort Sea in an effort to protect their interests in subsistence hunting, the stability of marine ecosystems, and especially the conservation of a healthy bowhead whale population. *Village of Kaktovik* v. *Corps of Engineers*, 12 E.R.C. 1740, 9 E.L.R. 20117 (D Alaska 1978), involved the drilling of an exploratory well on an artificially constructed gravel pad. *North Slope Borough* v. *Andrus*, 642 F. 2d 589 (D.C. Cir. 1980), involved the sale of oil and gas exploratory leases in the Beaufort Sea. The lower court's decision may be found at 486 F. Supp. 326 (D.D.C. 1979). In *North Slope Borough* v. *Watt*, Civil Action No. A82–421 (D. Alaska, Jan. 4, 1984), plaintiffs challenged then Secretary of the Interior Watt's exploratory drilling restrictions for tracts in the BF and No. 71 sale areas for failure to protect adequately the bowhead whales during migration periods. In *State of California* v. *Watt*, 668 F.2d 1290 (D.C. Cir. 1981), plaintiffs, including the state of Alaska, challenged then Secretary of the Interior Andrus's five-year (1980–1985) plan for leasing drilling rights on the outer continental shelf (OCS). Following revision of the five-year plan by Secretary Watt, new lawsuits against the plan were filed; these were consolidated with the original case and finally decided by the Supreme Court in *Secretary of the Interior* v. *California*, slip opinion no. 82–1326, 52 U.S.L.W. 4063 (Jan. 11, 1984). In *Inupiat Community of the Arctic Slope* v. *U.S.A.*, No. A81–19 (D. Alaska, filed Oct. 1, 1982), a federally recognized tribe together with an Inupiat village and individual plaintiffs claimed property rights to parts of the Beaufort Sea, including the OCS, based on aboriginal use and occupancy of the sea ice.

10. For a discussion of internal colonialism in the Arctic, see John Dryzek and Oran R. Young, "Internal Colonialism or Self-Sufficiency," in Robert S. Merrill and Dorothy Willner, eds., *Conflict and the Common Good*, Studies in Third World Societies Publication no. 24 (Williamsburg,

Va.: College of William and Mary, 1983), 115–34. A substantially revised version of this essay appears as chap. 1 of this volume.

11. See Kenneth J. Arrow, "The Organization of Economic Activity: Issues Pertinent to the Choice of Market Versus Nonmarket Allocation," in Robert H. Haveman and Julius Margolis, eds., *Public Expenditure and Policy Analysis*, 2d ed. (Boston: Houghton Mifflin, 1977), 67–81.

12. The Alaska Native Claims Settlement Act of 1971, 85 Stat. 688 *et seq.*, 43 U.S.C. Sec 1601 *et seq.*, granted about 12 percent of the land area of Alaska to a group of regional and village Native corporations. Virtually all of the remaining land in the state is owned either by the federal government or by the state of Alaska. Additionally, all of the marine areas adjacent to Alaska are effectively controlled by the state government or the federal government.

13. For a clear discussion of quasi-markets in the context of natural resource issues, see J. H. Dales, *Pollution, Property and Prices* (Toronto: University of Toronto Press, 1968).

14. The classic argument for private bargaining as a response to environmental externalities is set forth in R. H. Coase, "The Problem of Social Cost," *Journal of Law and Economics* 3 (1960): 1–44.

15. Alan Randall, "Coasian Externality Theory in a Policy Context," *Natural Resources Journal* 14 (1974): 35–54.

16. Derek C. Bok, "A Flawed System: Report to the Harvard University Board of Overseers for 1981–1982," *Harvard Magazine* 85 (May–June 1983): 38–45 and 70–71.

17. The resultant delays and uncertainty can be just as costly to industry interests as to environmentalist or Native interests. To illustrate, consider the protracted litigation over U.S. Borax and Chemical Corporation's attempt to develop a molybdenum mine in the Quartz Hill region of southeastern Alaska, *Southeast Alaska Conservation Council, Inc. (SEACC) v. Watson*, 526 F. Supp. 202 (D. Alaska 1981), appeal after remand, 535 F. Supp. 653 (D. Alaska 1982), affirmed 697 F.2d 1305 (9th Cir. 1983).

18. For a northern example, see Oran R. Young, *Natural Resources and the State* (Berkeley: University of California Press, 1981), chap. 2, which deals with Native claims in Alaska.

19. For a well-known examination of this proposition, consult Frances Fox Piven and Richard Cloward, *Regulating the Poor: The Functions of Public Welfare* (New York: Pantheon Books, 1971).

20. Market mechanisms and private bargaining are discussed in the preceding section, but these approaches can be treated as substantive solutions as well as procedural arrangements. Accordingly, they should be kept in mind in thinking about substantive solutions to Arctic resource conflicts.

21. This is one of the principal bases of support for the efforts that have been undertaken under the provisions of the Arctic Research and Policy Act of 1984.

22. These acts are the Multiple-Use and Sustained Yield Act of 1960

(74 Stat. 215, 16 U.S.C. Sec. 528–531) and the Federal Land Policy and Management Act of 1976 (90 Stat. 2743 *et seq.*, 43 U.S.C. Sec. 1701 *et seq.*).

23. This regime is set forth in Section 18 of the Outer Continental Shelf Lands Act Amendments of 1978 (92 Stat. 649, 43 U.S.C. Sec. 1344).

24. For a sophisticated discussion of techniques for choosing optimal mixes that is fully compatible with the perspective outlined in the text, see A. Myrick Freeman III, "Project Design and Evaluation with Multiple Objectives," Haveman and Margolis eds., *Public Expenditure*, 239–56.

25. See David Sheridan, *Hard Rock Mining on the Public Domain* (report prepared for the Council on Environmental Quality; Washington, D.C.: U.S. Government Printing Office, 1977).

26. See also Dales, *Pollution*, on the problems of delineating zones with regard to all ecosystems.

27. The idea of rights as trumps is developed in detail in Ronald Dworkin, *Taking Rights Seriously* (Cambridge, Mass.: Harvard University Press, 1977).

28. *Hamlet of Baker Lake et al.* v. *Minister of Indian Affairs and Northern Development*, 107 D.L.R. 3d 513 (1980).

29. There is no precise and generally accepted definition of problem solving. For relevant background, however, consult Rapoport, *Strategy and Conscience*; John Burton, *Deviance, Terrorism, and War* (New York: St. Martin's Press, 1979); and Oran R. Young, "Korean Unification: Alternative Theoretical Perspectives," *Korea and World Affairs* 7 (1983): 57–80.

30. For an extended analysis of the hazards and pitfalls of strategic thinking, consult Rapoport, *Strategy and Conscience*, pt. 2.

31. For the theoretical background relating to this proposition, see James M. Buchanan and Gordon Tullock, *The Calculus of Consent* (Ann Arbor: University of Michigan Press, 1962), and Robert Nozick, *Anarchy, State, and Utopia* (New York: Basic Books, 1974).

Chapter 6. The Politics of Animal Rights

1. Perhaps the most influential single effort to articulate an ethical basis for opposition to the killing of animals is Peter Singer, *Animal Liberation: A New Ethics for our Treatment of Animals* (New York: Avon, 1977). For an account of the animal rights movement that is sympathetic to the concerns of consumptive users, see Alan Herscovici, *Second Nature: The Animal Rights Controversy* (Ottawa: CBC Enterprises, 1985).

2. Western observers often find it difficult to grasp the significance of the consumptive use of wild animals as a focal point of cultural complexes in hunting and gathering societies. For some outstanding discussions of these cultural complexes, see Richard K. Nelson, *Hunters of the Northern Ice* (Chicago: University of Chicago Press, 1969); Rosita Worl, "The North Slope Inupiat Whaling Complex," in Y. Kotani and W. B. Workman, eds., *Alaska Native Culture and History* (Osaka: Senri Ethnological Studies, 1980), 305–20; and Peter Usher, "Sustenance or Recreation? The Future of Native Wildlife Harvesting in Northern Canada," in M. M. R. Freeman, ed., *Renewable Resources and the Economy of the North*

(Ottawa: CARC, 1981), 56–71. For a commentary on the implications of discounting the cultural significance of hunting and gathering activities, see George W. Wenzel, "Inuit Harvesting in the Animal Rights Era" (Paper presented at the Fifth Inuit Studies Conference, Montreal, 1986).

3. The history of this harvest is described in detail in Briton Cooper Busch, *The War against the Seals: A History of the North American Seal Fishery* (Kingston and Montreal: McGill–Queen's University Press, 1985).

4. For firsthand accounts, see Brian Davies, *Savage Luxury: The Slaughter of the Baby Seals* (New York: Taplinger, 1971), and Robert Hunter, *Warriors of the Rainbow: A Chronicle of the Greenpeace Movement* (New York: Holt, Rinehart, 1979).

5. For a description and critique of the role of the Canadian federal government, see Shelagh Jane Woods, "The Wolf at the Door," *Northern Perspectives* 14 (March–April 1986): 1–8.

6. This formal action was preceded by a "voluntary ban" in 1982, which had a significant impact on the spring 1983 harvest. For a more detailed account, consult Herscovici, *Second Nature*, 83–87.

7. For a contemporary account of developments regarding this issue, including a discussion of possible government actions in response to the report of the Royal Commission on Sealing and the Sealing Industry, see Douglas Martin, "Canada's Sealers Prepare for Reduced Hunt," *New York Times*, 10 Dec. 1986, A15.

8. George Wenzel has documented the impact of these side effects in the eastern Canadian Arctic in a series of significant papers. See George Wenzel, "The Harp-Seal Controversy and the Inuit Economy," *Arctic* 31 (1978): 3–6; "Marooned in a Blizzard of Contradictions: Inuit and the Anti-Sealing Movement," *Etudes/Inuit/Studies* 9 (1985): 77–92; and *Animal Rights, Human Rights: Ecology, Economy and Ideology in the Canadian Arctic* (Toronto: University of Toronto Press, 1991). For evidence that similar side effects have been occurring for some time, consult Don Charles Foote, "Remarks on Eskimo Sealing and the Harp Seal Controversy," *Arctic* 20 (1967): 267–68.

9. The harvest more than doubled from the 1960s to the period 1973–1977. Scientists were suggesting a range of 600–2,000 in their estimates of the western Arctic stock of bowheads in 1977. For a thorough discussion, see Edward Mitchell and Randall R. Reeves, "The Alaska Bowhead Problem: A Commentary," *Arctic* 33 (1980): 686–723.

10. For a helpful descriptive account, see Steve J. Langdon, "Alaskan Native Subsistence: Current Regulatory Regimes and Issues" (Paper prepared for the Alaska Native Review Commission, October 1984), 43–52.

11. Mark A. Fraker, *Balaena mysticetus: Whales, Oil, and Whaling in the Arctic* (Anchorage: Sohio Alaska Petroleum Company and BP Alaska Exploration, 1984).

12. The quotas for 1985–1987, for example, were an average of twenty-six strikes per year, with the provisos that no more than thirty-two strikes could be made in any one year and that unused strikes could

be carried over from one year to the next. For an account of the nego-
tiation of these quotas on a year-by-year basis, see Langdon, "Alaskan
Native Subsistence."

13. See Fraker, *Balaena mysticus,* and Edward Mitchell and Randall R.
Reeves, "Current Status of the Bering Sea Stock of Bowhead Whales,"
The Musk-Ox, no. 34 (1986): 57–76, for accounts of biological research on
the bowhead whale stock of the western Arctic.

14. This language is from the preamble of the 1957 Interim Convention on Conservation of North Pacific Fur Seals as Amended. The parties
to this convention are Canada, Japan, the Union of Soviet Socialist Re-
publics, and the United States of America. For the full text of the convention, see 8 UST 2282 or TIAS 3948.

15. Barbara Boyle Torrey, *Slaves of the Harvest: The Story of the Pribilof
Aleuts* (St. Paul, Alaska: Tanadgusix, 1978).

16. See the array of statements from preservationist groups included
in U.S. National Marine Fisheries Service, *Final Environmental Impact
Statement on the Interim Convention on Conservation of North Pacific Fur Seals*
(FEIS), (Washington, D.C.: Author, 1985).

17. For a discussion of the consequences of the Fur Seal Act Amendments of 1983, consult Oran R. Young, "The Pribilof Islands: A View
from the Periphery," *Anthropologica* 29 (1987): 149–67.

18. About 3,700 fur seals were harvested on the Pribilof Islands in
1985, largely for subsistence use. The comparable figure for the 1986 harvest was approximately 1,290. This compares with a harvest of 22,066
in 1984, the last year in which a regular commercial harvest was conducted. See Loretta Lure, "Update—Pribilof Seal Harvest Reduced,"
Bering Sea Fisherman 7 (October 1986): 11–12.

19. On these constraints, see U.S. National Advisory Committee on
Oceans and Atmosphere (NACOA), *North Pacific Fur Seals: Current Problems and Opportunities Concerning Conservation and Management* (Washington, D.C.: Author, 1985), as well as the 1985 FEIS (see n. 16, above).

20. For an up-to-date account, see Woods, "Wolf at the Door." For a
history of the growing opposition to fur trapping, consult Herscovici,
Second Nature.

21. See the articles in the special issue of *Information North,* published
by the Arctic Institute of North America (Winter 1985), titled "Our Land,
Our Life: The Role of the Subsistence Economy in Native Culture." For
a more analytic account of the role of trapping in the Canadian North,
consult Peter J. Usher, *The Bankslanders: Economy and Ecology of a Frontier
Trapping Community* (Ottawa: Department of Indian Affairs and Northern Development, 1971).

22. Woods, "Wolf at the Door," 6. Currently, Greenpeace International is embarking on a conscious effort to improve its relations with
northern indigenous peoples regarding a number of issues.

23. NACOA, *North Pacific Fur Seals,* 24–28. But see also Lure, "Update," for evidence that this view is not universally shared.

24. For an authoritative account of the fur trade in Canada, consult

Harold A. Innis, *The Fur Trade in Canada* (Toronto: University of Toronto Press, 1964).

25. Busch, *War against the Seals,* chap. 8.

26. See Martin, "Canada's Sealers," for indications that such a revival could even occur in the case of the eastern Canadian harp seal harvest.

27. George Wenzel, "'I Was Once Independent,' The Southern Seal Protest and Inuit" (Unpublished essay, n.d.).

28. The Income Security program for Cree Hunters and Trappers, mandated in Section 30 of the James Bay and Northern Quebec Agreement of 1975, is designed to provide a guaranteed annual income for Cree hunters and trappers. For an account of the program and an assessment of its first five years of operation, see I. LaRusic, *Income Security for Subsistence Hunters* (Ottawa: Department of Indian Affairs and Northern Development, 1984).

29. The Royal Commission on Sealing and the Sealing Industry, as expected, recommended that the Canadian federal government initiate an explicit program to bolster the sealing industry in Canada.

30. To take a dramatic example, Ted Stevens, the senior senator from Alaska, has played an active role in efforts to expand the amount of federally owned land in Alaska open to sport or recreational hunting.

31. For a helpful account of the administrative culture prevailing in federal agencies responsible for the management of natural resources, consult Paul J. Culhane, *Public Lands Politics* (Baltimore: Johns Hopkins University Press, 1981).

32. Woods, "Wolf at the Door."

33. On the use of the phrase "fourth world" to describe indigenous peoples locked into nations they can never hope to control, see Thomas R. Berger, *Village Journey* (New York: Hill and Wang, 1985).

34. In fact, there are some indications of an emerging link between indigenous peoples organizations and IUCN and WWF. Consider, for example, the ICC's adoption of an Inuit Regional Conservation Strategy modeled after the World Conservation Strategy.

35. Such threats trigger a persistent and influential concern in many quarters focusing on the protection of biological diversity. On the general idea of biological diversity, consult E. A. Norse and R. E. McManus, "Ecology and Living Resources—Biological Diversity," in *The Eleventh Annual Report of the Council on Environmental Quality* (Washington, D.C.: U.S. Government Printing Office, 1980), 31–80. For an account documenting the general decline of animal populations in North America over the past five hundred years and attributing this decline largely to the actions of human beings, see Farley Mowat, *Sea of Slaughter* (Boston: Atlantic Monthly Press, 1984).

36. Fraker, *Balaena mysticetus,* 24–29. Some scientists now believe that at one time there was one stock of bowheads that summered in the Bering and Chukchi Seas and a second stock that summered in the Canadian Beaufort Sea.

37. For a summary of the available scientific evidence, consult the

1985 FEIS (see n. 16, above). But see the statement in NACOA, *North Pacific Fur Seals*, 43, to the effect that "NACOA rejects the notion that when a population falls by 43,000, including the 22,066 harvested, the harvest is unrelated to the decline."

38. See D. E. Sargeant, "History and Present Status of Populations of Harp and Hooded Seals," *Biological Conservation*, [London] 10 (1976): 95–118. Consult also International Council for the Exploration of the Sea (ICES), "Report of the Meeting of the Ad Hoc Working Group on Assessment of Harp and Hooded Seals in the Northwest Atlantic" (4–7 Oct. 1982), and Northwest Atlantic Fisheries Organization (NAFO), "Assessment of Seal Stocks," Report of the Standing Committee on Fishery Science, approved by the Scientific Council, 23 June 1983. For a general account of the current status of living resources in the American Arctic, see John J. Burns, "Living Resources," in William E. Westermeyer and Kurt M. Shusterich, eds., *United States Arctic Interests: The 1980s and 1990s* (New York: Springer-Verlag, 1984), 75–104.

39. Though the animals involved in these conflicts are among the best studied in the world, great uncertainties remain regarding both the current status and the dynamics of these populations. Accordingly, parties to the conflicts under consideration here can almost always interpret available data in such a way as to support their views.

40. Under the terms of CITES, Appendix II includes species that, although not currently endangered, may become so in the absence of strict regulation of trade in their products.

41. Consider, for example, the statement in NACOA, *North Pacific Fur Seals*, 40, to the effect that "regardless of favorable or unfavorable market conditions, the U.S. government has no business as an entrepreneurial factor in a private-sector, worldwide marketing activity, and therefore in the commercial fur seal harvest."

42. For a discussion of the ecological effects of Arctic energy development, see M. M. R. Freeman, "Effects of Petroleum Activities on the Ecology of Arctic Man," in F. R. Engelhardt, ed., *Petroleum Effects in the Arctic Environment* (London: Elsevier, 1985), 245–71.

43. In 1986, a coalition of oil companies, environmentalists, fishermen, and Eskimos proposed the establishment of a Bering Sea Advisory Committee to resolve conflicts over oil and gas development in the Bering Sea. See "Disparate Groups Back Bering Sea Proposal," *New York Times*, 9 Sept. 1986, A21.

44. For a helpful account of the evolving place of hunters and gatherers within modern societies, consult Harvey A. Feit, "The Future of Hunters within Nation States: Anthropology and the James Bay Cree," in Eleanor B. Leacock and Richard B. Lee, eds., *Politics and History in Band Society* (Cambridge: Cambridge University Press, 1982), 373–411.

45. See George Mancel and Michael Posluns, *The Fourth World* (New York: The Free Press, 1974).

46. See Rice O'Dell, "Alaska: A Frontier Divided," *Environment* 28 (September 1986): 11–15, 34–37; and Thomas C. Meredith, "Institutional

Arrangements for the Management and Exploitation of the George River Caribou Herd," *Etudes/Inuit/Studies* 7 (1983): 95–112. Note also that the Canadian Arctic Resources Committee (CARC) organized a seminar during January 1987 that dealt with the growing controversies over the commercialization of northern wildlife.

47. The ability to form alliances on specific issues with those you are likely to oppose on other issues is one of the keys to success in any system of pluralist politics. But this can be a hard lesson to learn for those (like many indigenous groups) who have little experience with pluralist politics as well as for those (like many preservationist groups) who regard politics as an unsavory process requiring too many expediential compromises.

Chapter 7. The Petrodollar Trap

1. John G. Cross and Melvin J. Guyer, *Social Traps* (Ann Arbor: University of Michigan Press, 1980), 4.

2. Ibid., 11.

3. Ibid., 17.

4. See Figure 5 *infra* for data on state transfers to local governments in Alaska.

5. The national figure is computed from data in U.S. Bureau of the Census, *Statistical Abstract of the United States: 1987*, 107th ed. (Washington, D.C.: Government Printing Office, 1986).

6. This figure is derived from data in U.S. Bureau of the Census, *Statistical Abstract*.

7. The figure on nationwide spending per capita is from U.S. Bureau of the Census, *Statistical Abstract*.

8. The Permanent Fund, a pool of resources resulting from a policy of setting aside a portion of the oil revenues accruing to the state, is currently held in the form of an investment portfolio featuring relatively low-risk securities.

9. The state government subsidized the development of the Red Dog lead/zinc deposit in northwestern Alaska by providing loans on favorable terms for the construction of the necessary port facilities and haul road.

10. Although a sizable portion of this increase occurred at the local level, the bulk of local government employment in Alaska is heavily supported by transfers from the state government to local governments.

11. For figures on total Alaska employment, see Edward Eboch, "Alaska's Employment Outlook," *Alaska Economic Trends* 7 (April 1987): 1.

12. See Scott Goldsmith, "Sustainable Spending Levels from Alaska State Revenues," *Alaska Review of Social and Economic Conditions* 20 (February 1983): 1–21.

13. For a seminal account of governments as collective choice mechanisms, see Anthony Downs, *An Economic Theory of Government* (New York: Harper & Row, 1957), chap. 15.

14. By way of illustration, Alaska exports most of its crude oil and at

the same time imports a significant portion of its refined petroleum products. Even allowing for the generally high cost of labor in Alaska, savings on transportation costs may well make it profitable to expand the role of small, state-of-the-art refineries in the state.

Chapter 8. Arctic Shipping

1. Terence Armstrong, "The Northeast Passage as a Commercial Waterway, 1879–1979," *Ymer* [Stockholm] (1979): 86–130; Lawson W. Brigham, "Soviet Arctic Marine Transportation," *Northern Perspectives* 16 (July–August 1988): 20–23; and Alexander Arikainen, "Exchange of Experience in Arctic Marine Transportation" (Paper presented at the International Conference on Arctic Cooperation, Toronto, October 1988). According to Brigham, "A recent estimate of the annual level of operation of the [Northern Sea Route] shows approximately 600 freighting voyages carrying six million tons of cargo" (p. 20).

2. Franklyn Griffiths, ed., *Politics of the Northwest Passage* (Kingston and Montreal: McGill–Queen's University Press, 1987); Cynthia Lamson and David L. VanderZwaag, eds., *Transit Management in the Northwest Passage* (Cambridge: Cambridge University Press, 1988); David L. Vander-Zwaag and Cynthia Lamson, eds., *The Challenge of Arctic Shipping: Science, Environmental Assessment, and Human Values* (Montreal and Kingston: McGill–Queen's University Press, 1990).

3. Lawson W. Brigham, "Arctic Icebreakers—U.S., Canadian, Soviet," *Oceanus* 29 (Spring 1986): 47–58.

4. For a comprehensive account of these claims by a prominent Canadian lawyer, see Donat Pharand, *Canada's Arctic Waters in International Law* (Cambridge: Cambridge University Press, 1988).

5. William E. Butler, *Northeast Arctic Passage* (Alphen aan den Rijn, Netherlands: Sijthoff and Noordhoff, 1978); William E. Butler, "The Legal Regime of Soviet Arctic Marine Areas," Lawson W. Brigham, ed., *The Soviet Maritime Arctic* (London: Belhaven Press, 1991): 215–34; and Camil Simard, "Soviet Sovereignty in the Arctic Seas," *Northern Perspectives* 16 (July–August 1988): 24–28.

6. See Pharand, *Canada's Arctic Waters*, 107–10; and Erik Franckx, "Non-Soviet Shipping in the Northeast Passage and the Legal Status of Proliv Vil'kitskogo," *Polar Record* 24 (October 1988): 269–76.

7. Thus, paragraph 4 of the Agreement states that "nothing in this agreement . . . affects the respective positions of the Governments of the United States and of Canada on the Law of the Sea in this or other maritime areas."

8. Terence Armstrong, "From the Barents to the Bering: Coming to Grips with a Circumpolar Giant," *Northern Perspectives* 16 (July–August 1988): 4–5.

9. For a short but well-informed account of hydrocarbon development in northwestern Siberia, see John Hannigan, "Oil and Gas Activity in the Soviet North," *Northern Perspectives* 16 (July-August 1988): 14–16.

10. Armstrong, "The Northeast Passage."

11. For an account of the issues involved in efforts to transport natural gas southward from Alaska's North Slope and Canada's Mackenzie Delta, see Gurston Dacks, *A Choice of Futures* (Toronto: Methuen, 1981): 134–54.

12. Under conditions of uncertainty, investors are apt to use high discount rates in calculating the present value of future income streams. For an argument that social discount rates (of the sort used by government planners) may be lower than private discount rates, see Anthony Scott, *Natural Resources: The Economics of Conservation* (Toronto: McClelland and Stewart, 1973), chap. 8.

13. To be specific, Gorbachev spoke of opening "[t]he Northern Sea Route to foreign ships, with ourselves providing the services of icebreakers" (Mikhail S. Gorbachev, "The North: A Zone of Peace" [Speech delivered in Murmansk, 1 Oct. 1987]).

14. For a discussion of submarine tankers, see A. S. McLaren, "Transporting Arctic Petroleum: A Role for Commercial Submarines," *Polar Record* 22 (1984): 7–23.

15. Helge Ole Bergesen, Arild Moe, and Willy Ostreng, *Soviet Oil and Security Interests in the Barents Sea* (New York: St. Martin's Press, 1987), chap. 3.

16. W. Harriet Critchley, "Polar Deployment of Soviet Submarines," *International Journal* 39 (Autumn 1984): 828–65.

17. For a somewhat impassioned presentation regarding this situation, see John Honderich, *Arctic Imperative* (Toronto: University of Toronto Press, 1987).

18. For an argument that this poses potential dangers for Canada, see Douglas Ross, "Canada, the Arctic, and SDI: The Case for Early Disengagement from the Integrated Defense" (Paper presented at the Conference on Sovereignty, Security, and the Arctic, Toronto, May 1986).

19. Franklyn Griffiths, "The Arctic in the Russian Identity," in Lawrence W. Brigham, ed., *The Soviet Maritime Arctic* (London: Belhaven Press, 1991), 83–107.

20. For a seminal account of the notion of the Arctic sublime, see Chauncey C. Loomis, "The Arctic Sublime," in U. C. Knoepflmacher and G. B. Tennyson, eds., *Nature and the Victorian Imagination* (Berkeley: University of California Press, 1977): 95–112.

21. Griffiths, "The Arctic in the Russian Identity," esp. pp. 15–24.

22. On recent developments regarding this movement, with particular reference to the Northwest Territories, see John Merritt, Terry Fenge, Randy Ames, and Peter Jull, *Nunavut: Political Choices and Manifest Destiny* (Ottawa: Canadian Arctic Resources Committee, 1989).

23. T. C. Pullen, "That Polar Ice-breaker," *Northern Perspectives* 14 (September–October 1986): 9–10.

Chapter 9. The Arctic in World Affairs

1. For a more extended treatment of the issues discussed in this chapter, see Oran R. Young, "The Arctic in World Affairs" (The Donald L.

McKernan Lecture in Marine Affairs, University of Washington, Seattle, Washington, 10 May 1989).

2. For a short history of U.S. Arctic policy, consult William E. Westermeyer, "United States Arctic Interests: Background for Policy," in William E. Westermeyer and Kurt M. Shusterich, eds., *United States Arctic Interests: The 1980s and 1990s* (New York: Springer-Verlag, 1984), 1–18.

3. Joe Clark, secretary of state for external affairs (Speech delivered at the Norway–Canada Conference on Circumpolar Issues, Tromso, Norway, December 1987). The text is printed in *The Disarmament Bulletin* 7 (Spring 1988) (Ottawa: Department of External Affairs), 22–24.

4. A number of English translations of this speech are available. The quote is taken from Mikhail Gorbachev, "The North: A Zone of Peace" (Ottawa: USSR Embassy, 1988).

5. Gail Osherenko and Oran R. Young, *The Age of the Arctic Conflicts and Cold Realities* (Cambridge: Cambridge University Press, 1989), chap. 9 and Epilogue.

6. Oran R. Young and Gail Osherenko, eds., *Polar Politics: Creating International Environmental Regimes* (Ithaca, N.Y.: Cornell University Press, forthcoming).

7. For straightforward accounts of international cooperation regarding Antarctica, see Philip W. Quigg, *A Pole Apart: The Emerging Issue of Antarctica* (New York: McGraw-Hill, 1983), and Deborah Shapley, *The Seventh Continent: Antarctica in a Resource Age* (Washington, D.C.: Resources for the Future, 1985).

8. For a review of a series of recent bilateral Soviet/American agreements relating to the Bering Sea, consult David A. Shakespeare, "Recent US/USSR Agreements Relating to the Bering Region," *Arctic Research of the United States* 5 (Fall 1991): 37–47. There is every reason to expect that Russia, as the successor to the Soviet Union in the Circumpolar North, will take an interest in the continuation of these cooperative ventures.

9. N. I. Ryzhkov, speech delivered on 15 January 1988 in Oslo, Norway, in FBIS-SOV-88-011 (19 Jan. 1988), 53.

10. It is not surprising, under the circumstances, that Canada has become the principal proponent of the proposed international Arctic Council. For an extended discussion of this proposal, see Arctic Council Panel (Franklyn Griffiths and Rosemarie Kuptana, chairs), "To Establish an International Arctic Council: A Framework Report," Canadian Arctic Resources Committee, 14 May 1991.

Chapter 10. The Militarization of the Arctic

1. Parliament of Canada, Standing Committee on External Affairs and National Defense, *Fourth Report* (14 Feb. 1986), 47.

2. W. Harriet Critchley, "Polar Deployment of Soviet Submarines," *International Journal* 39 (Autumn 1984): 857.

3. Standing Committee on External Affairs and National Defense, *Fourth Report*, 52.

4. Ron Purver, "Security and Arms Control at the Poles," *International Journal* 39 (Autumn 1984): 897.

5. G. Leonard Johnson, David Bradley, and Robert S. Winokur, "United States Security Interests in the Arctic," in William E. Westermeyer and Kurt M. Shusterich, eds., *United States Arctic Interests: The 1980s and 1990s* (New York: Springer-Verlag, 1984), 289.

6. John Kirton, "Beyond Bilateralism: United States–Canadian Cooperation in the Arctic," in Westermeyer and Shusterich, eds., *United States Arctic Interests: The 1980s and 1990s* (New York: Springer-Verlag, 1984), 296.

7. Christopher S. Wren, "Weinberger Remark Adds Fuel to Canada Debate," *New York Times*, 19 Mar. 1985, A12.

8. Nils Orvik, "Greenland: The Politics of a New Northern Nation," *International Journal* 39 (Autumn 1984): 959–60.

9. Kirton, *Beyond Bilateralism*, 308.

10. Franklyn Griffiths, *A Northern Foreign Policy*, Wellesley Papers No. 7 (Toronto: Canadian Institute of International Affairs, 1979).

11. For a review of prior efforts to devise arms control arrangements for the Arctic, see Ronald G. Purver, *Arms Control in the North* (Kingston, Ont.: Queen's University, 1981).

12. Critchley, "Polar Deployment," 857.

13. A typical case occurred at the beginning of 1985 when a Soviet cruise missile strayed across northern Norway and fell to the earth in Finland.

14. Willy Østreng, *Politics in High Latitudes* (London: C. Hurst, 1977), chap. 6.

15. See Owen Wilkes, *A Proposal for a Demilitarized Zone in the Arctic*, Project Ploughshare Working Paper 84–4 (Waterloo, Ont.: Conrad Grebel College, 1984).

16. Johan J. Holst, "Norway's Search for a Nordpolitik," *Foreign Affairs* 60 (1981): 63–86.

17. The principal exception is the American airbase at Thule, Greenland. But even this arrangement is likely to become a focus of controversy in Greenland politics in the near future.

18. Johnson, Bradley, and Winokur, "United States Security," 282.

19. Parliament of Canada, *Fourth Report*, 73–74.

20. "Innu Fight Jets," *Alternatives* 13 (December 1985): 74.

Chapter 11. Sustainable Development in the Arctic

1. H. A. Innis, *The Fur Trade in Canada: An Introduction to Canadian Economic History* (New Haven: Yale University Press, 1962).

2. Interestingly, the World Conservation Strategy devotes particular attention to the Arctic. Section 19 of the Strategy states that "because the Arctic environment takes so long to recover from damage, the Arctic shall be considered a priority sea. Within their Arctic territories the Arctic nations should systematically map critical ecological areas (terrestrial as well as marine), draw up guidelines for their long term management, and establish a network of protected areas to safeguard representative, unique and critical ecosystems."

3. World Commission on Environment and Development, *Our Common Future* (New York: Oxford University Press, 1987), 43.

4. Thomas R. Berger, *Northern Frontier, Northern Homeland: The Report of the Mackenzie Valley Pipeline Inquiry* (Ottawa: Supply and Services Canada, 1977).

5. David P. Ross and Peter J. Usher, *From the Roots Up: Economic Development As If Community Mattered* (Croton-on-Hudson, N.Y.: The Bootstrap Press, 1986), 148.

6. Royal Commission on Seals and the Sealing Industry in Canada, *Seals and Sealing in Canada* (Ottawa: Supply and Services Canada, 1986).

7. Thomas R. Berger, *Village Journey: The Report of the Alaska Native Review Commission* (New York: Hill and Wang, 1985).

8. President Gorbachev, for example, called for "the cooperation of the northern countries in environmental protection" in his well-known "Arctic zone of peace" speech of 1 October 1987. Following up on this initiative, the Finnish government launched an effort to reach agreement on a multilateral strategy to protect the Arctic's environment. This effort bore fruit in June 1991, when the eight Arctic states signed a declaration establishing an Arctic Environmental Protection Strategy to safeguard the Arctic's ecosystems against a variety of environmental threats.

9. Mark A. Fraker, *Balaena mysticetus: Whales, Oil, and Whaling in the Arctic* (Anchorage: Sohio Alaska Production Company, 1984).

10. Ian Stirling, *Polar Bears* (Ann Arbor: University of Michigan Press, 1988), 187–204.

11. The United States failed to ratify a 1984 protocol that would have extended the Interim Convention on the Conservation of North Pacific Fur Seals of 1957 for another four years. This put an end to an international regime that originated in a 1911 agreement among Great Britain (on behalf of Canada), Japan, Russia, and the United States.

12. On the case of Prudhoe Bay, see Trustees for Alaska, Natural Resources Defense Council, and National Wildlife Federation, *Oil in the Arctic: The Environmental Record of Oil Development on Alaska's North Slope* (New York: Natural Resources Defense Council, 1988).

13. Michael S. Whittington, *Native Economic Development Corporations: Political and Economic Change in Canada's North*," CARC Policy Paper No. 4 (Ottawa: Canadian Arctic Resources Committee, 1986).

14. On reindeer herding in Fennoscandia, see Tim Ingold, *Hunters, Pastoralists and Ranchers: Reindeer Economies and Their Transformations* (Cambridge: Cambridge University Press, 1980); and Hugh Beach, *Reindeer-Herd Management: The Case of the Tuorpon Saameby in Northern Sweden* (Stockholm: Almqvist and Wiksell, 1981). On recent practices regarding reindeer herding in the Soviet North, consult P. S. Zhigunov, *Reindeer Husbandry* (Jerusalem: Israeli Program for Scientific Translations, 1968) and Vasilii Mikhailovich Kladkin and Aleksandr Danilovich Kurilyuk, *The Intensification of Reindeer Herding at Tompo Sovkhoz*, trans. Canadian Department of Indian Affairs and Northern Development. (Yakutsk: Yakutsk Publishing House, 1980).

15. George Manuel and M. Posluns, *The Fourth World: An Indian Reality* (Toronto: Collier-Macmillan, 1974), and Noel Dyck, ed., *Indigenous Peoples and the Nation-State: Fourth World Politics in Canada, Australia and Norway* (St. John's, Newfoundland: Institute of Social and Economic Research, 1985).

16. William Alonso and Edgar Rust, *The Evolving Pattern of Village Alaska* (Anchorage: Joint Federal-State Land Use Planning Commission, 1976).

17. Ernest S. Burch, Jr., "War and Trade," in William W. Fitzhugh and Aron Crowell, eds., *Crossroads of Continents: Cultures of Siberia and Alaska* (Washington, D.C.: Smithsonian Institution Press, 1988), 227–40.

18. Gerald A. McBeath and Thomas A. Morehouse, eds., *Dynamics of Alaska Native Self-Government* (Lanham, Md: University Press of America, 1980); Gurston Dacks, *A Choice of Futures* (Toronto: Methuen, 1981); and Jens Dahl, "Greenland: Political Structure of Self-Government," *Arctic Anthropology* 23 (1986): 315–24.

19. Shelagh Jane Woods, "The Wolf at the Door," *Northern Perspectives* 14 (March–April 1986): 1–6.

20. Gail Osherenko, "Can Comanagement Save Arctic Wildlife?" *Environment* 30 (July/August 1988): 6–13, 29–34.

21. Section 19 of the Strategy, in fact, directs attention specifically to the Arctic. It recommends "measures (including joint research) to improve protection of migratory species breeding within the Arctic and wintering inside or outside the region; studies of the impact of fisheries and other economic activities in the northern seas on ecosystems and non-target species; [and] the possibility of developing agreements among the Arctic nations on the conservation of the region's vital biological resources, based on the principles and experience of the Agreement on Conservation of Polar Bears."

22. Elizabeth Snyder, "The Arctic Marine Conservation Strategy," *Northern Perspectives* 15 (November 1987): 12.

Chapter 12. The Arctic

1. More precisely, choices among interpretive frameworks are based on *perceived* interests. It is possible, of course, to argue that individuals or groups of individuals are sometimes misinformed or deluded about their own interests. We may also come to think that certain actors define their interests in an excessively narrow or shortsighted fashion. This makes it feasible to debate the proper formulation of the interests of specific actors as well as to raise questions about phenomena like false consciousness. But it also poses serious normative and methodological problems because it requires procedures for identifying interests that are independent of what actors say their interests are and that apply even when actors openly disagree with the results.

2. Antinomies are statements or propositions that seem true when examined individually but that are inconsistent with one another.

3. This is by no means peculiar to democratic political systems. There is ample evidence of the operation of such interests in authoritarian systems, such as the former Soviet Union, as well.

INDEX

aboriginal movements, 7; *see also* indigenous peoples

Aboriginal Trappers Federation of Canada (ATFC), 130–31

Africa, 244, 245

Alaska, 1, 2, 20, 21, 240–41; accident rate, 73, 74; alcoholism, 73–74, 75–76, 84, 90; anomie, 75–76, 78–80, 83, 84; coal, 105; co-management, 81–82, 84; dependence mentality, 75–77, 80–82, 83, 84, 91–92; domestic production, 68–70; drug abuse, 74, 75–76, 77, 84, 92; economic problems, 82; economic returns and rents, securing, 64–65; education, 79–80, 91, 152; employment, 61, 62–63, 150–51; enclave development, 66–67; federal revenue, 145, 152–53; fishing, 56, 67, 68; fur trade, 64–65, 132; government revenue, 61, 142–58; health care, 44, 73–84, 91; homicide, 73; hunter/gatherers, 56, 57, 68–69; income security programs, 70–72, 80, 84; indigenous peoples, 41–42, 56–72, 88; infrastructure, 151–52; land claims settlement, 41, 51–52, 56, 88, 96, 220; local government revenue, 146, 147–48; mental illness, 73; mining, 62, 66, 150, 223; mixed economies, 56–72; natural resources, 41–42; oil, *xiii*, 56, 62, 64, 66, 94, 105, 109, 142–58, 161, 181; pathologies, 73–

84; political fragmentation, 82, 83; and popular culture, 92; Power Cost Equalization Program, 61; Rural Education Administrative Areas, 152; shipping, 161; state government growth, 143–48; state revenues, 61–62; subsistence economies, 56, 57–60, 63, 68–69, 71; suicide, 73, 74, 75; tax base, 65, 94, 157–58; timber industry, 56, 62, 67; trapping, 67; and United States government, 41, 45–46, 61, 62, 88; village corporations, 47, 56, 57, 82, 221; walrus ivory trade, 57; welfare programs, 76–77, 80, 91; whales, 225; wildlife management, 81–82; *see also* Alaska Eskimo Whaling Commission

Alaska Coalition, 109

Alaska Conservation Society, 136

Alaska Eskimo Whaling Commission (AEWC), 81, 128–29, 136, 139, 140

Alaska Federation of Natives, 82

Alaska National Interest Lands Conservation Act (1980), 88, 96

Alaska Native Claims Settlement Act (ANCSA), 41, 52, 56, 66, 69, 82, 88, 96, 221; land bank provisions, 97; and natural resources, 110

Alaska Native Coalition, 82

Alaska Natural Gas Transportation System, 165

Alcan Highway, 199

286   *Index*